THE GOSSIP PROJECT

LAUREN JONES

Copyright © 2024 by Lauren Jones

All rights reserved.

No part of this book may be reproduced in any form without written permission from the author.

This story is a work of fiction. Any reference to people, places or historical events are used fictitiously. Names, places, events and characters are products of the author's imaginations. Any similarities to real people, places or events is entirely coincidental.

For Sam,

This better be the peak.

A NOTE FOR READERS

Please note this story contains references to drug use, alcohol abuse and addiction. It also contains on-page depictions of anxiety and sexual harassment.

CHAPTER ONE

My back is screaming as I silently change positions on the floor of my best friend's closet. I've folded myself over a shoe rack for the last fifteen minutes, trying not to breathe while Eve's fiancé breaks up with her in the living room. The acoustically beneficial architecture of her loft means I can hear every word so she won't have to recount it over dinner later.

Darren draws an exaggerated breath, and there is a forced waver in his voice. "I'll always love you, but we both know this isn't working. If we go through with the wedding, we'll be wasting everyone's time."

He *is* a waste of time. She needs someone with a backbone. Someone who admires her tenacity and wildness. She needs an earthquake. Someone she can't live without because the sun doesn't shine as bright when they aren't around.

Darren falls short in every regard, but we ignored it because Eve's had too many failures, and she's owed a win.

Before Darren, there was Marco, a hedge fund manager who paid someone to iron his ties and spoke down to waitstaff. Before Marco was Delilah. She was lovely, but she believed that Eve's tumultuous relationship with her mother was because of a convoluted astrological theory that would solve itself if she wore a special crystal during solstice. Before Delilah were Cooper and Shae, whose marriage was never going to be saved by the addition of Eve. They separated a few months later, and Eve moved on to an engineer who thought women were property and was upset to learn that Eve couldn't be told what to do.

Darren is different, though. Against all odds, they made it to a proposal over a fifteen-dollar slice of cheesecake at a restaurant that requires men to wear dinner jackets. She called me from the car right after, and her voice was several octaves higher than normal. Apparently, she was ready to settle down with this meek office supply sales associate.

Now, here I am, trying not to crush her Jimmy Choo Dreece Kb 95s because Darren pushed back dinner with his parents to break up with her as soon as possible.

"We're on the same page. Right?" He forgets to add the whimper to his sentence, losing mass credibility and forcing me to roll my eyes in the darkness.

Eve and I were on this page before the asshole opened the book. We decided that she's entitled to half the gifts from the engagement party, and we're willing to fight him on that. Of course, she won't use three sets of crystal wine glasses, but it's more about being compensated for the emotional damage. They're also a bargaining chip to get the floor rug. It's one of those gigantic woven ones that really ties a room together.

"God, I can't believe how hard this is," Darren remembers to sniffle.

I bet Eve is wondering how much she can get for the bread maker on eBay. It's an obscure brand, and the instructions are in German, so she may as well hang onto it. We could make artisan loaves like the ones at the bakery down the block. They would go hand in hand with the compound butter her dad, Doug, has been making since he and Eve's mom, Elaine, split.

"I don't want either of us to be unhappy," Darren says. "I have so much on my plate, trying to move up to branch manager, and I think I'll get there in the next twelve months."

He's been saying that for the last twelve months. At some point, he needs to realize that he isn't management material. He can't even book his own doctor's appointments, and if a restaurant doesn't have an online booking system, he refuses to go. How can he negotiate wholesale discounts on office supplies when he has to call Eve to open the parking garage because he won't press the help button after forgetting his fob? It's a wonder he was able to pull off the affair he's having with the accounts clerk.

And because of that, we're keeping the bread maker and the rug. He can have the linens since Steph has spent more time naked in them than Eve has.

"Eve, there's something else." Darren sucks in a breath. "I want you to keep the ring. It's the least I can do."

I muffle a gasp. That is unexpected. I thought for sure he'd pin her down and twist that dust particle of a diamond off her finger.

"If you insist," she chokes out, and my god, it is the worst performance of her life. Thankfully, Darren, in all his inept glory, is buying it.

"I feel sick about this." He sighs as I shift the Jimmy Choos and suck in a much-needed breath. "You love this apartment."

We do love this apartment, especially when Darren isn't in it. Compared to my place, it's a palace, with its massive industrial-style windows, and an entire wall of exposed brick. The kitchen is stunning too. It has an enormous island counter and state-of-the-art appliances. It's the apartment we always dreamed of living in together when we were old enough to afford it. But of course, the generational wealth of Darren's parents rewarded him with this place because he graduated college with moderate grades.

"I can talk to your mom if you like," he offers. "Help her with canceling the wedding. She's going to be so upset."

He isn't wrong about that. Elaine loves Darren, and I can't figure out why. He's wholly unremarkable, and as I listen to him pretend to sob, his future plays out in my mind with pinpoint accuracy. In a few years, he'll get the coveted branch manager position and update his LinkedIn profile before the ink is dry on the contract. By then he'll have married Steph to justify the affair and they'll have two children that wear matching outfits to all family events. Of course, they'll live in a leafy suburb with an aging, mid-size mall where Steph can spend Darren's yearly bonus on the latest plastic organization bins for the French door refrigerator Darren strong-armed the salesman into reducing because there is a dent in the left side. Around forty, Steph will sleep with their kids' soccer coach, and Darren will wonder what he did to deserve such treachery.

My legs ache as more clichéd breakup lines fall from Darren's thin lips. I'm still pissed he did this tonight. Especially when he asked Eve to, in his words, "whip up something nice for dinner to impress his parents" knowing that she can't boil an egg and I'd be called in to help. We were hoping he'd do it next week with the rug safely at my apartment. I'd say Steph laid down the ultimatum and now, my beef and red wine casserole is in jeopardy. It has to be stirred at frequent intervals so the meat doesn't stick to the bottom of the pot.

"Eve, tell me you're alright." Darren sniffles.

A long silence stretches out and I picture the cogs turning in Eve's head. She can't tell him the truth despite the fact he was the one who started inappropriately texting his colleague and took her on a "work trip" to Portland. Eve, to her credit, handled it well. She wiped her tears, opened a separate account, and used their savings to buy "wedding essentials" with flexible return policies.

"My parents are on their way over. I thought it was best to tell them in person." Darren must have stood up because I can hear heavy footsteps on the polished timber floor.

"Okay." Eve's voice is devoid of the false emotion she was putting on earlier, and I hear her walking up the stairs. This isn't part of the plan. She is supposed to stay downstairs and I'm supposed to stay in the closet while she gets Darren out of the apartment. That's when we're going to roll up the floor rug and somehow wedge it into my hatchback.

"That went well," I say as Eve pulls open the wardrobe door and helps me out. She's heavy-lidded, and her cheeks lack their usual rosy glow.

"Can we get out of here?" She sighs.

I nod as I stretch my upper body. "Yeah, of course."

I follow her back down the stairs with a wide-eyed Darren staring up from that masterpiece of a kitchen.

"Spencer?" He raises an eyebrow and has the good sense to look embarrassed.

"Darren." I squeeze past him to get to the oven. Eve doesn't explain my presence and instead gets a towel from the hall cupboard and lays it on the counter. I open the oven, lift the lid off the ceramic baking dish, and stir the casserole. It's salvageable, but I internally curse Darren when I feel the meat sticking to the bottom.

I tell him to move, taking the dish and placing it on the towel. Eve wraps it in a neat bundle and jostles her handbag onto her shoulder before we leave without another word.

For the entire forty-five-minute drive to Eve's sister, Kit's place, she unleashes on Darren for dumping her at peak hour.

"Couldn't he dump me at seven? It's five-thirty. The traffic out of the city is a nightmare. We're getting every red light." She closes her eyes and takes a rattled breath. When all the cheating stuff came to light, she made me promise never to ask her if she was alright. She doesn't want to admit that he hurt her. Like the idea of it is embarrassing. I want to tell her she doesn't have to hide.

Upon our arrival, we're greeted by Kit's boyfriend, Danny, struggling to make tacos. The poor guy looks like he's run a marathon, been told his whole family was in a boating accident, and is undergoing a tax audit all at once. Not to mention, the place smells like burnt taco seasoning. Kit's on the couch, jaw clenched and resisting the urge to fix the disaster unfolding in her compact kitchen.

"We brought a casserole." Eve places the cloth-wrapped bundle on the counter, outside the culinary disaster zone.

I pat Danny on the arm before he whips the dish towel off his shoulder and drops it on the bench. "But it looks like you're doing a great job."

"No, I'm not." He ambles from the kitchen to the couch, looking defeated. Kit gives him a kiss on the cheek before she joins Eve and me in the kitchen.

"Is everything okay?" Kit looks at her sister as she gathers plates and silverware.

"I'm free!" Eve shouts. "Darren broke up with me."

Kit's abreast of the Darren situation and has been pushing for Eve to extricate herself for some time. She didn't see the sense in not confronting Darren about Steph, but we both know Eve needs to do this her own way.

"So we're celebrating with a casserole?"

"The casserole was already in the oven when he dumped her," I explain. "He's keeping the apartment, so he can't have the casserole."

"Sounds fair." Kit lifts the lid on the pot, replacing the charred taco smell with that of salty beef and rich red wine.

I help her dish up the food while Eve busies herself interrogating Danny. He and Kit haven't been together long, but she needs an update on his intentions. Nothing has changed since the last time she asked. And since they grew up as neighbors, she knows everything about him and his family.

"We're still in a relationship," he says. "I have nothing else to tell you."

As a former pro hockey player, he's gigantic compared to Eve, but like any self-respecting person with the full attention of Eve Reilly, he cowers under her scrutiny.

"Are you going to live together? Get married? Give me a niece or nephew?"

"You're already getting one," Kit calls out, referring to her twin, Bea, being pregnant. Her boyfriend, Jamie, never got this level of interrogation because they moved to his native London amid Doug and Elaine's divorce.

"Eve, get up here and eat the spite casserole before it gets cold," I say, placing two plates on the table.

"Saved by the casserole." She stares at Danny. "I'm watching you, though."

He nods and swallows hard as a few strands of his blond hair fall into his eyes.

"Okay, stop threatening Danny, please." Kit hands her boyfriend a plate and a fork. There are only three seats at the dining table, but he looks relieved to be relegated to the coffee table.

"What's the plan now, Eve?" Kit asks.

"We're getting the rug and the bread maker," she says.

"I was referring to your more substantial assets."

"It's a big rug," Eve says to her sister.

"We've been pilfering her money out of the joint account

for months. She's got first and last on a studio covered, and it is a big rug," I explain.

Kit nods, impressed that her sister has taken some initiative though it's questionable. She might be the youngest, but Kit is by far the most responsible of the Reilly siblings. She loves plans, lists, and organization. Eve, by comparison, is a plastic bag floating on the wind. No idea where she's going, just enjoying the ride.

"Do you need help with the rug?" Danny asks as he swallows a chunk of beef.

"Nah, we got it covered," Eve says.

I watch my friend beam and wipe gravy off her chin with a napkin that Kit, the ever-diligent host, laid out. Whatever anguish held her hostage in the car has dissolved, and I'm reminded of what it really takes to rattle her foundation. Darren's no earthquake, but what she's been through would fold anyone like a lawn chair.

I push a cube of potato around my plate, listening to Kit assassinate Darren's character while Eve soaks up her sister's unwavering support. It distracts me from the sound of the front door opening and my breath catches in my throat as Kit and Eve's older brother, Alex, enters the kitchen.

"Just in time." Kit springs up, handing him a plate. He accepts it with a smile, and my heart hammers in my chest when he looks at me across the rapidly shrinking space.

He's the same as I remember. Still carrying himself with confidence, like he's entirely at home in his skin. I've always envied that about him. That and his impossibly soft black hair that curls at his temples. And those fathomless blue eyes.

"Hey, Pen," he says in that velvety smooth, multi-million dollar voice.

Eve looks from her brother to me before suggesting Danny turn on the TV so we can watch whatever game is on. She's never made such a request in her life, but Danny does as he's told and soon the ambient noise of a basketball game and the scrape of silverware fills the small apartment. I can't stop looking at Alex, though, watching his every bite of the food I made, my chest constricting at how he closes his eyes to emphasize his enjoyment. His whole body loosens as he leans a hip on the edge of the counter, acting like no time has passed. Like seeing each other is of no consequence. I wish I could do that. I wish I could act like my cheeks aren't heating and my palms aren't sweating. Pretend my heart isn't racing and my legs aren't shaking. But I can't. And when he looks at me again, there is only one thought in my head.

He's back.
My earthquake.

CHAPTER TWO

I barely have my front door open when Eve barrels in and heads straight to the kitchen. With no preamble, she takes two wine glasses from the overhead cabinet and twists the lid off the bottle of red she bought on her way over. Her lip quivers as the wine splashes into the glass, so I'd say we've reached the breakdown portion of this breakup.

"Why is this upsetting me so much?" she grunts. "I wanted to leave."

She did.

"I hate him so much."

She doesn't.

"We could have had a great life together."

They couldn't.

"I would have been happy."

She wouldn't.

"What does Steph have that I don't?"

Darren.

"I should get her fired."

No.

"Or get Darren back."

Big no.

"Or move on and focus on myself."

Much better.

Her hands tremble as she lifts the brimming glass to her lips and takes a gulp.

She wants to hate him because of what he did, just like she wanted to love him because of what he represented: the cozy, stable life everyone else seems to have.

"I know it feels like the world is ending right now, but trust me, this is for the best," I soothe.

She takes another painful gulp and winces at the taste of her four-dollar purchase. "I rushed into things with Darren. It was a mistake."

She did. Of course she did because she was tired and wanted what she thought she needed at the tender age of thirty. It's not her though. Eve isn't a picket fence, two-kids kind of girl. She's the kind of girl who gets takeout at eleven p.m. because she put off making dinner for too long. The kind of girl who forgets to pack at least ten essential items when traveling and always needs to find a store upon arrival. Eve is that girl, a chaotic whirlwind who seems to thrive in any circumstance. That girl needs someone to challenge her. Someone who doesn't agree with everything she says for the sake of it. Someone with a streak of chaos.

"Yes, you did," I agree, and she pins me with a flat look.

"You agreed with that too fast."

"Of course you rushed into it. He was nice at the time and the complete opposite of anyone else you've dated."

Her teeth press into her bottom lip, and her hands shake. I relieve her of my wine glass, and she pouts. "I didn't want to be wrong about him."

"That's not a good reason to marry someone." I take hold

of her shoulders. "Now, we have to focus on the task ahead. I can help with canceling vendors, and we'll go back to the apartment to get your stuff."

She's only partially listening, staring at the ceiling, her mouth slack.

"That's the other thing I'm pissed about. I wasted four hours at IKEA last weekend trying to decide between the Landskrona and the Farlov, and he'll keep it because I don't have anywhere to store it." She waves her hands at nothing. "He gets a Farlov by default."

"The Kivik was better," I mumble as I take a sip of wine.

"I wanted the Kivik, but he said it was too boxy. He liked the curved armrests of the Ingatorp."

"That's a table."

"Is it? What am I thinking of then?" She takes the glass, pressing it to her cheek in contemplation.

"Ektorp."

"Ektorp." She chews on the word before chugging the wine like a freshman at their first college party. "Yeah, that sounds right."

A darkness settles over her again, her gaze shifting to the countertop as she wraps an arm around her midsection. *She doesn't deserve this.* She loves love, and I keep hoping that the next person to enter her life will give her the big, crazy, hopelessly debilitating love she is looking for.

"Fuck Darren, though." I exhale. "Fuck him and Steph and his parents for raising a human being with all the charisma of a wet cardboard box."

Eve's mouth lifts at the corner.

"And fuck him for not letting you get the Kivik. I can picture him in the showroom too. Hands in his pockets, wearing that stupid golfing invitational polo and casting aspersions on the boxy armrests. It would have been perfect with the area rug, adding a level of cozy sophistication to an industrial space."

Eve throws her hands up. "Yes. Thank you. That's what I kept saying. He was against the Borgeby from the start too. I forgot to tell you that."

I press a hand to my chest. "I'm sorry, did you say he was against the Borgeby? Does he know it comes in black?"

Eve nods vigorously. "Yes, he does. But we just had to get the Havsta because his mom likes the look of nested coffee tables. I'll tell you this, Spencer: it will be a cold day in hell before I take interior design advice from a woman who thinks patchwork corduroy is a stylish fabric choice for occasional chairs."

"I've had enough of this," I grunt as I stride over to the hall table by the front door and pull my tan leather bag onto my shoulder.

"Oh, where are we going?" Eve grins, delicate brows raised in anticipation.

"We're going to get that floor rug, and then we're getting noodles from that place you like that will probably give us food poisoning again."

"I love that place."

"I know you do." I fish out my keys. "Now get in the car."

Our verbal annihilation of Darren continues for the entire drive to his building. We systematically dissect every remotely selfish thing he's ever done, and Eve brings up all the red flags she ignored during the wedding planning. There are more than I realized.

"I should have known he wasn't the one," she says as we pull up outside. "He wanted to wear a tan belt with black shoes to the wedding. He didn't see a problem with it."

"Hell no," I scoff as I close the car door, and a fresh wave of hatred for Darren hits. If he gets the apartment, we won't be able to have breakfast at the cafe across the street anymore, and they have the best French toast in Seattle. I'll be damned if we lose that French toast and have nothing to show for it.

As we climb the stairs, I notice Eve's shaking hands and shallow breathing. I take the key, slide it into the lock, and we're met with the blank stares of Darren's parents, seated together on the Farlov.

"Eve?" Darren's bushy brows rise as he approaches us. "What are you doing here?"

"I need to get some things," she says as she traipses up to the bedroom, leaving me stranded with Darren and his parents.

He is a carbon copy of his dad, right down to the tiny eyes and wispy brown hair. They have the same irritating curve to their mouths. A perpetual smirk. His mother, an overbearing chore of a woman, is slack-jawed and clutching her necklace like she's a regency mother whose daughter is in the midst of another unsuccessful season.

"She could have called." Darren folds his arms over his chest, and I feel my lip curl.

We could have, but he doesn't deserve it. He's getting out without so much as a slap on the wrist when Eve is the kind of person who will covertly destroy your credit score if you cut her off in traffic.

"She'll only be a minute." I exhale, employing the calming techniques Eve taught me when she was a meditation guru for three months last year.

There is a loud clunk in the bedroom, and a few minutes later, my best friend emerges, dragging a battered yellow suitcase down the industrial-style loft stairs.

"Evelyn." Darren's mom narrows her eyes. "You can't storm into Darren's space like this without proper notice."

"Well, I still have a key, so technically, I can do whatever I want." She turns back to face me and gives the confirmation nod. "Take it."

I spring into action, marching across the apartment while Darren's parents sport twin looks of confusion.

"Spencer, what are you doing?" Darren watches on as I drag the Havsta to the side and begin rolling up the floor rug.

"Feet up," I bark at Darren's parents. His mother huffs but does as instructed. I hoist the rolled-up rug over my shoulder and head for the exit.

"Spencer!" Darren shouts, reaching for the rug, but I artfully dodge him. Eve grins as she opens the front door and ushers me out into the hall before letting the door slam behind us.

Half an hour later, we're sitting in my car holding containers of spicy beef noodles and satay chicken with a rolled-up rug poking the dashboard between us.

"I feel so much better now," Eve muses through a mouthful of beef. "Do you think finding peace in having this rug is a sign from God that leaving him was the right thing to do?"

"I don't think God has anything to do with it. He cheated on you, so you left him," I say as I twist my chopsticks into the densely packed container of noodles.

"You're right." Eve chuckles. "But seeing the look on his face when you told his parents to lift their feet felt like a gift from God."

She stretches her arm over the rug and swaps containers with me because her food envy has kicked in.

"So, what's the plan now?" I ask.

"No idea." Eve's shoulders sag, and she looks at me with empty eyes. "I was going to stay with Kit, but Alex is staying in Seattle for a while."

My spine locks, and ice crawls through my body. He's been back over the years, but only for a few days, and I've been able to avoid him. Seattle doesn't feel safe anymore.

"Are you okay with him being here?" Eve's bright blue eyes appear over the rug, the glow of the neon sign outside the noodle place making her skin glow.

"Yeah, it's been years, Eve." I swallow my mouthful of food. "You can stay with me."

"You live in a one-bedroom," she says. "I mean, we're close, but I don't think we can share a bed. Not with your involuntary spooning."

"I gravitate toward a heat source."

"I know, but you're like a furnace, and your limbs are pokey. And your hair ends up wrapped around my neck somehow like it grows ten feet when the sun goes down and becomes sentient with a bloodlust."

"You aren't much better. You hog the covers and snore."

"I do not," she snorts.

"You do, but you can have the couch."

She doesn't have another option. Since her parents' divorce, she's been more distant than usual with Elaine, and Doug is currently living above the bar our friend Miles owns. My couch is all she has.

"We'll be fine for a few weeks until Alex leaves," I say. "Bring the rug, though."

Eve agrees, and when we get home, she drags my couch to the side and rolls out the stolen rug. It's too big for my measly living space, but I'm assured it looks great, that having it doubled over itself on one side looks good.

"I'm sorry my brother is here," Eve says as she adjusts the pillows on my couch and lays down. "Mom and Dad have calmed down, and Kit is doing great, so I don't know why he wants to stay."

"Homesick, maybe." I shrug, even though I haven't stopped thinking about him relaxing in Kit's kitchen and acting like things between us didn't end the way they did. Our first time seeing each other in four years feels more important than a casual "hi" over a stolen casserole.

Eve frowns. "I can tell him to go back to New York or LA. I can book him a flight using the miles Darren was saving to take Steph to Fiji."

"Well, as much fun as it is screwing Darren over, that won't be necessary. I'm fine with having Alex here. I've moved on."

The lie passes my lips with ease, but the sting of tears is harder to hide. Eve doesn't push me, though, and when she disappears into the bathroom, I take a deep breath to shake off the unease and go to my room.

With my back pressed against the door, I listen to my best friend settle for the night. When the living room light clicks off, I slide into bed. My sheets are colder than usual, and the space beside me is bigger than before. The mere mention of him brings a hollow feeling to my chest, and loneliness creeps in.

An hour slips by as I watch the sheer gossamer curtain flutter in the breeze from the partially open window. He's never been here, but seeing him the other night has triggered some kind of nostalgic response. I loved him so deeply for so long, but I didn't think it would be so quick to resurface. Suddenly, I see him everywhere in my space. I can picture him beside me and trace his features in my mind.

It's devastating.

For another hour, I toss and turn, forcing myself not to dig up something I worked so hard to bury. But in the end, Alex wins. He usually does. I crawl out of bed and pad over to my closet. With only the dim glow of the city outside my window, I search around until my fingers brush the unmarked cardboard box.

I open the lid and pull out the tattered black hoodie, running my fingers over the fabric. His smell is fading, almost completely used up, but the hit of bergamot and wood smoke ignites twenty years of memories.

I bring it to my face, pressing my cheek against the soft fabric. Time was supposed to fix everything. I thought I'd wake up, and the burn in my chest would feel more like a warm breeze on a clear day. I thought I'd stop seeing him everywhere, that my existence wouldn't feel so empty. But the realization of moving on wasn't so poetic. I was in my kitchen. For the first time in over a year, I didn't instinctively get two coffee cups from the cabinet. I cried that night. Painful sobs wracked my body like I'd lost him all over again. My subconscious had moved on, and I feared what that meant for our past. I wondered if I'd forget him.

Hoodie in hand, I climb back into bed. The wind picks up, and the air thickens with the promise of rain. I love nights like this, waiting for a storm to cleanse the city and waking up to the smell of sodden earth and nourished plant life. Tonight is different, though. He isn't hundreds or even thousands of miles away. He's here, under the same stormy sky, listening to the same clap of thunder.

CHAPTER THREE

Ruby Heather Ward is the bane of my work existence. She is the rain on my metaphorical parade. The door handle that catches the belt loop on my jeans. The spatula that's perfectly angled to stop my utensil drawer from opening and makes my staff writer job at *The Gossip Project* as fun as moving apartments with a broken elevator.

She's a recent college graduate, and based on the personal phone calls I've overheard, Daddy worships the ground she walks on. She might be a wonderful daughter, but as a desk mate, she never puts her phone on silent, has an obnoxiously loud clicky pen, and drums those Barbie pink talons on her armrests whenever I'm on the phone.

Like any other day, Ruby arrives thirty minutes late, complaining about traffic and holding a coffee from that overpriced café that charges for Wi-Fi. Her voice is that of someone with zero responsibility, operating on eight hours of uninterrupted sleep. And from her dewy skin, she's squeezed in the eighteen-step skincare routine she submitted for last week's beauty wrap-up.

"Parking is a nightmare in that garage. I was looping around for ages, trying to get a space," she groans as she takes out her laptop, phone, and day planner from their monogrammed leather cases. I return to my task only to be interrupted again when Hazel, our boss' overworked PA, appears on the other side of the bullpen. Her wide brown eyes dart around the space like she's at Wimbledon. There is nothing commanding about Hazel. She's small, gentle, and has a different pastel cardigan for each day of the week.

"Staff meeting in five." Her voice is barely in the realm of normal speaking range, but everyone in the office observes the power she's proxy to and stops what they're doing.

If the meeting is in five, Natalia, the editor-in-chief, will arrive in thirty-five minutes. When she glides in like Aphrodite riding that pesky clam to shore, everyone needs to be at the conference room table, notepad and pen in hand. Hazel learned this the hard way when she started working for Natalia. She'd spent the first ten minutes of the meeting wrangling staff while Natalia tapped her Balmain slingback pumps on the leg of the conference table, her razor blade glare spiking everyone's blood pressure.

When the elevator dings, we're crowded around the boat-shaped boardroom table, backs straight, and nerves prematurely fried. No one wants to be singled out, and she'll take aim if she doesn't have your undivided attention. There is a collective intake of breath as Natalia drops her designer purse on the table and faces the group. She never sits during a meeting, and with heels that high, the structural integrity of her needle-thin ankles is at risk. It's strategic, though. From such a vantage point, she commands the room, radiating energy that is equally terrifying and inspiring.

It isn't just her demeanor that draws attention. Her hair is a decadent caramel color, and her skin is flawless, but she appears to wear no makeup. There is something wildly unnerving about her eyes, though. They are darker than the night sky. All the better to stare into your soul and make you tremble in fear of being punished for a crime you're yet to commit.

"Website traffic is down since last month, and we've seen a decline in post engagement across all socials." Natalia's voice is flat and even, hiding the disappointment. "I want ideas to increase our exposure."

One of the social media consultants, a twenty-something with thick eyebrows and an enthusiastic wardrobe color palette, raises her hand. Natalia's attention snaps to the young girl, and she lowers her hand slowly before speaking.

"We've had good engagement on the quiz posts. Maybe we could do more of those?"

Natalia sighs. "We're better than 'pick a vegetable' and 'we'll guess your ideal vacation destination'."

The girl clams up, her cheeks reddening as she picks at her multi-colored nail polish. The scrutiny doesn't last long because Ruby stands up and takes the spotlight. I'm already dreading whatever idea passes those shiny lips because as her desk clump buddy, I'll be roped into it. If it's a good idea, it's hers. If the suggestion doesn't land, it's mine. I'm already swamped with my usual clickbait articles, and I've been working on a passion project about a murdered actress from the forties. I want no part of what she's cooking up in that annoyingly proportionate head of hers.

"I think we should focus on celebrity news. I mean, we're called *The Gossip Project*, aren't we?" Ruby says this like Cher from *Clueless*, and I notice she's mimicking Natalia's pose: hands on hips, shoulders back, her pencil-thin neck straining to keep her thick blonde ponytail high.

"I've got a contact on that TV show, *Love Shack*." Dustin,

the content writer who takes three cigarette breaks every hour, jumps in. "There are three former TV actors on it this season."

"Is that the show where D-list celebrities spend a month hooking up in a rented mansion?" Natalia's pinched expression has Dustin scrambling. Fortunately, Ruby is on hand to take over.

"I heard there was a scandal involving a producer. He was sleeping with two contestants, and they found out about each other. Then, his wife caught him when she visited the set. They have some exclusive footage of it, and by the sound of it, they'll sell it to the highest bidder."

As if TGP *would be the highest bidder for something like that.* It's probably grainy cell phone footage that's already leaked on social media with the production company's watermark. It doesn't stop everyone at the table from nodding in agreement and turning Ruby's smile positively Cheshire.

I make the mistake of looking out the window to avoid entering the conversation. On average, we publish three reality TV scandal pieces a week, so none of this is new. If we run with it, we'll get a boilerplate cease and desist from the show, legal will order us to publish a retraction that expertly absolves us of all responsibility while never admitting fault, and Dustin will go back to his pack-a-day habit while *TGP* hangs onto its reputation as the least reputable gossip site in existence. *What a title to hold.*

"Spencer?" Natalia zeros in, and my stomach turns to stone. With each passing second, the intensity of her bird-black gaze has everything I know about journalism slipping out of my brain.

"Yes, Natalia?"

"Any ideas for content?" She rests her hands on the table,

fingers splayed, the sunlight from the window glinting off the dime-sized diamond on her left hand.

My throat constricts and an endless beat of silence holds the entire room hostage. I can feel everyone's eyes on me, thanking whichever god they pray to that they're not in my shoes right now. I could run. Just run from the building. Ditch my block-heeled Mary Janes in the elevator and never look back. Sure, without a job, I'd have to give up my apartment, but Eve and I could stay with Miles for a while. I could work at the bar. Polish glasses while telling anyone who'll listen about the time I interviewed a pediatric surgeon who saved babies in utero only to have the piece scrapped in favor of a former child star getting a DUI. I could do it. I could be free, and this crippling fear of Natalia's rejection under the watchful eyes of my colleagues could be a distant memory.

But I'm still here, stuck in this faux leather swivel chair, and my head is a black hole. Not a single thought materializes behind my dry eyes, and in this state of abject panic, I suggest the only idea that remains in the void.

"Florence Ritter." My voice is like heavy-tread hiking boots on the gravel of a mountainside. "I've been doing some research on Florence Ritter. Looking into different theories on her murder. Searching for any new evidence."

"The actress?" Natalia arches a brow. "What kind of story?"

"An investigative piece. I've already put together a timeline of events, and the case still has a big following online. Some mainstream media coverage might draw out a few new armchair detectives."

Natalia taps her chin, and the room holds its collective breath. To her credit, she is constantly trying to steer *TGP* away from red carpet nip slips. Unfortunately, the last time she rolled the dice on one of my ideas, the company got sued for defamation. It settled out of court, and she's never brought it up, but no matter how passive and nonverbal her disappointment is, it's still disappointment. It didn't matter that one of my sources called and apologized for publicly denying the accusations that were leveled in my article. She'd received an under-the-table payment to make the whole thing go away. It made me a liar and Natalia incompetent.

"We'll table it, Spencer," Natalia says, and a little wash of relief settles over me. I won't be called on for the duration of the meeting. Ruby, however, does not share the sentiment of wanting to remain invisible. She springs to her feet again, like she's already withering from not being the center of attention.

"How about celebrity profiles? We haven't done that in a while."

Natalia's eyes snap to her. "Do you have someone in mind?"

I don't know what comes over me, but I sit up, leaning past Ruby so I'm in Natalia's eyeline. Two ideas, no matter how flawed, might get me off the hook for our next content meeting.

"How about Camille Montgomery?" I offer. "She just signed a deal for an interior design reality show."

"*House and Garden* did a spread on that last week," Natalia replies, and I deflate back into my chair.

There are exactly three minutes of further discussion on the topic, but a lack of solid connection to an interesting celebrity means Ruby's second idea is shelved as well.

The rest of the meeting drags. Natalia's impatience grows, and office morale reaches basement-level. In the end, we're reduced to our usual product reviews and quizzes before she dismisses us to our cubicles to see what celebrity feuds we can recycle.

Even though she terrifies me, I have sympathy for Natalia.

THE GOSSIP PROJECT

She's forced to peddle clickbait and sell weight loss pills to people who don't need it so our engagement numbers look better at the quarterly meeting. Once upon a time, though, she was like me: hungry and searching for something bigger and better. She started as a cub reporter with *The Seattle Star*, and before long, she was covering political corruption scandals and exposing the heinous treatment of refugees on foreign shores. She's traveled to war zones and royal palaces and is the reason I applied for this job. But reading her old stories brings my career—or lack of—into harsh perspective, which is not helped by the terminally ill light bulb that flickers above my desk.

"Are you going to answer that?" Ruby waves her hand in front of my face. "It says it's the front desk."

I look down at my standard issue, gray desk phone, and scramble to pick up the receiver. From the look on Debra's face, the monotone ringing has caused grave upset to the neighboring desk clump.

"This is Spencer," I say, and the first thing I hear is Eve in the background, complaining about how ridiculous it is that she can't come up to my floor without permission.

"Hey, it's Owen. I've got a disgruntled realtor with black hair and scary eyes here to see you."

"Come on, Owen. I know that your whole job is security, but you know who I am," Eve groans. "I was at the Christmas party last year."

"You *crashed* the Christmas party." He pulls the phone from his mouth. "And I'll bounce you again if I have to. Don't think I won't."

Eve lets out an exaggerated sigh. "Why are you like this?"

"Because I'm doing my job. I can't let you up without permission from the office you're trying to enter."

There is some kind of scuffle, followed by Owen's muffled

protests before a crackle and several beeps tell me Eve put it on speaker.

"I was trying to surprise you, Spence, but apparently, I need sworn statements from several government officials and a rare amulet from a hidden cave to gain access to this stupid office building."

"I think you just need to sign the visitor book," I say.

"Exactly," Owen's frustrated voice calls out in the background.

"Can you put Owen back on the phone? We don't need a repeat of the Christmas party."

"Why does everyone keep bringing that up? I was in the neighborhood, and the old guy who runs the modeling agency on level sixteen said I have good bone structure. Owen bouncing me lost what could have been a lucrative contract."

"There is no modeling agency on level sixteen," Owen gripes. "And that guy doesn't even work in the building."

"Wow, you really let anyone into your Christmas party, don't you?" Eve scoffs. "Not great at security, are you, Owen?"

He says something I can't make out, and they fight over the phone again. Eventually, Owen wins. I'm taken off speaker and his voice comes down the line. "Can I bounce her, Spence? Please?"

"That depends." I sigh. "Does she have food?"

"Yeah. It looks like pasta or something."

"It's risotto," Eve shouts.

"Garlic bread?" I ask.

There's silence for a moment, followed by the rustle of a plastic bag.

"Yeah, she's got garlic bread. Looks like extra parmesan too."

There is another scuffle, and Owen is relieved of the

phone again. "Can you tell him to let me up? I promise I won't go up to sixteen and look for a modeling agency."

"Good, because that man was trying to kidnap you. Level sixteen is an audiologist and an art dealer—which is a scandal in the building because he doesn't deal much art. Owen and I think it's a front for something."

"That is interesting." Eve's voice sounds strained, and I picture her physically holding Owen at arm's length, even though he's twice her size. "Can we talk about this over risotto with extra parmesan?"

"Yeah, of course. Put Owen back on."

Eve's voice is distant when she speaks again. "Owen, stop dicking around over there and do your job. The journalist at *TGP* wants to speak with you."

"Spencer, I swear to God—"

I cut him off. "Send her up. Thanks, Owen."

A few minutes later, Eve arrives on my floor with the violent ding of our ancient elevator. It's been a while since she's graced my fluorescent prison with her presence, and since she commits almost nothing to memory, I hold my hand up over my cubicle wall so she can find me. Most of the bullpen watches her swan over, all long legs and shiny hair. She winks at Hamish from marketing, and he chokes on his tuna and rice. She'd eat that poor guy alive, and he knows it.

"To what do I owe the pleasure of this impromptu lunch?" I grin as Eve rounds the wall of the cubicle and sits on the edge of my desk. Ruby's eyes narrow over the partition.

"I'm showing an apartment two blocks away and thought I'd drop in." Eve looks over the wall. "Ruby, isn't it?"

They've met before—multiple times—but Eve enjoys this game, and Ruby is a worthy opponent. They always bristle at the sight of each other. It's like watching two clucky hens in designer pencil dresses fight over a nesting box.

"I am." Ruby Heather Ward straightens in her seat and pulls her ponytail over her shoulder. "Sorry, but I've forgotten your name?"

"Evelyn Reilly."

Eve never goes by Evelyn. If there is one thing she hates more than people texting during a movie, it's her legal name. Still, she puts stock in the power it seems to hold and uses it to assert dominance. What's more surprising is that it works. Especially when she completely ignores Ruby after their rerun of an introduction.

"This might not be exactly what you want right now, but I'm meeting Kit and Danny for dinner tonight. Alex will be there because Kit invited him, but you're welcome too. I can run interference, and we'll get Danny up to speed on the situation so he can help." Her sharp, flawless features soften. She won't push me on this.

"I'm working late," I say. "But I might stop by Kit's place after."

She accepts the lie and takes my hand, leaning down to exclude Ruby, who is doing a terrible job at pretending not to eavesdrop.

"Mom and Dad are good, so he won't be here much longer. Kit said the label is getting antsy from all the delays on the album, so he has to get back to New York. It will be like I don't have a brother again."

She says it for my benefit, but pretending her brother means nothing to her doesn't sit right. It's a reminder that I'm part of the reason they hardly speak. I downplayed my heartbreak and told her it was an amicable ending because he wasn't the only one I'd lose if it wasn't.

"Wait, wait." Ruby stands up, her spindly fingers gripping the partition. "The label?"

Eve turns her head slightly, not fully committing to giving her any attention.

"Is your brother Alex Reilly?" Ruby's eyes are wider than the distance I put between us daily, and my heart sinks. All this time, I've flown under the radar, and now she's a Google search away from discovering everything I'd like to keep buried.

"Wow. You are good at eavesdropping," Eve deadpans. "Now, back to spell-checking clickbait you go."

Ruby should look affronted, but she's wrapped up in a minor brush with fame, and it turns her cheeks pink. She's a hardcore fan of Alex's. The day she arrived, she had his first album playing on her phone. She'd forgotten her headphones but played it over and over, singing along to songs well outside her vocal range. She asked if it bothered me. I said I didn't care and then waited an appropriate amount of time before working from the supply closet.

"I could use Alex for my celebrity profile idea." Ruby ignores Eve's irritated stare. "He never does interviews. Shit, Spencer, why didn't you say something? This would be a game changer."

"There is a reason he doesn't do interviews," I say.

I'm pretty sure the reason is me.

"But if you know each other, he'll do it, right?" Ruby's full bottom lip rolls into a pout. It must be a reflex, but I'm not the target audience for it.

Eve swivels to face my coworker, and the smile she paints on has me cowering slightly. "Ruby, be a dear and go away. At no point were you invited to this conversation."

Her mouth hangs open, but Eve turns back to me.

"Can we have lunch now? I've got to let a bunch of childless millennials through an overpriced apartment."

CHAPTER FOUR

There is not, nor has there ever been, a shortage of parties in Bristol Court. Every milestone, holiday, and envelope opening is celebrated with a backyard barbeque that has at least three iterations of potato salad. Tonight, we're celebrating Judy and William Larson's fortieth wedding anniversary, and the potato salads include bacon and egg, spinach with herbs, and a vegan offering.

A few days ago, Mom called to say they were attending this barbeque and to avoid Dad. Clearly, she hoped I wasn't going so we could all pretend my relationship with my father was a functional one. It couldn't be further from that. Dad doesn't even acknowledge that he has a child. Not only did my Hail Mary article get *TGP* sued, but the subject of my feature was Dad's oldest friend, colleague, and confidant, Dr. Kirk Purcell, a slimy leech of a man who was harassing his staff. Of course, he's untouchable and paid off the victims, but my name on the byline made Dad the pariah in his professional and social circles. If Dad thinks I got away with the damage I caused, he couldn't be more wrong.

Over the last year, I've applied for multiple staff writer and beat reporter jobs at publications that actually populate a newsstand. I've never made it to an interview because while my Kirk Purcell article is good, I'm a liability. That's why my latest pursuit—a staff writer position at *The Herald*—is something I've only told Eve and Miles about so as not to get my hopes up.

The Herald is seven floors above my current desk. It's owned by the same media group, but it may as well be in a different dimension. Three weeks ago, I submitted an expression of interest for a position, and my email seems to have gotten lost somewhere between my sent folder and Nirvana. That, or they saw my name and weren't particularly interested in promoting the journalist who cost them a bundle in settlement money.

As curiosity about the application crosses my mind for the twentieth time today, my phone dings, and I scramble to grab it off the coffee table.

My heart sinks when I see it's an email for ten percent off at Market Street Stationery Emporium.

"Is this too much?" Eve asks as she tugs on the hem of her old sequin mini skirt.

"Yes." I nod. "It's the Larsons' backyard."

She huffs as she battles the invisible zipper on the side. "Jeans it is, then."

My meager living space is now buried under several suitcases containing Eve's entire wardrobe. Every day, she tells me she's looking for a place, and every day, I tell her she's welcome to stay as long as she wants. I really don't mind her being here. It's nice having someone to come home to, and we lived in each other's pockets growing up, so this feels normal. Except now we can legally drink, and no one can tell us we're spending too much on meal delivery services.

Actually, Kit can, and she does. Often.

My heart leaps at another phone ding, but it's Eve's this time. When she reads the screen, her face crumples. "Ah, shit. Alex is coming tonight. I thought he was going to sit this one out."

I raise a brow. "He knows Miles is going to be there, right?"

She types a reply as she talks. "Yeah, but I'm guessing Mom's forcing him to go. Alex will stay glued to her side, though. Dad's going, and she needs as many kids as she can get to act as buffers."

"Aren't you and Kit enough?"

She shakes her head. "Nope. Kit will hang off Danny all night, and the last thing I want to do is stand between my parents. Mom and I still aren't good."

"Bea really let the team down by moving to London."

"Tell me about it. You should have heard Mom going on about how her children are now scattered to the far reaches of the earth. Kit and Bea are identical twins. Just sit her next to a mirror and pretend Bea is there." Eve sighs as she wriggles into a pair of skintight black jeans and inspects herself in the mirror.

"I'm not sure you understand how maternal love works."

"And you're surprised? My brother is a rockstar, one of my sisters owns a business and does everyone's taxes, and the other one is giving Mom her first grandchild. I'm not exactly scoring goals in comparison, Spence."

Eve has these moments of unsolicited self-deprecation, but it's hard not to be envious of the woman. She's tall, perfectly curved, and walks like the world owes her a debt. There's a bit going on under the surface, but I'd give my left tit to have her posture and hair that healthy. Not to mention that she can seamlessly attach false eyelashes with unmatched precision and curl her hair with a flat iron. She says it's all about the angle, but I think she's just a wizard.

"I thought work was going well?"

"It's a job that I've held onto for more than six months. That's the yardstick that measures how well a job is going for me."

Eve rolls her shoulders back. This moment of vulnerability is a distant memory, and she resets herself and paints on a smile. I've heard of people lighting up a room, but I never fully grasped the concept until Eve grew up. Even though it's for show, she carries herself with an unattainable level of certainty. Despite her perceived societal failings, she exists for no one but herself. Alex is the same, but his confidence is quiet. You want to know him because when he looks at you, you're the only person in the room. You want to know what he's thinking because you know his thoughts are poetry.

"Are you ready?" Eve asks as she picks up her keys from the kitchen island. "Because I told Dad we'd pick him up ten minutes ago."

"I'm ready," I say as I gather my coat off the arm of the couch.

Doug Reilly has taken up residence in the post-separation cave that is the apartment above Whiskey Double. He seems to love it, but with Eve in need of accommodation, she's praying for the day he moves into a sparsely decorated one-bedroom beside a furniture clearance outlet. Eve says living above a bar means he's worse off in the divorce. He says he's being fiscally responsible and focusing on his career right now, though he seems to work fewer overtime shifts at the freight company and spends more time mixing drinks at Whiskey with Miles.

"Looking great, Doug." I give him a thumbs up, and he instinctively pats his hair down. It's more silver than black these days, but he's shaved and gotten himself a collection of new plaid button-downs. Tonight's offering is blue and red check, though it looks like he fished it out of a compacted laundry pile and lost interest after ironing the right sleeve.

Eve bolsters Doug's confidence on the drive over, and he accepts her positive affirmations, even though he doesn't understand them. Eve was very much in Doug's corner when they announced the divorce, and she's ensuring her dad prospers in his new single life. Many—myself included—would classify it as coddling. She has me pack up leftover meals for her to drop over four nights a week and requests updates from Miles about how his overhead tenant is going. Doug has little freedom under Eve's watch, and all he wants to do is eat cool ranch Doritos and watch World War II documentaries.

When we arrive at the Larsons' house, the party is in full swing. Coolers varying in size are lined up along the deck, and the fold-out tables have two more kinds of potato salad this time, which is a record for Bristol Court. The old plastic chairs are assembled in the same pattern as every backyard party that came before this one, and I feel like a kid again. Safe in the comfort of our cul-de-sac, and knowing to avoid Mrs. Hastings' gluten-free, dairy-free, and taste-free mud cake at all costs.

There's a break in every conversation as Eve, Doug, and I enter the backyard. It's only for a moment, but the residents of Bristol Court are trying to gauge an appropriate reaction to Doug and Elaine being in the same backyard at the same time. Elaine is busying herself with a stack of plates, and when she sees him, she puts the plates down and strolls over to say hello. This snaps the tension, and soon, Doug is pulled into the fold of dads critiquing imported beers and round-tabling when to flip the steaks on the grill. The Milfords from number six hijack Eve because they're looking at selling their apartment in Vail, and that leaves me, in plain sight, standing on the deck with my hands tucked into the pockets of my knock-off Burberry coat. I'm a sitting duck, and Mom zeros in immediately.

She saunters over in a white collared shirt adorned with strands of Chanel pearls that shine under the outdoor lighting. Her smile tests the limits of her latest Botox top-up, and when she's in reach, she brushes the ends of my hair with her fingertips before kissing my temple.

"Oh, darling, it might be time for a little trim," she says. "I've got some hydrating oil that can fix those ends if you'd like to pop over to the house before you leave."

The artificial pitch of her voice says more than her words. Namely, that I should fix my hair now and not return because the cardinal sin of using drugstore shampoo has blown my reputation in our neighborhood to smithereens.

I ignore the jab and crane my neck to scan the yard. "Where's Dad?"

"He'll be here soon. Surgery ran long." Mom is still smiling, but not for my benefit. She's told everyone Dad's in surgery, and she's ready to absorb the attention of being a surgeon's wife like gold coins in a video game. I can practically hear the cha-ching noise.

"Is he going to speak to me, or should I stay out of the way?"

Mom pats my forearm. "Best to give him space, I think, until you're ready to apologize."

My skin prickles. "I have apologized, even though I shouldn't, because him defending that predator is disgusting."

Mom puts her arm around me and rubs my shoulder. "Quiet now, darling. This isn't the place to talk like that."

She releases me and seamlessly joins another conversation. I'm not even out of earshot before she hijacks it with talk of an upcoming trip to Italy I know nothing about.

"Is your mom trying to start shit already? We've been here for five minutes," Eve grumbles as she takes my arm and guides me over to some vacant chairs at the side of the yard.

"It's fine. She said Dad's on his way." I exhale and smooth the ends of my hair.

Eve continues to grumble about my mother, but I miss the more cutting remarks because Alex has arrived. He nods politely and shakes Mr. Larson's hand before giving the rest of the yard a cursory glance. For a moment, I wonder if he's looking for me like he used to at these parties. Waiting to speak to me without prying eyes. After all these years, the tide has changed, and the piqued interest of our neighbors isn't an issue, so the moment he sees me, he walks over, head high.

"Hey, Pen. Can we talk?" he asks, voice even and body loose like he didn't break my heart four years ago.

"Not here, Alex. Leave her alone," Eve sighs, but I put my hand on her arm. Mom is watching from the deck, and I've already pissed her off with my subpar hair care. I don't need to cause a scene with Alex to further the judgment.

"It's fine. We can talk."

Eve looks at me for a long moment, worry knitting her brow. I share the concern, but he's here, standing in front of me, wanting to talk. It had to happen at some point.

With a huff, Eve vacates her seat, and Alex takes it as soon as she walks away. Not that she goes far. She lures Judy Larson into a conversation about stand mixers that's as deep as a kiddy pool so she can eavesdrop.

"I'm staying in Seattle for a while," he says matter-of-factly. "I just wanted to let you know."

"Eve told me, but you don't have to explain yourself. It's

not my business, Alex." The words come out pettier than intended, and I inwardly scold myself for it. *I'm better than this. And what happened the other night, with the hoodie, was nothing. I was tired.*

"Okay." Alex exhales slowly. "I didn't want to make you uncomfortable."

"I'm not uncomfortable."

"Good."

"It's very good." I fold my arms, then unfold them immediately.

Alex leans back in his seat and looks over at Eve, who's as relaxed as a cornered rattlesnake. We've also garnered the interest of a few other guests. Mostly my mother, with her eyes narrowed and pointed chin high, a lecture crawling up her throat. It's wasted because as far as the neighborhood knows, Alex and I had an amicable breakup.

I worked overtime to make it seem that way. In truth, it killed me, and I became so consumed with hurt and rage, I couldn't stand the mention of his name.

I also saved all the voicemails he left me, and I listened to them over and over, crying myself to sleep.

And I still have my wedding dress.

Everything I want to say to him dissolves as I picture that dress in the back of my closet. The pearl beadwork and champagne color I thought he'd love. Then I remember the smeared mascara on the neckline and the dirt on the hem from sitting on the curb outside the chapel.

He looks over at me, fingers digging into his denim-clad knees, and I can't articulate the thoughts that race through my mind.

"How's work?" he asks, eyes darting away.

"I write hard-hitting pieces about celebrities who edit their bikini photos and professional athletes getting into bar fights."

His mouth lifts slightly at the corner. "I'm sure it's more than that."

"It's not."

He shakes his head. "No. I read the piece you wrote about the doctor. It was great."

"It cost me my relationship with my dad."

"What relationship?" he asks.

I don't acknowledge the joke. "Well, it got me nowhere. I'm still writing fluff."

I don't know why we're doing this. Why we're pretending to be friends and making smalltalk under string lights with our neighbors watching. We aren't the same anymore, and if he's trying to smooth everything over, I don't want it. I don't want to talk about my floundering career, and I don't want his sympathy. It only invites a comparison between us, and it's a game I'll lose every time. Because he lost nothing, and I lost everything.

There is a cheer from the opposite corner of the yard, and I look up to see Dad has arrived. He's immediately accepted into the fold of dads without looking for Mom or me. He just takes the tumbler of scotch he's handed and begins telling an inflated story about his round of golf with the other heads of department last Saturday. The dads of Bristol Court eat it up, craving more and looking at him with adoration. Suddenly, a heavy realization hits. No matter what I do to gain his respect or even a hint of admiration, I'll never get it, just like everyone else in his life, because we're all in his shadow. Even at night.

Alex clears his throat, and I notice Eve is on her way over to us. She's timed the interaction, and Alex's two minutes are up.

"Time for a drink?" She directs the comment to me, but her brother takes the hint and stands up.

"It was good to see you," he says, his hand resting briefly on my shoulder.

The universe tilts for a second. He's touching me, and against my better judgment, I feel a sudden, fleeting high. Like a craving, however small, has been satisfied. A craving that has no business existing.

I miss the opportunity to respond because he's already making his way toward Elaine.

Eve watches him with eagle eyes as she slinks into the chair next to me. "What did he say?"

I wrap my arms around myself. "He just wanted to let me know he'll be in Seattle for a while."

Eve sighs, though her disgruntled stare is boring a hole in Alex's back. "You're so much better than me. I'd be keying his car or posting his phone number on social media."

I pat her hand and lie through my teeth. "Don't worry about it. He won't cause any problems."

"Speaking of causing problems." She inclines her head, and I follow her eyeline to see Miles step out into the yard.

There are shadows under his brown eyes, and he hasn't shaved in days. Whiskey has been taking it out of him since he lost a staff member to a long-distance romance and another one to a rather delusional dream of joining the pro poker circuit. His social life has also taken a hit; I really miss our heated Monopoly tournaments on Sundays. He somehow always ends up with a hotel on Mayfair while I have to liquidate my assets as he grins wickedly with his hand out.

That grin is a distant memory because he's spotted Alex at the other end of the deck, and you could cut the tension of their silent exchange with a knife. Their childhood friendship ended years ago, but The Larsons' anniversary party isn't the time to unpack that. Eve gets it and immediately lifts her hand, waving Miles over. He hesitates before crossing the deck, and

Alex sheepishly watches his every step, unsure whether to attempt a conversation. Thankfully, he turns his attention back to his mother and doesn't react when Miles bumps his shoulder on the way past.

"Why is he here?" Miles hisses under his breath when he reaches us. "It's my parents' party. He should know to stay away."

"He's leaving soon," I say.

"How soon?"

"I don't know." I shrug as I dig my vibrating phone out of my pocket.

It's a Seattle number I don't recognize, and that causes a sudden spike in my blood pressure. Eve and Miles both lean over to look at the screen, Alex forgotten.

"Is this it?" Miles shifts his weight from foot to foot.

I reach for Eve's hand, and she takes mine in both of hers, holding it up to her heart. "You got this. I know it."

I take a fortifying breath as I lift the phone to my ear. "Hi, this is Spencer."

"Spencer." A deep and vaguely familiar voice comes down the line. "Max Marlow from *The Herald* here. Have you got a second?"

I grin at Eve and nod my head. "Yes, of course. How are you, Max?"

Eve stamps her perfect little sample-sized feet and looks up at the heavens while Miles crosses his fingers and closes his eyes.

"Good, good," he says. "Listen, I read your EOI for the staff writer position. Are you still interested?"

"Yes. Very interested." I clench my jaw to steady my voice.

"Great. Come up and see me tomorrow at eleven, and we'll talk," Max says.

"I'll be there." I squeeze Eve's hand, and she winces a little. "Thank you, Max. I really appreciate—"

He hangs up before I finish speaking.

"Is it happening?" Eve squeals. "Is this the big one?"

"I think it might be." My whole body shakes, and my head is foggy. *No more Ruby. No more pointless quizzes. No more being a deer in the headlights at staff meetings. And no more walking on eggshells around Natalia.*

"Max Marlow wants to meet with me tomorrow." My voice rattles with excitement, and Eve whoops loudly, bringing the party's attention to us.

Miles scoops me up and spins me around. "Fuck yes! I told you this would happen."

I'm barely able to catch my breath, and my heart is thundering when he sets me back on the ground.

"We need more drinks." Eve claps her hands together and looks around for the nearest cooler, promptly relieving one of our neighbors of their imported beer.

CHAPTER FIVE

Dear Alex,

    We spoke tonight.

    In the Larsons' backyard.

    You looked at me like we're friends. It made my throat tighten and my palms sweat. We aren't friends, and I felt compelled to tell you that. I felt compelled to tell you a lot of things. The words were there, but I couldn't form a sentence to accurately explain how it felt to see you again. The drive home with Eve was silent, and now I'm in my room, thinking about you and how it's time we talked. Even if you never read this, it's time to share our story.

    The way I saw it.

    The way I lived it.

    So, let's go back to the start. Or close to it.

    I'll never forget the night you broke up with Gretchen. From my bedroom window, I saw the two of you parked outside your house. Gretchen was screaming, her hands flailing wildly, and her body turned in the passenger seat to face you.

You were staring straight ahead, your long body sunken and your mouth completely still.

She was too much for you. Too outgoing. Too demanding. Too obsessed.

She was also best friends with Eve and me.

She talked like she knew everything about you. Falsehoods she concocted to fill the spaces because she wanted your paper-thin relationship to be something bigger. She didn't know your favorite food was lasagna, but only the one your mother made. Or that you rubbed the pad of your thumb over your wrist bone when you were nervous. She didn't know you hated horror movies, listened to new songs three times in a row to decide if you liked them, or how rearranging your vinyl collection was your favorite way to unwind.

She didn't even bother to learn those things.

Your argument grew heated, and when you didn't fight back, Gretchen climbed out of the car, slammed the door, and shouted something as she smacked the hood with her palm. You didn't flinch. You didn't speak. You didn't do anything.

I watched Gretchen storm across the street toward my house and raced to my front door before she could knock. When I swung it open, she said nothing. She simply stood on my stoop, her heart-shaped face devoid of the rosy glow that made her shine with innocence. Her eyes were dull and bloodshot, and her cornsilk hair was knotted on top of her head. She wasn't angry. She was defeated.

She didn't see the error in her ways, though. She didn't see that she came on too strong. She showed you every extroverted part of herself and needed you to match her energy. That wasn't you. You were quiet and contemplative. Speaking only when you knew exactly what to say. Gretchen accepted that at the start because being in your orbit was satisfying enough.

She told everyone what it was like to sit beside you, run her hand through your dark hair, and drive around on Friday nights, listening to bands no one had ever heard of and never would. Gretchen told those same stories over and over. It filled me with irrational jealousy. I'd shake with irritation as she embellished each story until I realized they were the only stories she had. There was nothing below the surface. No chemistry, no desire. There were conversationless car rides and the occasional brush of your hair. She wanted you too much, and you didn't want her at all. It made me wonder why you dated her.

It took Gretchen hours to fall asleep that night, and when her breathing steadied and she rolled over to face the window, I snuck across the street and into your backyard to the place that would come to mean so much to us.

Do you remember your dad building that treehouse from the magazine lift out?

After seven arduous weekends, the small structure took shape. Doug was immensely proud, even though it looked like a distant cousin of the one in the picture. The ladder was flimsy, the windows were small, it was like sitting in a shipping crate, and that bent nail in the door frame ripped the sleeves of many jackets.

In spite of its structural flaws, it was still the happiest place on earth.

I climbed that rickety ladder, and you greeted me with soft eyes and called me Pen. To this day, you are the only one to ever call me that, and I loved the sound of it on your lips.

You moved to the side, your long legs stretching out as you settled back against the wall and steadied the guitar on your lap. Your leg pressed against mine, and I read into that more than you can imagine. You didn't move, and I felt like a magnet, completely incapable of separating myself from you. Forever tethered in some way.

I told you how devastated Gretchen was, and you delicately plucked the strings of your guitar. I didn't want to talk about her, but she was the elephant in that tiny wooden box. You ended it for the most obvious reason. You didn't care about her as much as she cared about you. I asked you why you dated her in the first place, and all you did was shrug.

For what it's worth, I do believe she loved you. But I also don't believe she knew what love was.

At the time, I couldn't attest to that either. I was eighteen and spent most of my adolescence watching you from across the room. You were bigger than me, though. Always greater and more impressive. Something to want but never have. I shrank in comparison, and you wanting me was impossible.

You continued to strum your guitar, lifting your knee slightly so less of us touched. I overthought that too. You changed the subject to my college acceptances. Talking about college felt like a waste of our limited time.

I told you my parents were mad that I was going to be a journalist. You said they were always mad and not to worry because I'd prove them wrong with my success.

My heart squeezed in my chest almost violently at those flippant words of yours. How could an off-the-cuff remark restore the faith I'd lost in myself?

I'd spent years thinking about what it would be like to kiss you. I'd wondered what your mouth tasted like and if your lips were soft. That was the first night I felt like I needed to know for sure. I ached to the point where I couldn't focus on what you were saying.

I should have listened, but I needed you.

I shifted so my leg touched yours again right before we heard the thump of sneaker-clad feet on the ladder. Gretchen appeared, her phone held high over her head to cast us in torchlight. I shielded my eyes, and you turned your face into my shoulder. I felt your hair brush my cheek, and it smelled like cinnamon. You'd used Eve's shampoo.

Gretchen demanded to know what we were doing, and even though we both denied any wrongdoing, she didn't believe us. For months to come, she retold that story, embellishing it more and more each time. We were kissing. We were naked. I was on your lap.

Gretchen spat vitriol at both of us before she ran off.

The next day, she told Eve her inflated version of her discovery. It was gratuitous and made me a monster. Thankfully, I calmed Eve down enough to explain. She said she believed me and told Gretchen that nothing was going on. Gretchen accused her of being party to my betrayal. Our friendship with her never recovered, and it broke Eve's heart. She'd done nothing wrong and lost one of her best friends.

That was when she made me promise to never get involved with you.

And I broke that promise a hundred times over.

CHAPTER SIX

At ten-forty a.m., I step out of the elevator into the luxurious 1920s hotel-style lobby of *The Herald.* Dark wood paneling lines the walls, and the brass wall sconces cast a soft yellow light over the space. Hartfield, our parent company, blew the decor budget up here. The heavy chocolate leather couches are a far cry from the molded plastic chair and IKEA table that sits outside our elevator. Behind *The Herald* reception desk is a backlit sign, bordered with an ostentatious gold frame. It's over the top, for sure, but I want it to be the first thing I see when I arrive at work every morning. As the thought sweeps through my jittery mind, I picture Natalia's look of disgust when I tell her I'm leaving *TGP* to work for Max Marlow.

Their long-standing rivalry is famous in the building, so naturally, Natalia undersold how impressive this office is. She also omitted the copious number of prestigious media awards bearing his name on display in a glass case beside the counter.

My hands are shaking even more when I say a quick hello to Ginny, the receptionist, and she directs me down a wide hallway. The same paneling and elaborate sconces line the wall to the executive offices, and the air smells fresher, lacking the artificial pine smell the *TGP* desks are slathered with each night. It's crisp, floral, and delicate. Like expensive perfume is being pumped through the ducting. It does nothing to ease my nerves. If anything, the pressure amps up. It's what I imagine drowning feels like; I can't catch my breath. Panic is washing over me in increasingly debilitating waves, and I'm suddenly nauseous.

I continue my walk toward Max's office and pass the carved archway leading to the bullpen, which, like the rest of the office, is high-end and minimalist. Every desk and chair matches, and the cubicles are impeccably neat, uncluttered. Soft music plays through an inbuilt speaker system, complimenting the sound of fingers skittering across keyboards. It's a modern architect's take on an old newspaper office, and I've never wanted anything more than the vacant desk in the front corner. I can picture my name on a little black plaque in fine gold lettering.

When I reach Max Marlow's door, I can see he's on the phone through a small section of unfrosted glass. He's wearing a dark navy suit, crisp white shirt, and a tie that's the exact shade of the suit. His impeccable dress sense and perfect posture contribute to the intimidation. Aside from the phone call, the only time we've spoken was in the elevator six months ago. I held the door, he said thank you and gave me three seconds of eye contact. I was not ready for it. He didn't look at me; he looked through me with intense gray eyes that made sharing his space feel criminal.

I hover at the door for a moment before he gestures for me to enter. His phone conversation isn't over, but he points at the seat opposite his desk, and I pretend not to listen to every word he is saying. He's approving funds for a reporter to cover an oil spill in the Gulf. It's the story I pitched to Natalia a week ago when the oil company refused to take responsibility for the damage. It was "shelved" in favor of a story about an influencer who got put on blast for demanding free accommodation for a social media post.

I guess I know where my pitch ended up.

Max is on the phone for another five minutes. He faces away for most of it, only turning occasionally to make sure I'm still here. When he wraps up the call and sits down behind his oversized cherrywood desk, my heart rattles my ribs all over again.

"Spencer." His voice is deep, firm, and infinitely more intimidating when paired with his icy gaze. I'm an imposter in this dark office with its leather-bound books, charcoal carpet, and the greatest investigative journalists in the country.

"Thank you for agreeing to meet with me, Mr. Marlow."

He doesn't ask me to call him Max, instead shuffling a collection of job applications on the desk in front of him. He's looking for mine because he doesn't know a thing about me outside of me being a current Hartfield employee.

I, on the other hand, know a lot about him. I know that he's twice divorced, and his second wife got way less than the first. He has no children; his desire not to have them is what ended his second marriage. He plays golf on Sunday afternoons, will only fly coach if the flight is under ninety minutes, and his favorite food is the medium-rare New York strip with garlic butter from the steak house three blocks away. Most days, he stays at the office until it's completely dark out. Except Thursdays, when he takes his aging golden retriever to her hydrotherapy appointment.

"I need a staff writer for general beat stories," he says.

"I can do that." The words come out in a rush, and I notice how far forward I'm sitting in his tufted burgundy leather guest chair. Max doesn't look up. He's focused on the applications in front of him, and mine has floated to the surface.

"I enjoyed your piece on that doctor. You write well. It's a shame he paid off the victims."

My brain momentarily stalls. When the article first went to print, I got a pat on the back from everyone at *TGP*, and a few of *The Herald* reporters praised it when I ran into them at the deli across the street. Even Natalia bought me a black coffee with no sugar—the way I hate it—as a subtle form of congratulations. I was the toast of the office until the suit. Then it was like my article and I didn't exist. Hearing Max comment on it so freely is jarring.

"Thank you. I worked hard on it."

"And to go after a close friend of your father's. That takes guts." Max looks up, and the corner of his mouth lifts slightly. "I'm sure Christmas was awkward for you."

I quickly realize I haven't given Max enough credit. Of course, he's done his research. He probably knows my date of birth, college grades, and every facet of my high school newspaper career. But he doesn't care about any of that. He wants to know what I'm made of. He wants to know what I'll do for a story.

"Dr. Purcell being a close friend of my dad doesn't make him immune to the consequences of his actions. Regardless of the retraction, he can't bribe his way out of the accusation. It'll forever be a mark on the reputation he paid a lot of money to maintain."

He studies me for a moment, sharp-jawed and crystal-eyed. The late morning sun streams in through the window, highlighting the slight copper tones in his hair. Honestly, it's a wonder he hasn't had more wives.

"I'm not in a rush to fill this position with just anyone. I want someone who deserves to be here. A reporter who can bring me something worth my time *and* the front page. What are you working on right now?"

My hands grow clammier when I think about the story I've been drafting this morning about a B-list actress who's made the jump to porn. It's not worthy of lining a birdcage, let alone gracing the front page of a newspaper housed in an office with three different sources of ambient lighting.

I straighten my back and smooth the front of my teal silk blouse. *I have something better. I always have something better, even though it's constantly crushed by Natalia.* "Have you heard of Florence Ritter?"

"The actress who was murdered in the forties?" He leans forward, thick fingers splayed on the smooth surface of his desk.

"There is a huge online community still investigating the case. A few weeks ago, the official case file was unsealed, and there might have been some police corruption."

Max is quiet for so long, my hands sweat again. *Maybe Florence isn't interesting enough.* A collective interest in true crime has over-saturated the internet with opinion over facts, and a mostly forgotten up-and-coming actress wouldn't get as many page reads as a state senator getting his nanny pregnant.

Max folds his arms across his chest. "Bring me the story. If I like it, we can talk about that vacant desk."

An astronomical wave of excitement hits me, and my words meet the perfumed air with a hurried whoosh. "Thank you for the opportunity. I won't let you down."

"Good," Max says. "I want quality, Spencer. Real investigative reporting. Facts with supporting evidence. Interviews. The works. I want it polished too."

I hold his gaze and dip my chin.

"I'll get you the story," I say it with conviction, even though my voice shakes.

When I arrive at my desk and sift through the folder on my desktop containing my Florence research, I realize how surface-level it is. It's all public records and theories from internet blogs. I'm going to have to try harder because I need this job more than oxygen. I was born for it. I believed that through every screaming match I had with Dad and every time Mom looked at me with disappointment in her eyes. I believed it when I walked across the stage at my college graduation and saw Doug, Elaine, Eve, Bea, Kit, and Alex cheering for me in the stands.

This is my chance, and I can dig deeper. I can give Max the article he wants.

"You look happy," Ruby says. "I take it you've heard the good news then?"

My smile disappears, because if Ruby says it's good, then it probably isn't. "What good news?"

She swivels her chair, dramatically folds one leg over the other, and lifts her shoulders. "Oh, it's nothing really."

She pauses for effect, but I shrug and get back to work. Last I heard, she was working on a piece about shopping for dogs that can be crossbred to make designer pets. It costs thousands, and there is no guarantee the dog will have the selected features from each breed. The actual story would be how it can go drastically wrong, and these poor animals end up with compromised skull cavities and respiratory problems.

"Natalia signed off on one of my ideas!" she screeches, sensing my lack of interest. "I'm doing a profile on Alex Reilly!"

She lets out a breathy scream before slapping her hand over her mouth. This over-the-top reaction is a tad premature. Alex doesn't do interviews, and just because Natalia gives something the green light doesn't mean she'll decide to run it. This whole thing will be an exercise in disappointment for Ruby.

"How do you know he'll do the profile?" I ask.

"Of course he will." She laughs it off. "No one says no to Natalia."

Sure, in this building, no one says no to Natalia, but I doubt Alex is going to give up his interview hiatus because an online gossip magazine asked him to. Still, I'm not thrilled about my work life and past romantic entanglement colliding.

"Has Natalia even spoken to him? Or his team?"

Ruby waves off my concern. "Probably. She said she was going to and then work out a time to meet."

This wouldn't be the first time Ruby has oversold something, but I'd like to hear exactly what's going on from the source.

Natalia is sitting at her desk, long legs crossed and her fingers dancing across her laptop keyboard. She's backlit by the midday sun, and she doesn't have a single flyaway. It's a scientific impossibility, as are the unblemished, bright red soles of her shoes. It's like she floated here.

I hold my breath as I knock gently on the door frame.

"Natalia, can we chat for a sec?"

She finishes whatever she is working on before she looks up at me. "Come in."

I close the door and take the seat opposite her, noticing this office has the same oppressive vibe as Max's, though its color palette is more coastal cool than luxurious smoker's lounge.

"How did your interview with Max go?" she asks, because

of course she knows about it, and it would be remiss of me to think she didn't.

"It went great. He's asked me to submit a story."

"Florence Ritter?" She closes the lid of her laptop and folds her hands on top of it, her fresh, black manicure shining under the recessed lighting.

I nod. "It's a really interesting case."

"It is, and I'm happy you're pursuing it. But you understand you'll be working on it in your own time. You still have a job to do here."

"Of course. It won't affect my work here."

"Good," she says, tilting her head like my allotted time has come to a close, and she's confused by my continued presence in her space.

I twist my fingers in my lap as Ruby's giddy expression fills my head, along with flashes of Alex in our conference room, sipping water from the fancy glassware that no one is allowed to touch. Ruby will playfully slap his forearm as he regales her with stories of his parties in the Hollywood Hills and tour antics.

"Ruby said you've signed off on a profile for Alex Reilly. Is that true?"

"It is. I've got a call scheduled with his manager in an hour to discuss it."

My heart stutters for a moment. There is no way Alex is actually considering this. He refuses to do lighthearted late-night talk show interviews. He won't sit down with Ruby and offer a play-by-play of every one of his mistakes. He hasn't changed that much.

"Is that a problem, Spencer?"

I shake my head and force a smile. "Great. I think it's wonderful. A great opportunity for Ruby too."

I wrap my fingers around the armrests, my trimmed nails pressing into the white leather.

"Do you want the profile?" Her head tilts to the side.

"No. Thank you. I'm doing red-carpet fashion reviews this week, so that will keep me busy."

Natalia's lips curve up in a smile, but her eyes don't reflect it. They tell a different story. Namely, that she's done her research, and the internet can't be scrubbed clean of all the photos of Alex that I'm in the background of.

CHAPTER SEVEN

Dear Alex,

    I've often wondered if my parents wanted me at all. I remember asking Mom why she became a mother. She said it was because that's what you did after you got married. I was young, but I knew that societal expectation wasn't a good enough reason to create a person. From then on, I noticed how other mothers behaved with their children. Elaine responded to Santa letters with handmade postage stamps from the North Pole Postal Service. Judy Larson was front and center at every hockey game, track meet, book event, and end-of-year concert. Eve and Miles always said how lucky I was that my parents gave me money for lunch each day while they ate turkey sandwiches and home-baked chocolate chip cookies. I didn't feel lucky when my mother slapped cash into my hand with a groan and told me to take care of myself.

    Feeding me was an inconvenience, and when I was included, they made no concessions for my age or personal preference. At five, I was eating lobster and drinking from crystal while being relentlessly scolded because my small hands couldn't grasp the glassware tightly enough. Meanwhile, across the street, Elaine was making mac and cheese and reading bedtime stories. At first, I found her nurturing strange. There was nothing transactional about it. She met basic parental requirements and expected nothing in return. My parents had expectations in exchange for food and shelter. I was to be quiet, clean, and present when it suited them. I was, for all intents and purposes, decoration.

I was supposed to follow in Dad's footsteps. Be great, but not better than him. Be amiable, but not a doormat. Be bold but not opinionated.

To Mom, I was designed to collect compliments because I wasn't my own person; I was a product of her, and her achievement was worthy of recognition. I looked like her, smiled like her, and barely spoke like her. I existed to elevate those around me, not steal focus. A doll. Perfect in every way. Never letting a single crack show.

That's why I spent every waking moment at your house. It felt like more of a home than mine. There were photos of Christmas Day, birthday parties, and school portraits. The soft furnishings were bought for comfort, not aesthetics, and there was always music and laughter. My house, comparatively, was a commercial office space, colorless and still. In place of dollhouses and toy boxes, there were bar carts and medical journals. I remember being told off for doing my homework on the floor of the living room instead of the dining table, for fear I would damage the rug. My mother called me selfish and ignorant.

My dad agreed.

I was seven.

Your family taught me what a family was supposed to be. Joy and love, pride in each other's achievements, and squabbles that were quickly forgotten. Elaine taught me how to cook. Doug taught me how to check the oil in my car. Eve taught me how to braid my hair. Everything I needed came from your family. Every night, after dinner, when I crossed the street and stepped through my own front door, neither of my parents asked where I'd been. They didn't ask if I'd eaten, done my homework, or if I'd had a good day. When Dad wasn't at the hospital, he was in his study, sipping scotch and discussing tee times over the phone with the other department heads. Mom was always pottering around her expansive walk-in closet, rearranging her designer clothes, jewelry, shoes, and purses. All those possessions made her so happy. I wondered if there was one thing in particular that made her happier than any other. She wore her Chanel pearls a lot and favored her YSL purse and Hermes belt. But it soon became clear that it wasn't any individual possession that made her happy. It was the collective, and the more she had, the better she felt.

I think that's what drove her to purchase things in excess for me. When her closet was full, she filled mine in her style. When I was old enough, she treated me like an extension of her. She took me to the salon and colored my hair the same shade as hers. I was primped and preened, molded into her replica, and expected to be grateful for the experience. I wanted to go to the hockey rink with Eve and the Larsons. I wanted to go to the mall and buy ripped jeans and flavored lip gloss. I wanted to be a teenage girl. Not a prop.

The most heartbreaking moment came with my college acceptance. I went from a minor inconvenience to a major disappointment. My mom took a break from criticizing the way I looked and switched to my career choice. The house went from passive indifference to outright hostility, and I questioned if what I wanted for my future was worth the pain.

After that, I relished the time I spent sleeping on the floor of Eve's bedroom. It became routine. While Mom and Dad were out of the house, I'd collect the things I needed before coming back to your place. On Wednesdays, I'd cook dinner using recipes from your grandmother's old cookbooks, and every night before bed, you and I stood side by side in the bathroom and cleaned our teeth.

After three nights, you laughed and asked if I came here often. From then on, we found ourselves on the same teeth-cleaning schedule. It wasn't a coincidence because when I heard your footsteps on the stairs, I'd sneak into the bathroom, put toothpaste on my brush, and wait.

One of my fondest memories at your house was after my second semester of college. Eve was throwing a party to celebrate her passing grade, and Jake Dennison, her then soul-crushing love, had shown up. He was leaning against the fence with his hands in the pockets of his jeans, and Eve insisted that never had a more handsome man existed.

After an hour of flirtatious conversation, Eve and Jake went to her room. I didn't want to go back to my place, and sitting alone in the living room while the party continued around me was sad. So, I wandered upstairs. When I passed your bedroom, I saw you lying on your bed, legs bent at the knees, eyes closed, and your fingers drumming against your stomach to the beat of the music you were listening to on the record player Kit and Bea had saved all their money to get you for your birthday. I leaned on the door frame, arms folded as I watched you. I wanted to lay there beside you, feel your body pressed against mine.

You opened an eye and looked at me with what I hoped was silent appreciation of the blue gingham mini dress I'd spent way too much on in the vain hope of a moment like this with you. You invited me in, and I watched from your bed as you flicked through your extensive vinyl collection. You selected *Tapestry* by Carole King. It was cute how you pressed your tongue between your teeth as you dropped the needle. It was like you were performing surgery.

I recognized the song. Elaine and Doug danced to it once after a boozy Thanksgiving dinner when they genuinely believed they would be together forever. We listened to every song on side A, and you hummed along. I watched your lips move and your eyes close. When it ended, and the room fell silent, you ushered me over to the turntable and showed me how to flip the record. Your hands guided mine, and we smiled at each other when "You've Got A Friend" started playing.

We returned to the bed and settled with our backs against the headboard. I watched you tap your foot along to "Where You Lead". As the song faded out, you turned to look at me. I didn't know what to do, but I couldn't look away.

You sang to me then. Not a low hum or mumbled lyrics under your breath. You sang "Will You Love Me Tomorrow?". And you sang it with feeling.

You didn't move closer, and even though the words weren't yours, the shift in our dynamic was seismic. It reminded me of the night in the treehouse and the guilt I felt afterward. Gretchen and Eve weren't friends anymore, and I'd made a promise that cost me a shot with you. A shot that I could have taken right then.

You looked down at my lips, and for a brief moment, I thought maybe this wouldn't end badly for us. We would be different, and Eve would be okay with it.

My skin prickled, and I glanced down at our hands. They were resting on the bed, barely an inch apart. I counted three little white scars across the back of your fingers and wondered how each of them came to be and if it had hurt at the time. When I lifted my eyes back to yours, there was something in them, an electricity that matched the way my body sang every time I was around you. We felt foreign to each other then like we'd changed shape right there on your dusty blue comforter in one of the oldest houses in Bristol Court. You'd evolved into something greater and more enchanting than before. You studied my face, and it made me acutely aware of the freckles across my nose and the eyeshadow that was a little darker on my right eye than my left.

You turned my hand over, singing beautifully as you traced the lines on my palm with your fingertips. The world quieted. We were both lost in the moment, and I was so thankful because it felt endless.

CHAPTER EIGHT

When I wake on Friday morning, everything is perfect. My hair sits the way I want it to. My favorite pants fit better than the last time I wore them, and there is no line at the coffee place on my way to work. I even snag the space closest to the elevator in the parking garage, and Eve texts to say she's taking care of dinner so I can relax after my long week at work.

All this good should be a sign that something bad is on the horizon, and I know exactly what that is when I reach the office and see Ruby already sitting at her desk. There is only one thing she would come in early for, and I'm sick at the thought.

He said yes.

Why would he say yes?

Ruby smiles politely as I sit down at my desk. I return the silent greeting, open my laptop, and take a deep breath, firmly believing that if I don't look at Ruby, Alex won't crash into my work life.

"I have a lead on a suburban housewife in Tacoma that's been running a coupon scam in the pickup line at her kid's school." Ruby hangs over the low wall that separates our desks. "It's more your speed than mine, and I need to prepare for my meeting with Alex."

I turn to face her, moving my neck from side to side to relieve the headache that's coming on. "I've got a lot going on right now, Ruby. Can't you give it to someone else?"

"But Natalia wants it ASAP," she whines. "And did you not hear me say I have to do interview prep for Alex?"

"I heard you. But you can't delegate your workload because you want to focus on one particular project." I frown at her as the elevator door opens, and Natalia steps out.

She's dressed in her usual all-black ensemble, her severe bob swishing as she moves through the office like a predator moves through a jungle. Watching this only reinforces how much I want to be her. I think it's the way she carries herself. Intimidating for sure, but the confidence that radiates off her is tangible.

"Ruby. Spencer." She snaps her fingers. "Let's go."

Ruby is off her chair so fast that it spins as we follow Natalia through the bullpen to her office. I'm assuming this meeting is to load me up with Ruby's work while she wines and dines my ex-boyfriend.

"I got another call from Alex's manager, Amalie Kent last night," Natalia says in a clipped tone before Ruby and I sit down. "Alex is on the fence about the profile. He doesn't like interviews, and with a new album in the works, his team isn't sure a profile that explores his past is the best image they want to put out there."

Ruby looks at me, doe-eyed, before she collapses into overwrought laughter that renders both Natalia and me speechless.

"Ahh, I'm sorry." Ruby wipes invisible tears as she stops laughing. "That's hilarious."

Natalia's microbladed brows draw together, and her blush pink lips press into a line.

"Ruby." Her tone has its usual edge. "Be quiet."

Ruby's cheeks flush, her almond-shaped nails dig into the back of the chair, and her synapses start to fire. It's a rapid build, but the rage she's poised to unleash comes out as a petulant whinge.

"That's so unfair. They said he'd do it. They can't just change their minds like that."

I think I'm witnessing the first time Ruby has been denied something, and from the slackness of Natalia's jaw, I'm guessing she is confused by this outburst as well.

"They can back out if they want to, Ruby," she says. "But I've convinced Amalie to have Alex attend the meeting today so we can discuss it and he can set boundaries on what he doesn't want mentioned."

Ruby's shoulders slump like a grumpy child's. "So you're saying he won't let me write about any of the interesting stuff. It will be an album promo."

Natalia grinds her teeth as she suppresses the urge to spit venom. It's the first time I've ever seen a wrinkle on her forehead, but it swiftly disappears when she takes a deep breath.

"This is still an opportunity. Now, pull yourself together. They'll be here in an hour."

On the walk back to our desks, I expect Ruby to unleash hell on Natalia under her breath, but she's dead quiet. Not a word of vitriol escapes her plumped lips, and as she sits down, I notice the flush of pink across her high cheekbones and the tears that swell in her eyes.

"Ruby?" I slide my chair closer and keep my voice low. "Are you okay?"

She shakes her head, looks up to the heavens, and fans her face with her hands. I've never seen her cry before. Only those exaggerated happy tears she cries when she's presented with the same pound cake everyone else gets on their birthday at *TGP*.

"It's just that... I... I thought... this was going to be a big break for me... you know?" She yanks a tissue from the box in her top drawer and pats her mascara-smudged eyes.

"It could be." I lie, knowing that Alex will never give her the juicy gossip she is looking for.

She looks at the crumpled tissue in her hand, shoulders slumped, and her slight frame sinking further down in her chair. She's small, withdrawn, and trying not to be noticed by the neighboring desk clump. It's unsettling because, under normal circumstances, she'd announce the slightest inconvenience to those around us to collect condolences before she moved on to the next minor injustice.

"You said he doesn't do interviews." She sniffles.

"I haven't spoken to him in years. He might have changed his mind."

She looks up at me, eyes red-rimmed and tears collecting on her fake lashes. "So you think he'll do it?"

"I don't know, Ruby. Is it really that big of a deal if he doesn't? We can find someone else."

"It is a big deal. He is a big deal, and this was supposed to..." She trails off, and a fresh wave of silent tears hits. I crane my head to peer over the partition. Everyone around us has headphones on while their fingers dance over their keyboards. I move a little closer to Ruby.

"What is this really about? Because it seems a lot bigger than not getting to interview a musician."

She blinks back more tears and shakes her head. "It's nothing. I'm fine."

It's obviously not fine, but Ruby effectively ends our conversation with a dash to the bathroom. A few minutes later, she returns looking as put together as usual and immediately returns to work, which in itself is alarming.

For the next forty-five minutes, Ruby and I pretend we aren't glancing at the elevator every few seconds. My stomach is already in knots, and when that violent ding echoes through our overcrowded, dimly lit office space, my heart crawls into my throat.

"He's here." Ruby jumps up from her chair, and in a moment of panicked weakness, I duck my head down so I can't be seen as he walks past my desk. I hear his voice, though, soft and low as he greets Ruby. The most meaningful words I've ever heard were spoken in that voice. Words that made my heart flutter, my skin tingle, and my world shatter.

And now that voice is thanking Ruby for the invitation to the offices of the least reputable news source in the Pacific Northwest.

When they're safely in the conference room, I sneak a peek over the partition behind my desk. He's standing by the door, hair perfectly pushed back and staying there as if held by magic. I hate how good he looks, and I hate that he's existing in my space while looking that good. It isn't fair that I have an eleven-step skincare routine, limit my greasy food intake, and have to dye my hair every six weeks to make sure I don't look anywhere near thirty. But here he is, thirty-two, flawless skin, midnight hair, and the same blinding smile that made me fall in love with him.

I turn back to my computer, busying myself with Florence's untimely demise while trying not to think about what Ruby is saying to Alex. I fail miserably, and after several glances toward the conference room, slip out of my cubicle and hurry off to battle with the ancient vending machine for some stale barbeque chips. As I pry them from the rusted flap, Ruby bursts into the room, chest heaving and patting her eyes with a tissue that has become paper mache in her delicate hand.

"He won't do it," she sobs as she drops onto a chair that has one leg slightly shorter than the other.

I lean my head out and see the conference room door is still closed. "Did he leave?"

Ruby shakes her head. "No. He's talking to his manager. But I can tell he doesn't want to do it. He kept looking over at Amalie, and she kept talking about press for his album and how he doesn't do interviews."

This is going exactly how I thought it would, and if I was Alex, I wouldn't want a gossip rag digging into my past either. I don't understand why Ruby is surprised by any of this. Did she think she'd get medical notes from the drug and alcohol treatment facilities? Or court documents relating to the money his old manager funneled out of his accounts for years while he was too messed up to notice?

Ruby slumps in her chair and releases a labored breath. "I need this, Spencer. My sister is a medical researcher, and she's discovered some treatment for this bacteria that eats people's skin. My brother owns a digital media company that just bought out two smaller companies, and his wife is an engineer who's in Germany, working on some project worth billions. My other brother is a vet and has this perfect family with three kids who are always well-behaved, and his wife takes Mom to lunch every week. That's what I'm dealing with at every family gathering. A table full of people who are all doing much better than I am. Mom's Christmas newsletter is full of my siblings' achievements, and when anybody asks what I'm doing, Mom and Dad avoid the question. Do you know what that's like? Being the ultimate disappointment to your family because your name is under a listicle for the top ten anti-dandruff shampoos you can get from the drugstore?"

For the first time in our working relationship, it doesn't feel like we live on different planets, and I understand why she wants Alex to be her big break. To be honest, I think she could pull it off. Granted, she's only done a handful of C and D list celebrity interviews, but she has a way of engaging with her subject, getting them comfortable, and drawing out interesting tidbits and quotables. Ruby was born to work for *TGP*; she thrives in this environment. She might be the only person here who sees this place as the start of something, not where careers come to die.

I shouldn't get involved, but if I have the power to do something, then I should probably do it. I've lied and acted selfishly in the past, so this might make up for some of that.

"Give me a second." I toss my chip packet in the bin and dust my hands on my pants as I stride out of the kitchen and down to the conference room. Alex sits up in his chair when I enter, but my focus is on Amalie.

"Can I talk to Alex for a moment?" My back is straight as an arrow, and I realize I may have come in a little hot. "Please."

Amalie's dark brown eyes dart to Alex, who gives a resigned nod. Her brow wrinkles under her wispy blonde bangs, but she collects her phone off the table and exits the room. Hazel is there to greet her with bottled water and directions to Natalia's office.

I wait until she's out of sight, and when I turn to Alex, he stands and moves toward me.

I hold up a finger. "Stay there."

His shoulders drop, and he steps back. "Okay."

The room is silent, save for the gentle hum of the ducted air conditioning, and it takes all my strength not to let every thought and feeling fall from my lips. If I was anywhere other than this office, I'm not sure I could hold back.

"Do the article," I say. "You can make it about your album. Just give Ruby something from the early days. The move to LA, or those bar gigs you used to play in Capitol Hill."

Alex shakes his head. "I don't want to."

I press my palms against my thighs and steady my breathing. "Why?"

"Because she's going to dig," he says. "I've done hundreds of interviews, Pen. I know what they're like, and Ruby wants more than I can give. She'll twist my words, and I've had enough bad press to last a lifetime."

His words push me so close to the edge that my stomach lurches at the drop. He is responsible for that bad press. He was the one who stumbled out of clubs at all hours of the morning with different women and bloodshot eyes. He was the one who missed deadlines and failed to show at the studio because he was too strung out to remember what day it was.

"You brought all of that on yourself."

"And I don't want to rehash it. Not when I have an album coming out."

I pace, hands on my hips and sweat beading on the back of my neck. "Then why would you take the meeting?"

"She's not going to respect my boundaries, Pen."

"Stop calling me Pen!" I shout.

Through the wall of windows that look out over the bullpen, I see heads pop up over their partitions. Knitted brows, wide eyes, and slack mouths. I turn my back, hands trembling as I grip the back of the leather chair Ruby sat in when she pitched this whole profile thing.

"I'm sorry," he whispers. "Force of habit."

My nails sink deeper into the leather, leaving half-moon impressions. "Ruby needs this, Alex. *TGP* needs it too."

He looks at the floor and drags his sneaker-clad foot over the carpet. "I can't risk it, Spencer."

"Risk what?"

"My reputation. I don't want certain things to get out, and I'm sure you don't want them to either."

"Then why are you here?"

"Because I thought it was with you." His voice shakes. "Amalie told me someone from Hartfield Media wanted an interview, and I thought it was you."

"Why would it be me?"

He swallows. "I don't know, but I knew you worked here, and I figured I could help you out."

I bark a laugh. "Help me out? Why would I need your help?"

"Spencer, don't make a big deal out of it. I was trying to do something for you."

"I don't need you to do anything for me. I don't need you."

He holds his hands up defensively. "Fine. Noted."

I turn and see more heads have surfaced above their partitions. Natalia notices and whispers to Hazel, who swiftly instructs everyone to return to work.

"Are you going to do the interview with Ruby or not? Because if you're not, then I think you should leave," I sigh. "We've drawn enough attention."

Alex tucks his hands into the pockets of his coat and rocks forward on the balls of his feet. When his eyes meet mine, I see the gears turning in his head.

"How long will it take?"

"Two one-hour face-to-face interviews and a photo shoot."

"Fine."

"And you don't say anything about me. Or us."

"Done."

"And you don't have the interviews here."

Alex frowns. "You're that desperate to avoid me?"

"Yes." I nod. "Do we have a deal?"

He extends his hand, and I shake it without thinking. It's a mistake. His touch is dangerous, charged with something that should be long dead. The spark warms my body, and I look into his eyes. It's an even worse mistake because my heart stutters.

"There's something else I want," he says.

"What?"

He's still holding my hand and my gaze. "Have dinner with me? So we can talk. That's all."

I pull my hand away. "No."

"Lunch?"

"No."

"Breakfast?"

"Stop listing meals."

His mouth lifts at the corner. "Brunch?"

"Alex."

"Sorry." His hands return to his pockets. "I thought we could clear the air without your entire office watching us."

Every employee in the bullpen is tempting fate by watching this exchange, and they know it. So does Hazel because she's failed her task and will face the wrath of Natalia, who takes professionalism as seriously as her cuticle care.

"When do you go back to LA or New York, or wherever you are now?"

"I'm going back to New York in a few months. I just wanted to be out here with Mom and Kit for a while."

My heart squeezes when I think of Kit and how happy she must be to have him back while I desperately want him on the next flight out.

"We can avoid each other for a few months."

His eyes settle on mine again, and the smirk on his lips has vanished, replaced with a flat line. "If that's what you want."

He steps past me, and I hold my breath, not wanting to

remember how good he smells. I don't want to remember anything about him. Not his touch, his voice. I want my memory scrubbed clean.

Once Alex is out of the building, I go back to Ruby with the good news. She wants to call Amalie immediately to arrange the interview times, but I tell her to give it a day because we're already on thin ice. She can't contain her smile. It splits her face in half as she texts her sister-in-law to tout that she'll be interviewing their favorite musician.

"Thank you so much, Spencer." Ruby pulls me into a lopsided hug before she bounds off to the break room to call her mom. It leaves me entirely unguarded, and when I see Bess and Elsa from ad sales strolling over, I grab my phone and hurry down to the lobby to avoid any questions.

As soon as I see Owen's smiling face behind the reception counter, I feel a pang of guilt.

"Shit. I'm sorry about lunch. I got held up."

"No sweat." He spins the spare chair to face me as an invitation. "I saved the second half of the turkey sandwich for you. But first, I have brownies."

He retrieves a small plastic container from a shelf under the desk. A smile tugs at his lips as he presents the perfectly cut squares, and the sugary sweet smell of baked chocolate fills my nose.

Owen is a baker, which I discovered on his second day on assignment in our building. I was waiting for Eve to pick me up for dinner, and he asked if I'd like to try some cookies he'd baked the night before. They were a little overdone, but he went back to the drawing board and offered a far more successful product the next day. Since then, he's had various baked goods available for collection each morning, provided I can assist him with whichever crossword clue has him stumped that day.

I take a brownie and sink my teeth into the perfectly soft, gooey slice of heaven.

"Good?" Owen asks. "Any notes?"

I shake my head and talk through my mouthful of brownie. "No notes. It's perfect."

He pumps his fist. "Yes! Because I've got plans to make a lemon meringue tart after work tonight."

He's kind-eyed and baby-faced, but very serious about whipping up a lemon meringue, judging by the set of his sharp jaw. I don't know what I'd do without him waiting for me every morning with a new treat to lift my spirits. I really hope the security company Owen works for doesn't assign him to another building in the future.

"What's going on in the office today?" Owen asks. "Any fresh scandals?"

"Sorry to disappoint, but no, we're incredibly boring for a gossip magazine."

"That's a lie, and you know it." Owen points an accusatory finger at me.

I swat it away. "What are you talking about?"

"There has been some hubbub in the lobby."

"I'm sorry, did you say hubbub?"

"Yes. Because there was a hubbub."

"Hubbub?"

"Yes. I'm going with hubbub."

"Not commotion? Ruckus? Rumpus, even?"

He shakes his head. "I'm sticking with hubbub."

"Cacophony?"

"Sorry, but I'm committed to hubbub."

The corner of my mouth lifts. "What was this brouhaha about then?"

Owen's eyes widen. "Oh, I like brouhaha."

"Thought you might."

"The brouhaha was over *TGP*'s visit from a musician. I didn't realize who it was because the lady he was with signed them in, but Garth from the accounting firm on twelve…"

"The one with the questionable mustache?" I interject.

"Yes, but not anymore. His husband made him shave it off because they have a big gathering on Sunday, and it's the first time Garth is meeting some of the extended family. Anyway, Garth told Mary on seven, and she told Jolene on nine, then somehow everyone on eighteen found out, so they all came down to watch Alex Reilly walk out of the building. You could have told me someone famous was coming in."

"I didn't realize you were a fan." I slump onto the marble counter.

"I don't know if I'd say fan. I mean, I've heard of him, and I've got a few of his songs on some old playlists."

I stand up straight again, roll my shoulders back, and yawn. "He's Eve's brother."

He snaps the lid back on the brownie container. "Wait, what?"

"I dated him too." I take the container, peel the lid off again, and stuff another brownie into my mouth. Owen's mind is clearly racing, and it takes a second for him to tune back in.

"Are you serious? How long did you date him for?"

"Not too long. On and off for four years, then very much on for another four years."

His mouth falls open. "Spencer, that's almost a decade."

I slump against the desk, brushing brownie crumbs off my charcoal wrap blouse. "Yeah, it felt longer than that."

Owen picks up his phone, types something, scrolls for a while, and then turns it to face me. Through the splintered glass, I see a photo of myself. Cheeks flushed, eyes red, and my hair partially covering my face. Five minutes before it was taken, Alex and I had one of the worst fights of our relationship. His manager, Howie, had kicked me out of the green room because some cut rate magazine wanted to interview Alex after the show, and Howie didn't want them to know he was in a relationship. It wasn't good for business.

"I can't believe this is you," Owen says.

"And look how happy I am." I laugh sardonically. "That tells you everything you need to know about what it was like to date a famous musician."

He places his phone back on the shelf under the desk, and I feel like I've disrupted the delicate balance of our low-maintenance, fun-filled friendship.

CHAPTER NINE

Dear Alex,

 Did you ever get tired of Bristol Court's brimming social calendar? Easter with the Stuarts at number seven, Christmas in July with the Rowlands at number eleven, Elaine and Doug hosting the neighborhood ping-pong tournament in August, and the Milfords taking New Year's Eve to a new level year on year. It was always themed and always inappropriate to have children there. Though, as unhinged as those parties got, one of them played host to the best night of my life.

 The neighborhood was circling Vince and Carla's backyard, drinks in their hands, all dressed like members of KISS. The theme was famous musicians, and no one communicated their outfit choices ahead of time.

 I spent most of the night leaning against the back wall of the house, wearing fingerless lace gloves and an oversized bow in my teased-up hair. I'd talked Eve out of dressing up as conebra Madonna, so she was happily eating mini quiches as Ziggy Stardust with a wonky lightning bolt across her eye. I felt ridiculous when you walked in wearing your usual black t-shirt, jeans, and that old hoodie that was far too light for the punishing December chill. Several of our neighbors accosted you, asking about your plans since you'd bailed on college to pursue music. It took some time for you to extricate yourself, but you eventually made your way over to me.

You settled against the wall, standing close enough that your shoulder pressed against mine. From there, it didn't matter how that night turned out; it was already perfect.

It did get better, though, and it started when you reached for my drink and pressed your lips to the spot on the cup that was stained with my cherry red lipstick. Your mouth tightened at the sweetness of the melon liqueur, and you said my outfit was cute.

A flush crawled up my neck and stained my already over-blushed cheeks. You shifted slightly and dropped your hand from the pocket of your jeans, so it rested beside mine. The brush of your fingers against the back of my hand was light, but it was there, and it was intentional. We'd found ourselves there—again. It had been six months since we'd listened to Carole King in your bedroom, and we hadn't had a repeat of that night. The fear of Eve finding out was enough to keep either of us from reliving it, and a lot had happened since then. Gretchen had gone nuclear. Her broken heart became Eve's responsibility, and every day was an exercise in how to irrevocably destroy a friendship. Gretchen wasn't just heart-broken. She was betrayed, angry, and spiteful. In one breath, she wanted to destroy you, and in the next, she was begging Eve to convince you to take her back. I stayed silent through all of it, and when Gretchen came knocking, the splinters of her heart in her outstretched hands, I didn't know what to do. I wasn't with you, but she didn't apologize for alleging I was. We all underestimated what you meant to her because it had been almost two years, and she still hadn't recovered. I told her you'd moved on, and you had. I saw you sneak a girl out of your house one night and felt sick thinking that moments earlier, her honey blonde hair was splayed across your pillow. The same pillow I laid on when you sang to me. It went nowhere, but I spiraled a little and made a couple of poor choices at college parties. I didn't care for either of them, but it was nice to feel wanted, even if it was only for a night or two. Though nothing seemed to stick for either of us and when you walked up to me at that party, I believed it was the universe making sure we'd end up in that exact place at that exact time.

That's what my optimistic little heart believed, anyway.

We said nothing to each other, but it felt exactly like that night in your room. It emboldened me, and I hooked my index and middle finger around your thumb. You wanted more, though, threading your fingers through mine completely and shifting so the black tulle of my skirt hid our hands from view. Every inch of my skin heated, the feeling heightening as neither of us said a word. We were just holding hands, but it mattered. To me, it mattered.

I wanted to tell Eve how I felt, and if you were anyone else, I would have. I would have poured my heart out because I craved your touch like it was a drop of water in the desert. Seeing you for even a second was the best part of my day.

I smiled at the thought before you pulled your hand away. Elaine was holding up an open jar of salsa, and her face was panic-stricken. She'd run out of chips, and you were the only child near enough to solve the problem. I hardly saw you for the rest of the night. Every time we neared each other, someone wanting to engage in inane conversation ripped us apart. I gave up trying to nonchalantly find myself beside you and joined Eve on some folding chairs in the back corner of the yard. We ate neatly cubed cheese and overcooked hotdogs while Eve told me about the number of unanswered texts she'd sent Gretchen.

On those folding chairs, Eve's frustration morphed into sadness as she reminisced about the three of us camping out in the treehouse and playing bingo in math. I was thankful she didn't make it to midnight because my conscience was in tatters. I couldn't stop thinking about your hand in mine. I still felt your touch as I walked Eve home and created even more intense scenarios in my head on my way back to the party.

What if I waited for you? What if we were alone? What if I made the first real move?

That's exactly what I did. I didn't go back to the party. Instead, I went straight to the treehouse and found you already waiting for me.

You held out your hand and helped me up the ladder. When we settled side by side in the cramped wooden box, your shoulder pressed against mine, and I shifted my weight so our hips touched as well. You looked at me, and when you smiled, your eyes crinkled at the corners. I was breathless and thought what a privilege it was to hold that much of your attention. The next moment, I remember with the clarity of cut crystal because I still think about the rush of it all to this day. You lifted your arm and pulled me into your side. We fit perfectly, and I'd never felt that way before. It was the anticipation. This feeling that I couldn't wait any longer, mixed with the dread that this moment together would be over too soon. In the distance, countdowns echoed through the neighborhood.

It was the longest ten seconds of my life—a painfully drawn-out chant—and I'd been staring at you for so long that if you hadn't kissed me, I'd have crumbled into a million pieces. Never to be put back together the same way again.

Midnight finally struck, and amid the cheers from

surrounding houses, you leaned down and pressed your closed lips briefly to mine. It was sweet but chaste. Almost platonic.

It killed me.

You said Happy New Year and relaxed back against the wall, your breathing even. My world shattered because I thought I'd read the whole situation wrong. Was I just your little sister's best friend who followed you around like a lovesick puppy, begging for a scrap of your attention? We were only two years apart, but at that moment, you seemed so much older than me. Worldly and experienced, while I was small and reckless.

I knew what I wanted, though, and it was more than hand brushes and the silence that always seemed to hang between us. I wanted you. All of you.

I asked what we were doing, and when you turned to look up at me, there was a sharpness in your gaze. Things were about to change, and I didn't know if it was going to be better or worse. We'd toed the line but not yet fully crossed it. I was still innocent. I hadn't broken my promise to Eve. Yet.

You said Eve would kill you if she knew the thoughts you had about me, and as your fingertips skated over my shoulder, I had those same thoughts. You were magnetic, inescapable, and the way you looked into my eyes coaxed honesty. I knew I loved you, and you were the person I wanted to share all my secrets with.

You asked if you could kiss me again, and I begged you to.

That was our real first kiss. Your arm around me, holding our bodies together. Your other hand was on my cheek, moving down to my throat as your tongue parted my lips. It was a surreal feeling to want something so badly and have the blissful expectation met. I decided we shouldn't talk about Eve or Gretchen. It was the only way I could survive the guilt of wanting you so badly.

CHAPTER TEN

Avoiding Alex does wonders for my productivity at work. All of my current assignments are in Natalia's inbox, awaiting approval, and I've dived headlong into advanced Florence Ritter research. I've been charting her life, noting down and fact-checking every drop of information I can find on her untimely demise. It has me staying late at the office most nights. Something about the second-hand office chair with no lumbar support and a terminally ill fluorescent light flickering overhead gets my creative juices flowing. Tonight, though, I'm taking a break and have been on the receiving end of Miles' pity face for two hours. After serving each customer, he looks over, draws his dark brows together, pushes his bottom lip out, and mouths, "You okay?". He's doing damage control to ensure that pesky broken heart of mine doesn't bust its stitches. I've told him several times that I'm fine because I'm certainly not going to tell him that most nights, I go home and cry in the shower.

"Alright, kid." Miles strolls over, needlessly polishing a

hurricane glass. "I can't have you warming a seat and not sampling something off my new cocktail menu."

I lean forward, resting my elbows on the bar. "What have you got?"

With a wink, Miles reaches under the bar and pulls out a tattered hardback book with a pixelated photo of a gelatin meat log on the front. "Check this out."

I reach for the book and read the cover. "*Sensational Seventies: Dinner Party Host Guide*. Yikes."

"I found this behind the file cabinet last week."

"Maybe it should have stayed behind the file cabinet?" I hand it back, and as he flips it open, the spine makes an audible crack.

"Sit tight, Spence. I've got the perfect drink for you."

He plants the hurricane glass in front of me, tongue pressed between his teeth as he fetches bottles from every shelf. He's so fast that I don't have time to read the labels as he splashes way too many types of liquor into the glass and finishes it with three splashes of orange juice.

"And what is this called?" I ask as he pushes the glass toward me.

"A Slippery Deck Chair." He beams with pride, though beaming might not be a strong enough word. More like radiating because this is the holy grail of cocktails, and he's the only bartender in the world who can make it.

My brows draw together as I look at the glass. "A what?"

"Try it."

I do as I'm told, spluttering as the orangey rocket fuel coats my tongue and sears my throat.

"How good is it?" Miles' eyes are wide, and his grin is debilitating.

"So good." I suck in a breath, reigniting the burn. "You can barely taste the alcohol."

He slaps his hand on the bar in triumph, and a few seconds later, when he's dragged away to serve a group of guys who want to sample all the whiskey, I pour the Slippery Deck Chair into a nearby potted plant and pray Miles doesn't ask why it's dead in a few days.

Leaving the now-empty glass on the bar, I settle at a small table against the wall. With my distraction being distracted by paying customers, I take out my notebook and trace the last few words with my index finger.

It was the only way that I could survive the guilt of wanting you so badly.

After seeing Alex at the Larsons' party, I lay in bed, staring up at my criminally low ceiling and mentally digging through my past. Memories of Alex that have lived in darkness for years drifted to the surface, so I climbed out of bed, grabbed one of the twenty unused notebooks from my desk drawer, and started writing. They were little notes. Reflections and musings. Now they're letters.

Letters to Alex.

And I haven't stopped writing them.

"What are you writing?" Miles' hands grip the back of my chair, and his mouth is close to my ear.

"Nothing. Just some journaling." I flip the notebook closed, but Miles has already seen the "Dear Alex" part.

"About him?"

His voice is low, agitated and it feels like he's turned the volume down on the world, and I'm a deer caught in the headlights.

"Yes," I whisper.

"Why?"

"Because it helps."

Miles stands upright and glances around for a moment, gathering his thoughts.

"Come with me." He nods toward the back room, and I stand from the table, stuffing the notebook into my bag as I follow him.

The back room is roughly the size of a commercial elevator, with a small desk, swivel chair, and the file cabinet that's been holding that gem of a dinner party book hostage for over fifty years. It smells like stale beer with a hint of lavender from the candle Judy Larson bought when she offered to help Miles with his books last year.

Miles closes the door behind us and steers me toward the swivel chair before perching himself on the stool in the corner with the broken footrest. "We need to talk."

"About what?" My voice climbs an octave, and I fold my hands in my lap. Guilt about everything from my conversation with Alex at *TGP* to ditching the Slippery Deck Chair ripples through me.

"Come on, Spence." He frowns as he leans forward and rests his elbows on his knees like a camp counselor who's really trying to connect with the campers. I could feign ignorance, but it would be a waste of time.

"*TGP* contacted Alex for a profile while he's in town. Ruby is writing it, but Alex was reluctant. I convinced him to do it."

Miles drags his hands down his face and groans. "That's obviously a ploy. He's trying to weasel his way back into your life."

"I'm not letting him back in," I say. "All I did was help Ruby."

Miles chews on his lip for a second, and a crease forms between his eyebrows. He has all the features of his brothers: Danny's hooded eyes, Nolan's sharp jaw, and Fletcher's dark hair. His kindness comes from his mother, and his desire to meddle comes from his sister, Leah.

I understand his concern, but this is the first contact I've had with Alex since the breakup. My record is clean.

"I still think this is a bad idea," he says.

"He'll probably stop by the office, but I'll be keeping my distance."

"Why are you writing him letters, then?"

I sigh. "They're not really for him. They're for me. It's cathartic to get everything out of my head."

Miles' eyes narrow, and he's poised to say something when a knock rattles the battered wooden door. He sticks his head out, and urgent whispers ensue before he looks back at me.

"They need help. But I think we still need to talk about this."

I feel like a scolded child. "We don't, Miles. Everything is fine, and I have to go. I'm meeting Owen for a drink tonight."

"Good." Miles nods sharply.. "Whatever keeps you away from Alex."

I sigh as I fold my arms across my chest. "There is nothing to worry about. I can exist in the same city as him and not relapse."

Miles lowers his voice, and his amber-brown eyes soften. "I know you, Spence, and I know him. You two are like magnets. You always have been."

He steps out of the room, returning to his post behind the bar without a backward glance. I lean on the desk, my fingers tapping the keg delivery schedule and Miles' words ricocheting around in my head.

Magnets.

We've always been magnets.

Twenty minutes later, I meet Owen in the courtyard of a tavern a few blocks from Whiskey. The compact space is surrounded by red brick buildings on all sides, but the twisted ivy that crawls up the walls, the soft string lights overhead, and the guy playing folk music on his guitar make it more romantic than expected. Beers in hand, we slide onto the bench seats on either side of a rustic farmhouse table and take in the magic.

"I love the lights. I've always wanted to live somewhere with a courtyard so I could do that." I point upward, and his eyes follow before settling back on me.

He tells me about the townhome he bought a few months ago. His self-deprecating laugh is melodic when he jokes about how much debt he's now in, not to mention the money he is pouring into the renovation.

"I used to work in construction, so I have some idea what I'm doing," he explains. "It's been a while, though."

"I've heard a full-scale home renovation is like riding a bike," I smirk and sip my drink. He laughs at my joke, and the lights overhead highlight the soft, golden shade of his hair.

I want to know more about him. Something other than his baking skill and the fact that he's financially stable enough to get a mortgage. I want to know about his family, what he does on weekends, and which foods he can't stand. I want to fill my head with the intricacies of another person so I can force others out.

"Do you have any siblings?"

He nods. "A sister. You?"

"Only child."

"I bet your parents are proud of you."

A bitter laugh escapes me. "You're wrong about that."

"You're a successful journalist."

I force a shallow laugh, and he looks at me with a softness I can't place. Like I'm something impressive. Fascinating, even.

"You're wrong about that too."

He tilts his head, and his mouth slackens. "Why would you say that?"

"Because my father is a surgeon and my mother works in finance. Either of those career paths would have made them proud of me. Instead, I'm peddling lies and selling scandals. The opposite of what they wanted."

Owen drags his fingers through the condensation on the side of his glass as he surveys me. I've never been this candid with him before because, for the last year, we've existed inside the Hartfield Media building. We're built on polite greetings, shared turkey sandwiches, and building gossip.

"Your job is important too," Owen assures me.

"Last week, I wrote an article on a grocery store in Bellevue with a haunted produce section."

"I read that." His tone lifts. "It was good."

I hold up my glass. "Yes. I'm doing God's work."

He laughs but takes a large gulp of his beer. I open my mouth to apologize for bringing down our evening with my most recent career failure when the musician in the corner plays the opening chords of a familiar song.

The music curls around me like a restrictive plastic film as a table of women who look barely old enough to be here let out giddy sighs. One of them closes her eyes and sways from side to side. Another clutches her heart and loudly wishes she was the woman he sings about.

I ignore them and focus on Owen, but it's entirely unsuccessful. The singer doesn't hit the right note as he goes into the second verse, and the tempo is off. It's like having my ears dragged over a cheese grater.

"It's gin, not beer." I scrunch my eyes shut like it will stop the song.

"What?" Owen's brow wrinkles when I lift my face to look at him again.

"The song is a cover," I say. "He fucked up the line, though. It's supposed to be 'the treehouse felt right, drinking stolen gin and chasing this night'. He said beer, not gin."

I sound ridiculous, and Owen doesn't know how to react, so he says nothing as he takes another long sip of his drink.

"Sorry. I get annoyed when people get the lyrics wrong."

"It's fine. It's a great song, and that guy's a professional. He should get the words right."

I appreciate that he's trying to placate me, but we've both noticed the shift as we listen to the soundtrack of my early twenties. After three more incorrect lyrics, the musician takes a break from butchering Alex's back catalog. It's too late, though, because whatever energy there was in the space has been sucked out and replaced with stagnant air.

"Do you want to get out of here?" Owen offers. "There's beer at my place and no live music."

I laugh. "That sounds perfect."

After battling some evening traffic, I pull up outside the address Owen sent me. His block is neat rows of townhomes, all with matching storm gray siding and tall wooden fences. The leafy trees planted in perfectly spaced lines along the street have grown tall, creating a canopy above the sidewalk.

Owen meets me out the front, eyes shining as he ushers me into his home. I hover on the threshold, watching as he drops his keys on the scratched wooden table by the door, flicks on a lamp, and moves to the side to allow me to enter. When I brush past him, I notice his rapid breathing and that he's fiddling with the zipper of his coat.

"It's a work in progress." The words tumble out in a rush as I look at the unvarnished floors and missing cabinet doors in the kitchen at the back of the open living area. Fresh paint permeates the room, and a sheet covers the modest amount of living room furniture, which is clustered in the center of the space.

"But it's a slow process." Owen rushes past me, whips the protective sheet off the couch, and haphazardly fluffs the lone cushion. His hand shakes as he presents the seat to me.

"I love the cabinets. Sage green is a good choice." I sit on the couch and reach up to take his shaking hand and pull him down next to me. It takes him by surprise, and he drops ungracefully. He's never been this scattered before, and I feel I've invaded his space.

"Yeah. The green." He looks toward the kitchen, but I see the color in his cheeks. "My sister, Whitney, picked it."

"She chose well."

"Yeah. Turns out she has a lot of opinions about paint colors." He drags his hands down his thighs.

"Are you okay?" I lean away from him slightly, thinking distance is what he needs. Apparently, it's not because he inches closer.

"I'm fine," he says. "I just wish I'd made the place a bit more presentable before I brought you here."

"Don't worry about it. I know you're renovating."

I reach over and squeeze his hand. His palms are slightly clammy, but his fingers aren't shaking anymore, and the blush in his cheeks has faded, replaced with a wide smile that brightens his features. He's younger than me—by how many years, I don't know—and there is an innocence to his eyes and the fine angles of his face. He isn't worn or beaten down yet, and I subconsciously compare every inch of him to Alex. He's shorter, but not by much. His hair is blond compared to Alex's black, and his eyes are dark gray. A storm cloud compared to Alex's indigo.

I make other comparisons too. Ones I shouldn't because

they only serve as a distraction. Still, I wonder what it would be like to stay with him all night. Be touched by him and wake up in the morning to his youthful smile and a gentle kiss on the temple. It would feel nice, I'm sure. And I want to feel nice again. I want to have someone look at me and want me, expecting nothing in return. I want someone to choose me over everything else.

Would that be enough? Or would I find a way for it not to be?

"How old are you?" I ask, softening my tone as I study his features. He has a slight bump on the bridge of his nose, and the wash of warm light across his skin highlights the pale freckles on his cheeks.

"Twenty-five."

"Twenty-five," I parrot. "That's young."

"How old are you?"

"I'm about to turn thirty."

It feels like a sinful confession, but he doesn't even flinch. "That's young too."

I remember being twenty-five. I felt like I was aging too fast. Barreling toward this milestone like a freight train, and I didn't have a thing to show for it. I still have nothing to show for it. Just a collection of poor decisions and the ghost of a love with roots so deep, my heart doesn't beat like it should anymore.

Owen inches closer and leans forward. I read his every movement. The positioning of his hand beside my hip to support himself while he tilts forward.

"I kind of had an ulterior motive when I invited you here," he says. "I need to ask you something."

I tilt my head, trying to read what hides in his expression. "What do you have to ask me?"

"Whitney is getting married soon, and I was wondering if

you'd be my date for her wedding. It's at this estate out of the city, so I get it if that's too much trouble."

The blush has returned to his cheeks, and he looks down at his hand beside my hip. The occasional creak of the house settling and the rumble of street traffic don't mask how rapid his breathing is.

"I'd love to go with you." I smile. "It'll be fun."

He exhales, shoulders dropping and a laugh escaping him. "Thank God. I've been trying to ask you that for days."

"I'm not that scary." I fix my expression to one of mock indignation. "You can ask me anything you like."

He's quiet for a moment, the broken tension sewn right back up as he runs his hand through his hair and sinks back against the couch.

"Anything?" he asks, staring at the plastic-covered coffee table.

I lean back into the couch cushions as well. "Yeah."

Owen drags his hands down his thighs. "That song that was playing at the bar. The one where they got the lyrics wrong. It's about you, isn't it?"

"Yes." I nod, taking a deep breath and staring at my hands. "Most of them are about me."

CHAPTER ELEVEN

Dear Alex,

 Keeping our secret was thrilling and romantic, with a side of bone-aching guilt. I could barely look at Eve, and when she asked about my love life, I lied through my teeth. I lived in fear that she'd notice how often I'd find excuses to stand close to you. Being near you was like having a nervous system made of butterflies, but Eve wouldn't understand. She'd see a repeat of Gretchen, and even if I swore it was different, why would she trust another promise from me? Mine were clearly empty.

 I convinced myself that everything would work out because we were real and forever. It didn't matter that we'd never confirmed that. All that mattered was the evolution of our long conversations. We planned how I'd sneak into your gigs around Seattle, then we talked about the kind of couch we'd buy when we got our own place. We went on long drives, kissed in dark corners, and used an alias in our cell phones. I dealt with the heartache that took over every time I looked at Eve. Reasoned that it was the cost of loving you.

 It wasn't until the night a bleary-eyed Doug caught us

sneaking down to the treehouse that the guilt really buried me. You said it was nothing, and thankfully, Doug could hardly remember what he'd had for breakfast, so our secret remained undiscovered. It was too close for me, though, and I put a temporary ban on treehouse meetups. We still texted each other, and every night, I looked forward to reading the song lyrics you'd send me. Perfect poetry that I scrolled through whenever we were apart.

We weren't good at staying away from each other, and one afternoon, you were sitting on the couch watching a football game you had no interest in while Eve and I sat at the table, dropping chocolates into chiffon bags for Kit and Bea's upcoming birthday party. My cheeks heated when you turned around to look at me. It was dangerous, so eventually, you strolled over, sat in the vacant chair, and picked up a handful of chocolates. Of course, you bagged them wrong and were swiftly reprimanded by your sister. You made a second failed attempt before you slouched in the chair and rested your hand on my knee under the table. You walked your fingers up my thigh, and I squirmed. Thankfully, Eve didn't notice because a girl she'd met the week prior at one of your gigs texted to meet up. I'd never seen her leave the house so quickly, and the moment that front door closed, you were on your feet, pulling me up and sitting me on the edge of the dining table. My breath left my body when you kissed me, and a second later, you were leading me up to your bedroom.

We were completely alone in the house for the first time, and we both wanted to make the most of it. We didn't listen to *Tapestry* or aimlessly trace each other's skin with trembling fingertips. We didn't have time for it. You pulled my dress off, and I made quick work of your Henley and jeans before we fell into your bed. I saw God twice that afternoon, and when we collapsed against each other in an exhausted heap, I remember thinking that you were too beautiful to exist. That anyone else I'd ever love could never compare to you. That even in our secret world, you'd taken a piece of me I'd never get back. I wanted to give you more.

That's when you told me you were playing The Palace in three weeks' time as the opening act for Nine Acre.

I gripped your shoulders, stared into your brilliant blue eyes, and asked if you were serious. You nodded, that infectious grin spreading as you kissed me again. It's funny to think about it now. How Nine Acre ceased to exist not long after that show, and your fame eclipsed them to such a degree. Last I heard, their lead singer taught woodworking classes on his ranch in Texas, and the drummer went to jail for a laundry list of drug offenses.

I put my hand on your cheek, leaning in so our foreheads touched. I was so proud of you, but an odd sensation spread through my chest. A twitching feeling, like my muscles didn't know how to react to the news. You whispered in my ear that you were going to play the song you wrote for me on stage at The Palace.

I felt it then. Elation and fear because I knew it was the start of it all. You were going to be a big deal, and we'd never be able to hide from it. You ran your fingers down my arm and took my hand. I already missed you, and it made no sense. I had you right then. I had you.

I hitched my leg over yours and pulled your mouth to mine. I didn't have the future you had, so I held you tight, breathed in your scent, and whispered in your ear how excited I was to see you play and that you deserved this. You'd earned it. We were so wrapped up in each other, we didn't hear the footsteps on the stairs, and the new carpeting in the hallway muffled any noise. Which had served us well until that point.

Miles opened your bedroom door and promptly choked on

the donut he was eating. Glaze coated his lips as sprinkles fell onto Elaine's pristine floor. We broke apart, and I yanked the covers up to my neck like it would erase what he had seen from his memory.

Miles paced for a moment, alternating between bites of donut and the stressful rubbing of his forehead. He begged us to tell him that what we were doing was nothing. A lapse in judgment that would end right then.

But it was something, and Miles could tell.

He could never keep a secret, though, especially from Eve. She had a way of getting information. She was a bloodhound, and this was juicy. You talked Miles down, though, and he promised to keep our secret.

He stayed true to his word.

I was the one who ruined it all because I couldn't stop myself from wanting you.

CHAPTER TWELVE

For years, Florence Ritter's tragic life has piqued my morbid curiosity. There is something about 1940s Hollywood and its underbelly that's as interesting as it is unsettling. It's even more intriguing when a struggling actress finally lands a major film role and someone kills her before the first day of the shoot, leaving her hacked-up body in the bathtub of an abandoned mansion in the northern suburbs of LA.

I heard about the case at the tender age of fourteen, courtesy of a true crime show rerun that Dad was watching one night. The case has never been solved, so the episode's ending was a letdown, but it sent me down a rabbit hole, and I had to know everything about her. Now, I know her favorite drink was a Manhattan, and she wore a shade of red lipstick called "Femme Fatale". That she frequented a hair salon on 6th Street in downtown Los Angeles that was often paid for by rich male benefactors or possible murder suspects. And, thanks to the autopsy report, I know how much her kidneys weighed.

It's one in the morning, and my eyes are stinging when I click the save button on my *Herald* submission for the seventieth time. After many rewrites, I'm finally happy with it. The opening is lush and poetic, painting 1940s LA with all the beauty and promise Florence would have seen through her rose-colored glasses. It's easy to imagine how giddy she would have been when she bought that one-way bus ticket to Hollywoodland. Only to have the luster of it all fade after countless failed auditions.

"It's red velvet," Owen says as he places a small white box on the partition above my desk. There's a tag hanging off it with my name scrawled in blue ink.

I look up and meet his gentle gaze. "For me?"

"No. It's for Spencer from Medford Refrigeration on the second floor. I just wanted to show you."

"Spencer from Medford Refrigeration will be thrilled."

Owen gently pulls open the lid. "It's a thank you for agreeing to come to the wedding with me."

My heart skips a beat, and I inspect the most aesthetically pleasing cupcake I've ever seen. The frosting is a perfectly smooth swirl dotted with little sugar pearls. "You made this?"

"Just the cupcake. Not the box," he says. "I got that from the bakery across the street. They made me buy a cupcake too. I couldn't buy the box on its own."

"Sounds like a scam to me." I lower my voice. "Using the demand for cupcake boxes to hock their inferior product."

"Well, you haven't tasted this one yet. This might be the inferior product."

His jaw tenses, and he watches as I remove the cupcake from the box and take a bite as gracefully as I can. It is absolutely sinful. Perfectly moist, sweet, and the tang from the cream cheese frosting makes my eyelids flutter.

"Oh my God," I exhale through the mouthful of cake.

"Notes?"

I shake my head. "No notes."

Owen tips an imaginary hat and winks.

"I'm not kidding. This is incredible."

"Okay, calm down. You're making me blush."

It's true. His cheeks are a little pink, but his expression changes slightly, his mouth pressing into a line as I swallow the bite.

"You have frosting on your lip," he says, and before I can react, he brings his hand to my mouth and gently wipes it away with his index finger. The earth stops revolving, and I watch him put his finger in his mouth to suck the frosting off.

"It's pretty good," he says, casually tapping the partition and stepping back. "Anyway. I better get back to the desk."

I take a deep breath, the cold, recycled air filling my lungs and making me lightheaded.

"Okay." My voice is higher than usual because I'm not entirely sure what's happening.

"See you around." He smiles before strolling back to the elevator with the cool confidence of an attractive twenty-five-year-old who can make a woman melt with a cupcake and a smile.

An hour later, with a flirtatious cupcake sitting in my stomach, I step into the apartment to find Eve doing the most shocking thing I can imagine.

She's vacuuming.

"What happened?" I drop my bag on the kitchen counter and wave my hands dramatically.

"What?" she shouts as she tugs the earphones out of her ears.

"What are you doing?" I scan the apartment. It's pristine.

Like, cleaner than when I moved in. "Wait. Did you use the good streak-free glass cleaner on the upper cabinets?"

She kicks the switch on the vacuum, and it shuts off. "Steph moved into the apartment today."

I drop my bag on the dust-free floor. "Oh, shit."

"Yeah." Her mouth presses into a line. "I snaked the drain in the shower too."

"You know how to snake a drain?"

She shakes her head. "No. I think I made it worse."

There is a sharp thump on my front door, followed by a stream of muffled expletives and more banging. Eve grunts, stepping over the vacuum cord on her way to answer it. She swings it open with such force that a rush of air blows my hair back.

"It's two o'clock in the fucking morning," my neighbor, a middle-aged man with four kids and a dwindling life force, screams from the threshold. "Turn off the vacuum."

Eve's hand is on her hip, and her jaw is set. *I already feel sorry for this guy.*

"I'm sorry about the noise, but my fiancé's mistress moved into my apartment today."

My neighbor's thick eyebrows bunch and his mouth opens, but Eve cuts him off.

"And, for your information, I've done my due diligence, and I know for a fact that she loves mismatched furniture with candy-colored chalk paint jobs. Do you understand how serious this is? My apartment is an industrial-style loft in South Lake Union. A converted warehouse that pays homage to the original architecture of the building. Do you think a peacock green coffee table is going to complement all the exposed brick? What about the polished concrete countertops? Do you think they'll look chic and luxurious under mismatched coffee cups with chipped sides and stupid puns?"

I stifle a laugh. I've seen Steph's Instagram, and the assessment is accurate.

The wind goes out of his sails, and he doesn't have the energy to decipher anything Eve has said. "Just keep it down. I have to be at work in five hours."

"You should get to bed then." Eve folds her arms, and my neighbor's eyes narrow. "Kind of irresponsible of you to stay up late, accosting your neighbors when you have work in the morning."

His eyes narrow, and his tone is venomous. "I'll report this to the building manager."

"Go ahead. While you're at it, let him know my band will practice here every Monday night from now on," she chides. "I'm the drummer, and I'm terrible."

He grits his teeth, looking past her to me, and I shake my head to ease his concern. His thin lips press together, and he looks back to Eve. "I'm done with you."

"Yeah, whatever." She waves him off. "You aren't even the first man to say that to me this month."

She closes the door in his face and strolls back to the couch, dropping with a grunt.

"So, I'm definitely getting a strongly worded letter in my mailbox tomorrow."

"Sorry. I'm just pissed about the Steph thing." Eve sighs. "I'll call the building manager and say it was a misunderstanding."

I sit down next to her, resting my head on her shoulder. She's been too good lately. Too happy. Something had to bring her down. I see now that her nesting instinct—new throw cushions on my couch, clean laundry, and four home-cooked, albeit terrible, meals a week—has been a diversionary tactic.

"It's fine. I've never had a warning before. This might

make me cooler in the eyes of the seven college kids renting the one-bedroom on the ground floor."

We chuckle in unison, and when I look up at her, I notice the dark circles under her eyes. "I'm sorry about the Steph thing."

"Me too." She sighs. "I'm more sorry I ever met Darren."

"At least you didn't marry him."

Eve's head leans to the side and rests on mine. "For sure."

We sit in silence for a beat, listening to the occasional hum of a car driving by. It's peaceful, and my eyes grow heavy. I'm almost asleep when Eve's voice brings me back from the brink.

"Sorry about Alex, by the way. Kit said he's doing the interview with Ruby."

"I asked him to. Ruby was really excited, and it turns out her parents don't think her career in journalism is that impressive, either. She needed the win."

"That's nice of you. Are you going to be okay if you have to see him occasionally?"

"I think so." I sit up, shifting so I'm facing her. "There is something else I should probably tell you, though."

"What's going on?" Eve's voice lowers, and her head tilts. "Is it bad?"

"Alex asked me to dinner. He wants to talk through some things."

Her shoulders fall, and she presses her hand to her chest. "God, I thought he kissed you or something."

"No. He just wants to talk."

"Do you want to talk? Get some closure?" She arches a dark brow.

"I've survived this long without it."

She chews on her lower lip, her teeth leaving indents. I wonder if she knows something I don't. Since their parents split, Alex and Eve have been talking more. They have both tried to be there for Bea and Kit, and it has repaired some of their own damage.

"It's up to you." She settles back into the couch cushions. "Whether you speak to him or not, I'll support you."

I stew on her sentiment for a moment, my heart stinging and my head growing foggy. When I cut myself off from him, I hoped the wound would heal, but seeing him—even just for that moment at Kit's apartment or the meeting at *TGP*—made me realize that underneath, that wound is festering.

Eve blinks, rolls her shoulders back, and stands up. "I understand if you don't want to, though. It's your decision."

She pulls me off the couch and into a hug. We share a contagious yawn and say goodnight, so Eve can get to scrolling through Steph's Instagram before she falls asleep.

I'm no better because I scroll through Alex's until my eyes sting.

CHAPTER THIRTEEN

Dear Alex,

    I was twenty-two, ten pounds lighter, and there were flowers in my hair on the night you played at The Palace. Eve had attended a flower crown workshop the week before, and I was the guinea pig. I didn't mind because I looked like the carefree and vibrant woman you sang about. My strict wardrobe of neutral tones didn't lend to that at all. I was hardened so as not to crumble under the immense weight of my father's expectations. Everything about me was rigid. I wondered if you mistook that for confidence. That's what I found most magical about your lyrics. You saw me so differently than how I saw myself and how my parents wanted the world to see me.

    On the drive to The Palace, I kept fussing with the flowers. I wasn't perfect enough. I should have dressed better. I should have worn that lemon yellow knit dress. You loved it, and it would have matched the flowers. Instead, I wore jeans and a gray sweater. I thought it would throw Eve off, making her think I didn't care that it was your first actual show. I regretted the decision when I saw Eve in her floor-length, pastel-toned dress. She decorated her hair with the same flowers. Your mom said we both looked beautiful and insisted on taking photos of me and your sisters under your name on the marquee. I love that photo, and I'm glad Elaine got a copy framed for Doug to hang on the wall in his new apartment.

When I looked up at the sign, I couldn't fathom that six months prior, we were sitting in your car when one of your songs was being played on an alternative radio station. The late-night announcer said you were one to watch, and we screamed. You had that air about you, and your talent spoke for itself. There was no way you were going to play dive bars forever.

We entered the venue and were directed to a roped-off section that barely contained the Larsons. Miles was front and center, beaming with pride. He was always selfless—probably to a fault, but he wanted this for you. Even if the infancy of your success didn't include him. He commented on my flowers, and Eve took several photos of us before seeking approval from all parties on which one was fine to post. I didn't care because all that pride and excitement had morphed into sympathetic nerves. I wanted to see you before the show, but I didn't know how. You were backstage somewhere, and with the number of people filling the venue, I could barely move as it was.

The anticipation built to a worrying degree when a stagehand brought out a stool and sat it behind the microphone. The stage was expansive. It felt too big for you. Your music was deep, lovely, and soulful. More suited to the intimate atmosphere of the treehouse on freezing winter nights when it was only the two of us.

I excused myself and worked my way back to the ground floor. It was easier than I thought, and when I introduced myself as a close friend of yours, the security guard couldn't have cared less about my intention to get backstage. He passed me over to a woman with a headset, who then directed me to a guy around my age who was dressed head-to-toe in black. I spun some lies about urgently needing to speak with you, and he showed me to a small room at the end of a long hallway. There was no security there, probably because they were all hovering around an adjacent hallway where Nine Acre was housed.

When you opened the door and pulled me against your body, you were shaking. You spoke into my hair, saying you couldn't do it. You were worried the audience wouldn't like you. I held you tighter, pressing myself close in the hope I could take on whatever held you back from what you'd dreamed of your whole life.

You touched your forehead against mine, and I closed my eyes, waiting for your courage to manifest. Did I ground you? Did I make you feel safe? I wanted to make you feel that way, but you were a man of few words. Though they always seemed to be the right ones.

Then you said you loved me.

And I said I loved you too.

That was a night of firsts for you and me. Our first "I love you". The first time you graced the stage at The Palace. The first time you played "A Girl Made of Stars". It was also the first time I wanted everyone to know that you wrote that song about me.

It was the first time I felt ready to tell Eve.

Sometimes, I wonder what I would have done if I knew it wasn't going to last. Would I have been there that night?

Would I have held back tears while you sang those beautiful words?

Maybe if I had known, I wouldn't have let you hold me so tight. Maybe I would have kept part of me for myself instead of giving you everything.

CHAPTER FOURTEEN

A post-break-up Eve is a diabolical force of nature. Common sense? Don't know her. Inhibitions? What are those? Getting absolutely wrecked on red wine, listening to Avril Lavigne, and cutting wedding invitations into confetti? Completely normal. And you can't change her mind. Admittedly, listening to her thought process as we squeeze into tight dresses on this Wednesday night is entertaining. It's like being on a roller-coaster in the dark. I have no idea when the next turn is coming. Maybe she should talk to Darren and find out why he cheated? Maybe she should pour sugar in his gas tank? Maybe what they need is some time apart to reflect on what they both really want? If it's meant to be, then it will be?

"Am I supposed to sit around and be miserable? Fuck Darren," she slurs. "God, men are the worst. Honestly, Spence. Don't get me started on my brother. He keeps trying to get me to come to these family dinners that Kit organizes. Maybe I don't want to go to an overpriced restaurant and pretend my parents' marriage didn't fall apart. I mean, it's weird, right? They act like they have this budding friendship and aren't sure where the line is yet. It's all so fake and polite. 'How's work, Doug?' 'Great. How's the new place, Elaine? Kit said you had the floors redone. What stain did you end up settling on? Walnut or Beech?' 'Yeah, walnut is a good choice.' Like, for fuck's sake, I had a deeper conversation with the guy trying to sell us weed outside the CVS last weekend."

"To be fair, he was trying to make a sale." I slip my right shoe on and wiggle my heel into it. "Throwing in the bag of tortilla chips was a nice touch."

"Yes, yes. The weed dealer was a shrewd businessman, but you get what I'm saying, right?"

I press my mouth into a line and give her a firm nod. "Of course, and I think you should tell Kit you want to cool it on the pity dinners for a while."

"Alex won't have that. He wants us to be a family again, which is a joke on his part. He's barely been in our lives for the better part of a decade, and now he's back, making demands and acting like a garlic bread for the table is going to act as a Band-Aid for our broken family." She grabs her purse off the counter. "And he's showing up at your work because he's got to stick his finger in every pie. Also, don't tell Kit I said any of this."

I mimic zipping my lips shut, then pretend to unzip them. "The work thing isn't a big deal. I'll only see him in passing."

That is the plan, anyway. In truth, my liquor-addled mind is becoming an issue. I can't stop myself from thinking about him. Our entire history is covered in this candy-colored fog. Beautiful and sweet, but terrible for me.

"Still. Don't tell Kit. She doesn't like people dissing Alex." Eve attempts to tap her nose knowingly but misses and pokes herself in the eye. It's still watering when we crawl out of the cab and enter a club with a flashing neon sign and a sticky floor. It's loud, overcrowded, and the weight of preemptive regret is on my shoulders as we sidle up to the bar. *I shouldn't be here. I have a staff meeting at eight in the morning, and I know my body won't recover from this the way it used to.*

"Are you okay?" I shout over the music as I hand Eve a glass of vodka with what looks like a pre-chewed lime wedge floating on top. "You didn't say much in the cab."

She takes a big gulp of the vodka and squeezes her eyes shut until the burning subsides. When she opens them, her forehead wrinkles with concern.

"Things aren't going well at work."

I lean a bit closer. "What do you mean?"

She looks regretful at bringing the issue up, especially with an older couple grinding on each other not three feet away.

"I've been there for months and haven't made a sale yet. There's lots of pressure to perform, and I'm just not good at it."

"You're not selling graphic tees at a mall kiosk, Evie. You're selling multi-million dollar properties that require time and financing. I don't think they expect you to be selling a listing a week or anything."

She looks down at her shoes. "I know. I thought I'd be better at it, though."

"Give yourself some time." I wrap my arm around her shoulder, and she leans into me.

"You're so lucky, Spence. You've always known what you want to do with your life."

She has a far-off look in her eyes, and it's the first time I feel like she's envious of me. Journalism has always been my pursuit, even though it hasn't been easy. When I was nine, I started a newspaper for the street called *Bristol Court Bugle*. I interviewed our neighbors about the pothole at the mouth of the street and the paint job on the Rowlands' mailbox. Eve helped me draw up fake ads for toys we wanted, and Doug took my masterpiece to his office and made copies for me to distribute to every house on the street. I released thirteen editions before my math grade slipped, and my parents decided tutoring sessions were a better use of my free time. But I persisted. And when I was on the cusp of something life-changing, I threw it away.

"I made a lot of mistakes, Eve." My voice is so small that I'm surprised she catches it.

"I'm sure many people have made mistakes with my brother." She pats my arm. This isn't the comfort she thinks it is, and my mind races with all the tabloid photos of Alex with other women that have surfaced over the years.

"We should dance," I shout over the noise.

Eve nods, finishing her drink in one painful gulp and shimmying out onto the dance floor.

It's an uncomfortable crush of overheated bodies, and the floor pulses with the bass-heavy music. Eve relaxes almost immediately, holding my hands as she sways. Her head falls back, and her eyes close. I follow her lead, loosen my shoulders, and feel every beat. It reverberates through my aching feet, up my legs, and down to the tips of my fingers.

We have several more drinks, and after a few more songs, her feet are hurting, and she says she needs to sit down. She drops my hands, leaving me completely untethered, floating on a cheap vodka buzz and over-sampled, unintelligible music. I raise my arms toward the disco lights overhead and move my hips as I watch the colors seamlessly change from one to the next. Pink melting into purple and blue. Green melting into yellow and red.

Distracted by the lights, I stumble back, and the heel of my shoe digs into something soft. A loud hiss rings in my ear, and I spin around, locking eyes with a complete stranger whose face momentarily contorts with pain.

"I'm so sorry." I hold up my hands, waiting for him to hurl an insult at me. But he smiles lazily and leans down to speak in my ear.

"No need to apologize."

His accent is thick, but I don't catch enough of it to determine where he's from. Somewhere in Europe, maybe. He has a trimmed beard and unfairly full lashes that frame his deep brown eyes. He's mesmerizing, and I'm completely captivated as he moves. It's gentle, languid, and when I move closer and lift my arms to rest on his shoulders, his hands find my hips. He moves me to the music, and I lose track of time and space.

He's from Spain. Madrid, to be exact, and he's in town visiting a friend.

That's what he whispers in my ear while I stand between his legs at the bar. He doesn't ask my name, and even though he tells me his, I don't commit it to memory. I watch his mouth as he sips a beer and casually rests his hand against the side of my leg, rubbing slow circles like he's done it for years. *It's oddly comforting, pretending like this.*

"Would you like a drink?" he asks as I lean into him, bracing myself on his shoulder and sitting on his thigh. He snakes his arm around my waist and smells of hotel soap and chemically cleaned linen.

"I'm fine, thank you." I put my mouth to his ear. "But I'd like you to kiss me."

He turns, immediately placing his hand on the side of my neck before his mouth is on mine. He tastes sweet, and the way he moves his tongue against mine makes my knees weak. I press into him, my hand on his chest and my head empty. *This is a man I could make mistakes with. Mistakes that have me waking up in his hotel room and missing my meeting in the morning.*

When we break apart, he grins as he takes my hand and leads me back to the dance floor. My limbs are liquid again, and I'm still dizzy from the kiss. He takes me in his arms, moving me to the music, and it's incredibly freeing to exist with this stranger and have no expectations. There are no stakes because it doesn't matter what we do. I won't see him after tonight. There won't be any lengthy conversations about the future or fear that it won't work out. I don't have to sacrifice anything, and neither does he.

So I let him hold me. I let him press his body into mine, and I kiss him every chance I get. The beer taste is fading, but the sweetness lingers. It's maraschino cherries and a hint of fruit-flavored chewing gum. I relish it as his hands travel across my body, holding my hips and moving them in time with the music. I let my head fall back against his chest and laugh as he kisses the shell of my ear and continues to move my body. He's teaching me to dance, whispering instructions in Spanish.

We do this for some time before I notice Eve waving wildly from the edge of the dance floor. The strobe light is dizzying as I push my way to her.

"Is everything okay?" I ask, my words slightly slurred.

"Yeah. I'm just tired," she says. "You can stay, though. I've tried to get an Uber, but they keep canceling, so Kit is on her way."

The stranger has followed, and wraps his arm around my body, saying something in Spanish that makes my toes curl.

"You should stay," Eve encourages with a wink, but I shake my head, and some clarity returns. I'm also aware of my aching feet and how hot the club has gotten.

"No. I have a meeting in six hours." I feel the release of the stranger's grip as his friend comes over and says something to him. I imagine their conversation is the same as Eve's and mine.

"Make the most of your time, then." Eve winks as she

settles on the bar stool, phone in hand, waiting for Kit's arrival text.

I turn to face the stranger, and his hand slides into my hair at the nape of my neck. I barely suck in a breath before he kisses me. His tongue pushes past my lips, and his entire body envelopes me. It isn't invasive. It's passionate and sends shockwaves through my system.

"I have to go," I say against his lips. His response is a deeper kiss and the promise that we can run away together. I will want for nothing and live in one of his family's many villas. I laugh, plant my hands on his solid chest, and give him a final kiss, so devastating it deprives him of the ability to form a sentence in English or Spanish.

"Goodnight," I say as I pull away.

He presses both his hands to his heart as he watches me back away. "My dream girl."

I turn away from my stranger before rational thought leaves my head and see Alex standing behind Eve at the bar. Her eyes are wide, and she mouths an apology. His face is impassive, but he saw everything.

"Alex was still up, so he offered to pick me up so Kit could go back to sleep," Eve's words come out in a hurried jumble. "You can stay, though. That man seems really great."

"I'm ready to leave," I say as a shameful blush creeps up my neck.

"You can stay if you want to," Alex says. "I can come back later."

He buries his hands in the pockets of his coat and looks over my shoulder toward my stranger.

"It's fine. I need to get some sleep." I direct my response to Eve, who shoots up from the bar stool and walks me out of the bar with her arm linked through mine.

The ride home is torturous. I feel like I'm about to pay for my night of freedom with more than just a hangover in the morning. Eve, to her credit, keeps the conversation rolling. She doesn't mention the Spanish guy, instead focusing on how nice it is to get out of the apartment and enjoy life every once in a while. This spirals into talking about Darren, and Alex asks if Eve has spoken to Elaine recently. Aside from giving him my address, I say nothing, but I can't help myself from occasionally glancing at his profile from the passenger's seat. He's still as perfect as he always has been, though his defined jaw now has a light dusting of dark stubble, and his eyes have creases at the corners.

"Here you go," Alex says as he pulls up outside my building. The entire block is deserted, and the night is cold and clear. A fierce wind whips down the street, chilling me when Eve opens the car door.

"Can I talk to Spence for a sec?" Alex looks back at his sister. I can't see her face, but the long beat of silence means she doesn't want to say yes. He continues to stare at her, and eventually, she climbs out of the car and closes the door.

Alex sighs and looks over at me. "Hang on."

He gets out of the car and chases after her, stopping her before she enters the building. I watch through Kit's pristine car window as Eve turns the key in the lock and chocks the door with her foot before turning to her brother. I wish I could read lips, but the subject of the discussion is obvious when Eve's arm sweeps out in my direction. Alex keeps his hands firmly tucked in his coat pockets, and his broad shoulders fall slightly as she continues to talk.

They say so much in a matter of seconds, and it quickly becomes heated, only to end with folded arms and matching scowls. When Alex gets back in the car, he lets out a labored breath.

"What do you have to say?" I ask as I reach down to

unlatch my seatbelt. The button sticks, and no matter how hard I press, it doesn't release. The belt tightens, pressing against my chest and caging me in.

"Here. There's a trick to it." Alex leans over, his face inches from mine, and extends his arm over my shoulder. I hold my breath, hoping it slows my heartbeat, because I can't be this close to him.

He gently pulls on the seatbelt. It releases easily, and his hand brushes my hip as he presses the button. My breath catches at the contact, my skin feeling tight all over my body. I shamelessly drink in the smell of him, my heart still racing. He doesn't smell like he used to. The oceanic body spray and fabric softener smell is replaced with Kit's lavender body wash and a hint of spiced cologne.

"Do you do this a lot?" he asks as he leans back in the driver's seat. "Drink on a Wednesday, I mean."

"No," I say. "Eve needed cheering up."

"And was it successful?"

"I don't think so." I shrug.

He's quiet for a few beats, and I study his hands resting on the base of the steering wheel. His fingers are calloused from guitar strings, and a thin, white scar is visible on the side of his hand. He fell off the stage at a gig in San Francisco and ended up with a displaced fracture. The bones had to be wired back together, and when he woke up from the surgery, he kissed my hand and told me that all he dreamed about was me while under anesthetic. I wonder if that's true. I didn't question it.

"I didn't know you were seeing someone." His voice has a forced lightness to it.

"I'm not," I answer immediately. "I was just having fun."

"That's good. You deserve to have fun."

I chew on the inside of my cheek. "Yes. I do."

We used to have fun together, and that brush of his hand

on my hip when he unbuckled my seatbelt did more to me than the stranger did when he pressed his whole body against me on the dance floor.

"Have you been seeing anyone since," he swallows, "since us?"

"You don't have the right to ask me that."

"No. I don't." The words tumble from his mouth. "I'm sorry."

There hasn't been anyone since him. I was too destroyed for too long and refused to let anyone in. He didn't have that problem, though. We splashed every one of his conquests across the *TGP* homepage. While I cried myself to sleep, unable to breathe without him, he left clubs with a different woman on his arm every night of the week. My pain and anger were visceral, but I couldn't bring myself to hate him. There was too much love. And it had nowhere to go.

"No," I say, pressing my back into the seat. "You were it for me."

He looks at the steering wheel, breathing slowly. "I'm sorry about that too."

"What do you want from me, Alex?"

"I don't want anything. Just to apologize," he says.

"Okay, well, you've done that. Can I go?"

"I'm not holding you hostage, Pen."

I swing open the car door, and when my heel hits the pavement, I can't stop the words that tumble from my swollen lips in a poisonous tone. "No, you're not anymore."

CHAPTER FIFTEEN

Dear Alex,

    Even with Miles keeping our secret, we took too many risks. We stole kisses in dark hallways, brushed hands under the table at dinner, and spent nights in the treehouse after the street had gone to sleep. The thrill of chaste moments wore thin, though. Sometimes, I wanted to cuddle up with you on the couch and watch a movie, or go to a restaurant that wasn't five suburbs away. The desire for this had me testing the waters with Eve. I asked her to invite you to my twenty-first birthday. She raised an eyebrow and asked why I wanted you there. I brushed it off, saying you'd been present for most of my other birthdays, and I didn't want you to feel left out. Her eyebrow crept higher. She told me we weren't kids, and I didn't have to invite you anymore. I agreed but didn't feel the usual tug of guilt I felt when lying to Eve. This time, I felt like I'd let *you* down.

    We stood at Elaine's kitchen sink, washing dishes, when you asked me where the party was. It was a bar downtown with enough high-end decor to justify the drink prices. You frowned and continued scrubbing oil and chicken bits off a pan. I told you about my conversation with Eve, and your suddenly pinched expression meant you wanted to give her a piece of your mind. It wasn't her fault, though. She didn't know how much I wanted you there.

You chewed on your bottom lip for a second before flicking on the faucet and rinsing the pan. What were we meant to do? I was weak and beholden to a promise I had no intention of keeping.

You slid your hand under the surface of the water and entwined your fingers with mine, saying you'd go to my party anyway and pretend it was a coincidence.

It was the best we could do, and I agreed by gently bumping my shoulder against yours. We stared at each other for a second, listening for movement in the house. We'd become adept at locating each of the family members by sound alone. Eve was upstairs in the shower. The pipes groaned so that was an easy one. Doug was on the couch, commenting on how the renovation show contestants knew nothing about garden edging. The constant smacking sound in the neighboring yard meant Kit was with Danny, firing hockey pucks at the fence. And Bea was at a friend's house. Elaine was a little challenging, but we tracked her from the laundry room, and when the muffled sound of her weight on the stairs reached our ears, I leaned into your side, and you kissed the top of my head.

It was a rush. Followed by intense sadness because the pipes stopped groaning and we had to separate again.

On the night of my twenty-first birthday, Eve and I swanned into the venue, slightly buzzed on pregame champagne, and ready to forget how much we'd spent on our dresses, hair, and makeup.

The space was narrow, with ceilings so high that I strained

to look up. Heavy black velvet curtains hung from the front walls beside the stage, and a crystal chandelier gave off minimal light. It hid the scratches on the hardwood floors and the cigarette burns in the tufted furniture.

Eve had reserved the balcony that overlooked the rest of the hall for my special night. The papered walls were deep blue with gold drapes hanging from curled metal rods. There were several small tables, all low and surrounded by black velvet stools. At the far side, along the balcony railing, was a settee of matching velvet. Walking over, my hand grazed the back of the couch as I glanced down at the stage. There was a smattering of instruments and an innocuous wooden stool, but pop music was being pumped in through the sound system.

The private section filled up with old friends from school, new friends from college, and our neighbors. I watched Eve for most of it. She'd been nursing a broken heart the month before when she'd turned twenty-one. She said it made her lap around the sun less meaningful. It was a brief affair, but Eve loves hard and takes heartbreak even harder. This heartbreak opened a few old wounds, and she spent her birthday listing the failures of her great loves, wishing Gretchen was with us, and cursing your name in equal measure.

So, I had that twenty-first party for Eve. I got dressed to the nines and painted on the biggest smile I could because I wanted her to have a good night. I didn't make her night, though; an attractive man with sleeve tattoos up both of his arms did.

I was dancing with some college friends when the sugary pop music faded out and a clattering noise sounded from below. Leaning over the railing, I watched you cross the stage, guitar in hand. Your black hair shone under the overhead lighting, and you introduced yourself to a chorus of cheers from our balcony. At the sound of your voice, Eve scurried over and stared down at the stage, her confusion shifting to annoyance. She thought you were stealing my thunder and making my birthday about yourself.

Her anger reached a fever pitch when you looked up to the balcony and wished me a happy birthday into the microphone. It felt illicit, but I melted, and the balcony erupted into another round of applause before you began playing the opening chords of "Will You Love Me Tomorrow?". That night was about me. And in that moment, I knew our days of secrecy were numbered, because I wanted to be down there, telling you how much I loved you.

Eve dropped onto the lounge, arms folded across her chest as some of our guests migrated down to the main part of the hall to watch you. I told her I was fine with you being there, but it didn't matter. She was living in your shadow, but you weren't extroverted. You kept to yourself, and that was part of your charm. It's what drew people to you, and it was something Eve didn't know how to replicate. It drove her mad that you did the bare minimum and everyone liked you. It would have devastated her to know that I'd fallen under the same spell. I was just like everyone else in her life who seemed to love you more.

You played for another fifteen minutes to a thunderous round of applause, and when you walked off the stage, a man in a black button-down pulled you aside. I scanned the section for Eve. With the pop music playing again, she'd returned to her tattooed stranger. I used the opportunity to sneak down from the balcony, slipping through the press of drunk and sweaty bodies until I reached the bar. You'd finished your conversation with the man in black and leaned toward the bartender, asking for water. I stopped behind you, pressed my nose between your shoulder blades, and hummed into your back. It was a rush to touch you so carelessly in public.

You whispered my nickname as you turned to face me. After a quick scan of the crowd, you kissed my temple and wished me a happy birthday. My pulse thrummed, and I wrapped my hands around your forearms and felt your muscles tense. I wanted to leave. I wanted the safety of the treehouse, or your car, or the cheap hotel across the street.

I asked why you didn't tell me you had a gig, and you said you didn't until four hours beforehand. You'd called the manager, told him you were with the private function and wanted to play for me. I couldn't believe they'd let you do that. You laughed and told me they hadn't, and you had to pay for the privilege of singing to me. My stomach flipped as you looked down and tucked a strand of hair behind my ear. I wanted to kiss you, but instead, I grinned like a maniac and closed my eyes when you leaned down, placed a kiss on my jaw, and asked to meet up in the treehouse later.

I didn't have time to answer before you spotted Eve barreling toward us, parting the crowd like the Red Sea. She demanded answers, and I realized your hand was on the side of my neck.

My party ended with the three of us fighting outside in the alley. You swore nothing was going on, and she threw Gretchen back in your face. I leaned against the brick wall, my skin slick with sweat and lie after lie falling from my mouth. I told her we were talking. That you wished me a happy birthday, and I couldn't hear you over the noise, so you leaned down. She didn't believe a word you said, but she believed me, and I felt wretched for it.

By the time Eve and I got home, I was stone-cold sober. She was a mess and apologized for causing a scene with you. Every time she said she believed me, that she trusted that I'd keep my promise was a red hot poker through my chest. You were an addiction, though, and when she was asleep, I met you in the hallway. We locked eyes for a long moment, listening and accounting for every person in the house. I nodded, and you stepped forward, wrapped your arms around me, and kissed me so fiercely that it felt like my heart was going to crack my ribs. You stepped me back against the wall, pressed your leg between my thighs, and slid your hand under the hem of my t-shirt.

You suggested we go to the treehouse, and I pressed myself harder against you.

We didn't make it to the treehouse because a moment later, we heard the creak of a door opening down the hall.

CHAPTER SIXTEEN

The icy ammonia smell is thick in the air as the other volunteers and I listen attentively while Kit refers to the spreadsheet on her laptop. She and Danny bought the community ice rink recently, but even Kit's project management skills and Danny's robust work ethic aren't enough to meet the refurbishment challenge. As a result, every Larson relative by blood and marriage is here to help. Eve said she's on her way, but I doubt it. Elaine and Doug have shown up for their daughter, though. They look happy, sitting side by side on wobbly plastic chairs, with Elaine giving Kit an enthusiastic thumbs up after each instruction.

At the end of orientation, Kit assigns me to the snack bar. It's in dire need of a thorough cleaning, so I set to work scrubbing the cold stainless steel benches with lemon-scented disinfectant. My back has barely started aching when I look up and see Kit and Alex walking over.

I figured he'd be here.

I thought about it as I washed, blow-dried, and curled my hair. I thought about it again when I put on a full face of makeup and tried on seven different outfits, inspecting each of them in the full-length mirror on the back of my bedroom door. Every option was too much or not enough. It looked like I was trying too hard because I was. Ultimately, I settled for black leggings and a navy sweater.

I still don't feel comfortable, and my palms are sweating in my rubber dish gloves.

"You can fill in here for now," Kit says, picking up a clean cloth and handing it to her brother. "Once Eve gets here, head back to the skate room to help Nolan."

He's never going to get back to the skate room because Eve is allergic to manual labor, and she assumes everyone will forget that she promised to help.

"Hey, Spencer," Alex says in this cool, monosyllabic tone as he folds the cloth in his hand.

"You can clean that." I point at the glass door refrigerator that's humming in the corner. It is easily the cleanest and newest appliance in this snack bar, but it's the furthest from me. His eyes move from me to the fridge, and he scratches his stubbled jaw.

"There's cleaning supplies in that cupboard there." I tap the cabinet under the coffee machine with my sneaker-clad foot. "I'm going to keep going on this bench."

He does as he's told, crouching down and retrieving a plastic bucket overflowing with various rags and spray bottles. He wipes both the doors with glass cleaner before something grabs his attention, and he comes over to stand beside me. A charge shoots up my spine at his proximity.

"I'm not sure how I feel about this," he grumbles, and I follow his sightline to Kit and Danny in the dining area. Kit is explaining something to him and referring to her laptop. He stares at her, a slight smile on his lips, and when she breaks for a moment, he takes the laptop, sits it on the nearest table, and pulls her against his chest. She melts into him, her shoulders loosening and her confusion turning to a grin before he kisses her.

My chest constricts. *I remember that love. I had that love. And it was crushing.*

"They're perfect for each other," I say as I look down at where Alex's hand rests beside mine. "They always have been."

"She's my little sister, though. She deserves the world." He speaks so casually. Like we're friends, and confiding in me about his concerns for Kit is run of the mill.

"Danny would do anything for her," I say before slipping away into the small kitchen and beginning to fill the stainless steel sink with hot water. I don't need to turn around to know he's there. I can feel him in the doorway, watching as I squeeze dish soap into the water and stir it around with my hand. He joins me at the sink, and the industrial vacuum being dragged across the threadbare carpet of the upstairs offices fades away.

"Pen." His voice shakes as his hands disappear beneath the surface of the water. His fingers find mine, brushing gently, and my blood pressure spikes. "I want to talk."

I pull my hands from the sink and grip the cold metal edge. Something comes over me, a wildness, a rage. Flames lick at the walls of my stomach while my veins pump acid through my body. *Where was he when I needed to talk? Where was he when I was suffering?*

"Why? So you can feel better about what you did?"

He stares at the water, swallowing hard. "I'll never feel better about what I did."

I turn to face him. Every empty, endless moment I spent waiting for him floods my mind. *When I needed him, he wasn't there.* "Then why bring it up?"

"Because I want us to be okay," he says.

"We're never going to be okay."

He takes a dish towel from the rail beside the sink and dries his hands. There is no tension in his shoulders nor the usual press of his lips when he's annoyed. If anything, he looks tired, and that makes me angrier. I want to fight. I want to say all the things I should have said when he left me outside that chapel. I want to watch his heart break. *No, I want to watch it shatter.*

"Did I mean that little to you?"

He looks up, his lips part, and his face falls. "Spencer. You were everything to me. You know that."

I scoff as I push myself back from the sink. "It didn't feel like it when I sat at home looking at pictures of you online, drunkenly stumbling out of clubs every night."

"It wasn't like that," he says. "You know how overwhelming it was for me. I was trying to launch my career."

My throat burns, and I suck in a breath. *I need this fight. I need to say what I should have said years ago.*

"And you did everything you swore you wouldn't do. Do you know what it was like for your family? Kit still doesn't know how bad it got." I lower my voice. "I gave up everything to be there for you, and you didn't care."

"Of course I fucking cared."

We're closer now, chest to chest.

"Then why didn't it kill you when I left? I cried every day for months when we broke up, and all I saw was you, out on the town, drinking yourself into oblivion again."

His eyes are wild. "I wanted to get so drunk, I'd forget you."

"How did that go? Was it worth the three stints in rehab while I was busy holding your family together? Promising them that things were fine, and that LA was where you needed to be?" I drag my hands down my face. "And I'm still hiding everything that you are. Because your reputation has always been the most precious thing about you. When people ask me what you're like, I still lie."

"I didn't ask you to do that."

"I did it for Eve and Kit and Bea. Because they looked up to you and couldn't understand how the life you wanted so badly was killing you."

My heart is racing, and I can feel the anger rolling off my skin in heated waves. *He deserves to hear this. He needs to know the damage he caused.* I open my mouth, pure vitriol resting on my tongue, waiting. A silent moment stretches out before us, and his shoulders slump. I take in his morose expression. The disappointment he has in himself causes me to swallow those hurtful words.

"I can't stop thinking about what you turned into," I whisper. "You weren't the same, Alex. I didn't recognize you at all."

For a brief second, he looks like the old Alex. The young kid too talented for his own good and in way over his head.

"I am so deeply sorry for everything that happened. I know there's no excuse, but I was not okay. My head was a mess, and I lost sight of everything. I should have listened to you and cared for you, but I was selfish and surrounded by people telling me I could do anything."

"I told you that every day," I say. "So, why did you only believe it when it came from someone else?"

He meets my gaze, eyes shining, and the tether I've worked so hard to break seems to reattach, one delicate fiber at a time. All those painful, desperate memories blur at the edges, and I see glimpses of the times we made each other happy.

Alex lifts his hand and gently brushes a tear from my cheek. A familiar warmth spreads across my skin from the point of contact, and we're back to that night on his bed after the party when he hooked his finger around mine for the first time.

"I wish I'd held you longer when I had the chance," he says.

There is a pulling sensation in my chest. A rawness that makes my blood hotter and my muscles ache. *I can't do this to myself again. This should end now.* Still, I don't protest when he steps closer and brushes another tear off my cheek.

"Spencer?" A gruff voice echoes through the kitchen, and I look past Alex to see Miles standing in the doorway. "What are you doing?"

I step around him, wiping my face and blinking away the lingering tears. Miles is already seething, his furious gaze fixed on Alex, who steps forward. It's a small space, so he's almost pressed against my back.

"Hey, Miles," Alex says.

Miles doesn't acknowledge him at all. His attention is fixed on me. "What's going on, Spence?"

"We were talking," I assure him. "That's it."

"Why are you crying then?"

Miles scans me, looking for injury, which prompts Alex to interrupt. "I just wanted to talk."

"Why do you need to talk to her?" Miles' eyes flash with irritation. "You've done enough damage."

"Hey. Let's walk away, okay?" I reach out to take his arm. "This isn't the time or the place."

"It didn't look like talking," Miles hisses. "He was touching you."

"I know, but I'm fine. Everything's fine."

Miles isn't placated in the slightest and looks over my head to Alex. "Leave her the fuck alone."

Alex doesn't so much as blink at the harshness of Miles'

words or the acidic tone of his voice. Instead, he takes a deep breath and rocks back on his heels.

"She can do what she wants, man," he sighs. "And like she said, we were just talking."

Miles steps forward, and I block him with my body, my forehead bumping into his chin. "Hey, hey. Look at me."

He doesn't push forward, but every muscle in his body is coiled tight. Our shared history doesn't need to be unpacked through harsh words and violent glances in the dark kitchen of a community ice rink.

"This isn't you," I say when Miles' eyes finally meet mine.

I take his arm, gently guiding him out of the kitchen. The rest of the volunteers are on task, so we slip out of the building without alerting anyone, though Miles seems poised to shake me off and give Alex a piece of his mind.

I force him into my car, and though he's silent for the drive, he keeps crossing and uncrossing his arms. It isn't until I pull up down the block from his apartment building that he lets out a telling grunt.

"Just say it," I sigh. "You're about as good at hiding your feelings as Eve."

"Why'd he touch your face?"

"I was upset," I explain. "Are you sure this isn't about your issues with him?"

He releases an exaggerated breath and balls his hands into fists, dragging them down his thighs. "It's not about that."

"Miles."

His focus shifts to the gentle rain that falls against the car window. "I don't want to talk about it, Spence."

"Maybe we should. What he did to you was really shitty."

Miles' chest rises and falls, his knuckles still running tracks in his jeans. Their time in LA together started great, but like everything relating to Alex and his career, it didn't take long to spiral. It would be remiss of us to think that seeing him again wouldn't open old wounds for Miles as well.

I reach over, placing my hand on his forearm. "You've let me complain about him more times than I can count. Let me return the favor."

Miles looks at me, his warm brown eyes bringing our past to the surface. He wasn't made for LA, but my heartbreak overshadowed the pain of losing his best friend to a dream they'd shared.

"Promise me you won't get involved with him again," he says. "Your heart can't take it, and neither can mine."

"I promise I won't," I say before he climbs out of the car and walks into his building.

CHAPTER SEVENTEEN

Dear Alex,

After The Palace and my birthday, your star was on the rise. Every weekend, you, Miles, and the rest of the band played multiple shows around Seattle and occasionally down in Portland. It was exhilarating to see you on stage in the early days. Your thoughts and feelings, once relegated to the confines of the treehouse, were shared with the world. You sang with your whole heart, and you sang about me.

Your future took shape, and I couldn't see what that meant for us. You and Miles were talking about making a demo, finding a manager, and record deals. You were auditioning permanent musicians to join the band because you'd been surviving on favors until that point. There was action, and it was as exciting as it was scary.

Then came the night I couldn't keep the fear to myself. I waited for Eve to fall asleep and snuck down the flagstone path to the treehouse. When I hoisted myself up into the wooden box, you were already lounging in the corner on a stack of cushions Bea had thrifted to make treehouse sleepovers more comfortable. You opened your arms, and I laid down with my head on your chest. My skin rippled when you nuzzled your face into my hair and made this contented humming sound. The smell of the dive bar you'd played at stuck to your clothes. Smoke and warm liquor.

I shifted so I could look at your face. Your stunning blue eyes glistened in the moonlight that streamed in between the narrow wall slats. I said you were going to be a big deal, and I meant it because seeing you on stage was proof that what was coming for you was bigger than me.

You were silent, and your body tense because any talk about our future was off-limits. It was a childish, ignorant agreement, and it was the first time I'd broken it. We didn't know where you'd end up, but that night, I knew you were moving. And I was standing still.

You ran your hand down the side of my body, and I leaned forward to kiss you. Your fingers tangled in my hair as you maneuvered me underneath you. It was a dance we'd done many times before, under cover of darkness while the neighborhood slept. That night was different, though. We didn't rush. We weren't desperate for a stolen moment together. We took our time, skin to skin, feeling like nothing could tear us apart.

I fell infinitely more in love with you.

When we came back to earth, I placed my head on your chest, closed my eyes, and listened to your deep, soothing voice sing one of the many songs you wrote about me. You, the boy made of night, and me, the girl made of stars, living together in the darkness.

The lyrics were crushing, but I loved listening to you artfully tangle the love you had for me into a song. Our secret hid in plain sight. "A Girl Made of Stars" didn't have an ending, and that was my favorite thing about it.

Tears pricked my eyes when I told you I was worried we wouldn't last. You pulled back and tilted my chin up with your index finger, asking why I was talking like that. I told you I was terrified of the end, and it was barreling toward us like a freight train. What if no one ever made me feel the way you did?

You kissed the crown of my head and assured me we would be fine.

That was the night we started lying to each other.

We both knew you were destined for greatness, and I'd applied for a prestigious internship at *The Sentinel*. If I was good enough to be accepted, I couldn't leave Seattle.

There was a crease between your eyebrows. It was the look you gave me when I wasn't making any sense. But you felt it too. The end. Because you were holding me like you knew it wouldn't last.

CHAPTER EIGHTEEN

"Have you spoken to Miles?" Eve asks, her cheeks pink from her second glass of wine. Danny and Kit are picking us up for Fletcher's book launch in half an hour, and splitting a twelve-dollar bottle of wine felt like a good way to pass the time.

"He was supposed to get back to me about hosting this work event at the bar, but he's dodging my calls."

"I haven't talked to him since I dropped him home after helping at the rink." I take another sip from my glass, and Eve zeros in. I've also texted Miles a few times, but he hasn't responded.

"You'd tell me if something happened, wouldn't you?" She shifts on the couch, her long legs crossed with her foot tapping against my shin. "It's not like him to ignore us, and Kit said he and Alex were both at the rink."

"Yeah, they were. Things got a little heated, so Miles and I left."

"That's it?"

"That's it," I say.

She nods, but the way her teeth press into her lip makes

me think we aren't done with this conversation. "Did you talk to my brother?"

"Yeah. I got some things off my chest."

I don't want to get into my discussion with Alex because in truth, there have been more pressing matters on my mind. Yesterday, a sudden and honestly baffling restructure shook up the *TGP* office. Natalia called us all into the boardroom on an innocuous Thursday morning to inform the team that Parkhurst Entertainment has acquired *The Gossip Project* from Hartfield Media. Our new entertainment conglomerate overlords promised no layoffs before three department heads got fired. This prompted Ruby to make the Alex article as shocking as possible. Which is challenging, considering he's canceled on her three times due to scheduling issues. Ruby begged me to find out if he's avoiding the interview, but I firmly told her she can find that out on her own. I'm not his keeper, and if my job is on the line, then I need to get a desk at *The Herald*.

Twenty minutes later, Danny and Kit pick us up to head to the launch. This is Fletcher's second solo novel, but it is the first novel released under his wife, Hallie's publishing house. Hallie and her business partner, Jordan, wanted to go all out, so the launch is at an upscale art gallery. Kit helped Hallie organize the event and proudly fills us in on the canape selection and order of events for the evening while Danny looks for a parking space.

When we arrive outside Fawcett and Moore Gallery in the center of downtown, a knot forms in my stomach. It's an expansive, modern industrial building, and through the large, square windows, I see Alex posing for a photo with two women around my age. They each have an arm around his waist and grin at the phone being held by the third member of their group. I'm all too familiar with the fake smile he's sporting. Pursed lips, clenched jaw, his eyes praying for the moment to be over. It's been years, but I still hate this. They're all so pushy. Like they're entitled to his body. Putting their hands on his chest and stomach as they tuck under his arm when posing for photos. He is used to the attention and hides his discomfort like he's been trained to do.

Elaine puts an end to it, though, ushering him out of the clutches of his rabid fans.

"Is it weird to have your book launch at your ex-wife's workplace?" Eve whispers as we enter the gallery. "I know Fletch and Mia are on good terms, but if I were Hallie, I don't think I'd want to have it here."

"It shows maturity, I guess," I say, spotting Hallie and Fletcher across the room, hand in hand.

I avert my gaze around the gallery, pretending to take in the high ceilings with their network of rustic timber beams and the crisp walls covered in understated canvases lit by angular gold sconces. Eve, flutes of champagne in hand, ushers me to an unused corner of the gallery where we can set up camp for the evening. Fletcher's notoriety has packed the house, which thankfully saves me from having to interact with Alex. That and Eve is intimidatingly pretty with a resting bitch face, and if I stand slightly behind her, it wards people off.

"Aside from Mia, exes shouldn't exist. Once it's over, they should all fall into a volcano."

I ponder it for a second and take a sip of champagne. "That's dark."

She raises a brow. "Get a disease that's treatable, but it's touch and go for a hot second?"

"Better," I confirm.

"How about moving to another country with no Wi-Fi or cell service?"

"No cell service is a nice touch. That way, you don't have to watch them splash their weekends in wine country with their new girlfriend all over your feed," I agree.

"And you can pilfer money out of their bank account using the new ATM card that arrived at the house after you gaslit them into thinking it got lost in the mail."

I frown at my dearest and slightly unhinged friend. "Have you done that?"

Eve sips her drink and wrinkles her nose. "Fuck no. But I have been watching this docu-series about women who screw over their cheating spouses, and it's giving me ideas."

"I think we might have to circle back to this, Eve," I speak through a forced smile. "I don't want to testify against you should any of this come to fruition, and one of these nice folks ends up in an interrogation room, singing like a canary about the two women who were openly plotting the demise of an ex-lover."

Eve's eyebrows dance. "Oh, ex-lover? That sounds so scandalous. I love it."

I turn and giggle into her shoulder before taking another gulp of champagne.

"What are you two doing?" Miles points an accusatory finger at us as he approaches.

He looks handsome tonight, though he is wearing his dad's old suit that's slightly too small in the sleeves, and his thick, dark hair is slicked back with an overzealous amount of gel.

"Oh, so you are alive," Eve chides. "And we were talking about punishing ex-lovers."

Miles shakes his head. "Nope. Not interested in that. Thanks."

The sharp tap of silverware on glass echoes through the

open space, and we all look over to see Hallie waving to get everyone's attention. She's positively beaming and looking incredibly sleek in a blush pink suit with her waist-length dark hair pinned back on one side. Slowly, the crowd shifts, all converging on the central location as Fletcher, proud as anything, stands between his wife and Jordan. Eve elbows me when Fletcher's ex-wife, Mia, steps over to stand beside Hallie.

"Weird," she murmurs.

"Yeah, I see it now," I say.

Miles leans down between us to whisper, "What's weird?"

"Mia hosting a party for Hallie," Eve confirms. "It's a bit weird."

"But you like Mia," Miles says.

Eve looks at me. "He doesn't get it."

I shake my head. "Not even a little."

Miles' brow creases. "So you don't like Mia?"

"I love Mia," Eve confirms.

"Mia is the best," I add. "Remember that time she spent her entire Saturday sewing our ketchup and mustard Halloween costumes?"

"She's honestly the best," Eve sighs. "And she always has snacks on her. Like, any kind of snack you can imagine. Crackers, little cut up bits of apple, and cheese."

"Different types of cheese too," I say. "Not just cheddar."

Miles grunts. "What's the problem, then?"

Eve and I both turn to look at him. Eve gives him a tap on the nose. "Nothing, silly."

Miles' thick eyebrows creep toward his hairline. "Okay...I think."

He takes a gulp of his beer and wanders over to join Danny and Kit.

"I think we broke his brain." I giggle. "Love Mia, though."

"Love, love, love Mia. No volcano for her. And she can

have all the Wi-Fi and cell service she needs." Eve clinks her glass with mine, and we each take a sip.

We watch on as Fletcher thanks everyone involved with his book and does a short reading. Hallie and Jordan each make a quick speech before a fresh wave of canapes circles. My gaze lingers on the back of Alex's head throughout the entire proceedings, and I wonder why he had to be my great love. *Why does everything seem to begin and end with him? Every one of my sleepless nights are because of him, and now, four years on from the end, he so often haunts my thoughts.*

But he isn't a ghost tonight. He's flesh and blood and painful memories. So painful that Miles disappears after the speeches so he doesn't have to be subjected to breathing the same oxygen as him. I don't have that luxury because the second Eve excuses herself to use the bathroom, Alex strolls over.

"Hey," he says cooly. "How are you?"

"Good." I down the last of my champagne and hand the glass to a passing server. "And you?"

"Yeah. Good." He rolls onto the balls of his feet. He's standing close. If I sway an inch to my right, our shoulders will be touching.

"I'm sorry about the other day," he says. "I didn't mean to upset you or Miles."

"I'm fine. But I don't think Miles is interested in clearing the air, so please stay away from him."

"I will." He takes a sip of his soda, and our shoulders finally brush. It sends a little jolt up my arm, but thankfully, we're interrupted when Mia approaches. She smiles warmly as she tucks some errant strands of her chin-length dark hair behind her ear. She's seven years older than me, and I crave her level of refinery. She's the very definition of grace, and there is nothing she can't handle. I watched her enter Fletcher's life, become a mother to their son, Luca, and move on from their marriage without a single spiteful word. If it crushed her, we wouldn't know because she still looks at Fletcher like he is the sun and Hallie like she is deserving of his rays.

"I'm sorry to interrupt, Spencer, but I need to steal Alex for a moment," Mia says as she links arms with him. "Hallie's corralling everyone into the Crofton Gallery where the piano is set up. Are you ready?"

"Let's do it." Alex beams and pats Mia's hand. "I'll see you later, Spence."

The crowd moves through the gallery into the neighboring space, and Eve and I sidle up beside Kit and Danny in the corner of the room. I have a decent view of Alex in his tailored charcoal suit. As he sits down on the piano bench, excited chatter ripples through the crowd. He plays the opening notes of a song called "Malibu Sunset", and it feels like I've swallowed a shard of ice. His eyes close, and the nostalgia is clear in the lightness of his voice. Without a band, his vocals are on display. They're raw and perfect, and I fight the urge to close my eyes and take it in. His voice captivates the audience, but so much of his talent lies in the lyrics. It's poetry.

I look over at Doug and Elaine. They're swelling with pride, and Elaine leans her head on Doug's shoulder for a moment before she catches herself. There is a wisp of disappointment on Doug's face, and his focus returns to the show as Alex transitions into playing "Home at Midnight". His smooth voice continues to wrap around each word like they're something to be savored. When he reaches the chorus, our history comes rushing back in a dizzying flood. He sings about my beauty and what a privilege it was to be with me that night. To kiss me for the first time. My chest aches, and I remember that night with detail so sharp, it could draw blood.

If I knew then what I know now, would I have gone to the treehouse?

I close my eyes, and his words wash over me.

When the song ends, Alex searches the crowd. My heartbreak dulls for a moment as we lock eyes, and I'm hurtled back in time. He winks like he used to when he'd spot me from the stage. It was never just a wink, though. It was a question. Had he done okay? Did he make me proud? Was I happy? I would tap my nose and smile to let him know everything was perfect.

For everyone else in the room, it's a fraction of a second, but to me, it feels like time has slowed. I don't tap my nose. I just look at him. Mapping his features and remembering how much I loved tracing his cupid's bow with my fingertip and brushing his hair out of his eyes when it got too long.

"Alright. I have time for one more, and this one isn't an original," Alex says, his eyes still fixed on me. To my right, Eve bristles, and I feel her gaze move between Alex and me.

My heart sinks at the opening chords of "Will You Love Me Tomorrow?" by Carole King.

It's my twenty-first birthday again, and we're seven blocks from here. I'm watching him from the balcony and knowing for certain that he is all I'll ever need, and to be without him is a devastation I would not survive. It's the nights I stayed awake until he called from LA and sang every song on *Tapestry* until I fell asleep. It's the record player he bought when I moved into the apartment, so we could listen to it on vinyl while lying on his bed, our bodies sticky from the California heat.

This song is every tiny moment between us. The good and the bad. This song is our history, and every note is a scratch on my threadbare heart.

I reach for Eve's arm. "I have to go."

"I'll come with you."

"No," I whisper, my shaking voice drowned out by the music. "You should stay."

I slip through the crowd, my heels clunking on the wooden floor as I hurry to the exit. Tears are already streaming down my cheeks, and my heart is pounding. I round the corner of the gallery and suck in as much of the night air as my lungs can handle. It tastes rancid, like car exhaust and stale weed. My chest heaves, and I look down at the uneven pavement beneath these overpriced shoes that pinch my feet. *I'm out of my depth. This neighborhood isn't mine. This city isn't mine. Not as long as he's in it.*

I wipe my eyes and look around. The street is alive, cars whizzing by and people crowded at the crosswalk, waiting for the light to change. I cover my mouth to muffle the sobs as I lean back against the red brick wall of the gallery.

"Spence." Alex's voice carries down the street, and the sound tightens every muscle in my neck and shoulders. *Not him. Anyone but him.*

I frantically wipe my eyes as his footsteps grow closer.

"I'd like to be left alone, please." I turn my back to him, hearing the whispers of the people at the crosswalk who have realized who he is.

"Spencer. I'm sorry," he says. "I shouldn't have played the song."

My head falls back, my eyes stinging as the cool night air brushes my cheeks. He knew what it would do to me, and he did it anyway.

I turn to face him, arms pressed to my sides. "Then why did you play it?"

He's aware that most of the people at the crosswalk have their phones trained on him, so he steps closer. We're only inches apart. The sound of the crowded street and the howl of the wind whipping between the buildings fades away until all that's left are our shallow breaths.

"I wanted to play it for you."

My head falls back as an exaggerated sigh escapes me. "You wanted to? Of course, you did it because you wanted to. Did you think maybe I didn't want to hear it? That I haven't listened to that song since we broke up because it hurts me too much? No, you didn't. Because nothing has changed. You still only think about yourself."

I step around him and march off down the street, half expecting him to call after me. To offer some kind of defense. But he doesn't utter a word, and when I round the corner of the gallery, I know he isn't following me this time.

CHAPTER NINETEEN

Dear Alex,

 I expected my internship acceptance to be more exciting than a three-line email. I also expected my parents to be slightly more enthused than my mother saying, "That's nice, dear," and rushing off to a bridge game. Though, that was preferable to my father's musings about paying so much for my education, only for me to want an unpaid job out of college. I was already freelancing, writing articles for a Seattle entertainment blog and product reviews for some lifestyle websites. I was making money. Not much, but it was something.

 Still, my father criticized every choice I'd ever made, and I hated that I cared what he thought. The overly optimistic and obviously delusional part of me thought he would be proud that I'd secured one of the three spots on offer to recent graduates, that this was an opportunity that would set up the rest of my career. Not only had I worked hard, I was good. Exceptional, even. My submission was an investigative piece on wage disparity between male and female executives across a number of industries, and I aced the in-person interview.

I was proud of myself and great at something. But according to my father, what I was great at was the wrong thing.

Thankfully, I didn't have to put up with either of my parents that night. Dad was being schmoozed by a medical supply company and Mom was at post-bridge drinks. I'd been lying on my bed for hours, noticing there was not a single spiderweb on any of the ceiling beams. There were also no paint chips in the window frames or even a scuff on the hardwood floors. Everything was sharp and angled. Heavy and cold. I lived in a museum dedicated to the absence of comfort. My bedroom looked more like the untouched guest quarters of a palatial manor. A queen-sized bed with a cream, tufted headboard, and mauve linens with a thread count that had more zeros than most people's bank accounts. I had a carved wooden desk with deep drawers that Mom swept my belongings into because our house had to be in pristine condition for the three cleaners who attended twice a week.

We could not, for a single second, have the outside world know we were human beings.

It wasn't a happy place, and I didn't want to be there, but I can't explain the joy I felt when you barreled in, out of breath from running over, asking if I'd heard from *The Sentinel*.

I told you I got it, and you pulled me against you, kissed the top of my head, and said you never doubted me for a second. You didn't know how much I needed that. Because I had doubted myself so much in the months prior. When you told me to come to your place because we needed to celebrate as a family, my heart doubled in size. I wanted to be with you and Eve and the rest of the Reillys that night. I wanted to share my achievement with all of you in a place that made me feel secure and loved.

On the threshold, Eve threw her arms around me and

screamed before dragging me into the house. Doug and Elaine rushed in from the garage and kitchen respectively with twin looks of concern. Eve shouted that I'd got the internship, and one by one, your parents and siblings held me close and offered their congratulations. You hugged me last, and my whole body tingled with the understated brush of your hand on my back.

It wasn't just you that I loved. It was your family, and I needed all of them as much as I needed you and Eve.

Elaine shuffled us all into the dining room and sent Doug off to get the special occasion tablecloth with the gravy stain we'd all been covering up for years. As the guest of honor, I sat at the head of the table. I watched you send Kit off to get an extra fork we didn't need so you could casually slink into the chair to my right. Elaine dished up an immaculate home-cooked meal of roast chicken with lemon and thyme stuffing and five different vegetable dishes. Before we ate, Bea raised her cream soda in a toast to my success, and your dad told me he was proud.

I wanted to cry, and you knew because you squeezed my hand under the table.

That was when the bullshit with my parents didn't seem so important. I didn't need Dad to pat me on the back, and I didn't need Mom to gush about my achievements to her friends. I didn't need that sterile house that proudly displayed every variant of the color beige.

I didn't need my family because I had yours.

I was home.

CHAPTER TWENTY

After abandoning the book launch, I compose myself on the cab ride and send an apologetic text to Eve. She tries to call, but I silence the phone as we pull up outside my parents' renovated craftsman-style home. The vicious rattle of anxiety builds in my system as I stare at the well-lit living room window, the champagne curtains perfectly pressed, not a single smudge on the panes of glass.

"It's late," Dad grunts as I step through the door. It's ten after eight, and the whiskey tumbler in his right hand is empty. "You could have called."

"Sorry, Dad. Is Mom awake?" I place my clutch on the entry table as Mom appears on the landing. She's swathed in a silk robe the color of a clear winter sky and folds her rail-thin arms over her chest.

"That's quite an outfit," she says as she inspects me, eyes narrowed and lips pursed. It was the fifth option I tried, and until three seconds ago, I felt confident in my high-waisted white trousers, matching white blazer, and black lace bustier top.

Mom doesn't move from the landing, and I realize it was remiss of me to think I could turn to my mother for support after the night I've had.

I pull the blazer closed and button it up.

"Much better," Mom says. "But why are you here so late? Has something happened?"

Her tone harbors no concern, and the increasing depth of her forehead wrinkles will have her explaining to her esthetician that I'm the reason for her increased number of appointments.

I shake my head. "No. I just thought I'd stop by. I was in the neighborhood."

Mom trots down the stairs, halts at the bottom, and brings her hand to my face, lightly pressing on the bags under my eyes. "You know how important it is to get a full eight hours. It keeps you looking fresh."

I ignore her words and lean into the touch. Her hand is cold but soft against my cheek. I close my eyes, only to have her pull her hand away.

"Well, if you're not here for any real purpose, Spencer, then perhaps you should be getting home. Don't want to be late to write drivel for your gossip rag because you overslept," Dad chimes in from his perch on the Oxford sofa, refilled glass balanced on his knee. "It might not be a real job, but it's the only one you've got."

My skin heats, and I clench my teeth so hard it sends a sharp pain through my jaw. The jab is pointless, and it's become something of a game. He's condescending about my career choice, and he enjoys watching me scramble to justify it. Around and around it goes until I give in and let him have the last word. Tonight is no different, and I fall into the trap all over again.

"I've interviewed for a job at *The Herald*," I say. "And the article I'm working on for my submission means I have a good shot at it."

My tone is weak and desperate—exactly what he wants—but I stand up straight and roll my shoulders back anyway.

"Well, that's nice. Isn't it, Don?" Mom says as she strolls over to the couch and fluffs one of the overpriced pillows.

Dad doesn't acknowledge her. Instead, he stands up, crosses the living room, and splashes more whiskey into his glass from the vintage liquor cart in the corner. He grunts when some of the amber liquid splashes onto his hand. "Yes, how nice that you'll be working for a different gossip rag."

"It's not a gossip rag. It's a reputable media outlet," I bite back. "But once again, I'm incredibly sorry that my career and interests don't align with yours."

Dad drops the liquor bottle back onto the cart with a clang, and Mom flinches at the sound. When her eyes meet mine, they widen, and she tilts her head toward Dad. A silent warning that a genuine apology better be the next thing out of my mouth, or I'll be lucky to set foot in this house again.

Maybe it is time I give him an apology. But it won't be the one Mom is looking for. Her shoulders drop when I open my mouth.

"I'm sorry that my article affected your friendship with Dr. Purcell, but you're better off not being associated with him."

Dad grunts as he lifts his glass and takes a large gulp.

"Let's not get into that now," Mom says through gritted veneers.

I ignore her and look at Dad, my hands on my hips and my fingers digging in to stop them from shaking. "We should talk about it. You can finally get it all off your chest and go back to pretending you don't have a child."

"You ruined that man's life," he spits. "He's a good man. He doesn't deserve what you did."

"He harassed his staff members. Three receptionists quit.

He paid off another two, and he fired the sixth one because she wanted to report him."

Dad turns to face me. "There is no proof of that."

"I interviewed all six of his victims. The man is a pig."

"Money-hungry liars. All of them. They saw an opportunity, and they took it. And how embarrassing that it was my daughter who bought into their narrative. I've never held you to a high standard, Spencer, but I thought you were better than that."

My mouth is agape. "Are you serious?"

"Making up disgusting lies to turn your failures into a career," he grunts. "You ruined his marriage too. Poor Sheila."

"Don," Mom tries to interject, but her voice is weak.

"I don't know why I'm surprised. The only thing you've ever truly been successful at is disappointing me." Dad sighs. "I mean, studying journalism instead of medicine was bad enough, then quitting your internship to follow the deadbeat to Los Angeles. What a waste of money and a favor that turned out to be."

"Don!" Mom shouts. "That is enough."

My mouth goes dry, and my breathing slows as I look at my father. "What did you just say?"

He scoffs. "Come on, Spencer. Did you think that internship resulted from your hard work? If you refused to get into medicine, I would not suffer the embarrassment of having you fail at being a journalist as well."

"Don." Mom's tone is stern, but the tide hasn't turned. She's not springing to my defense. She just doesn't like the noise and unpleasantness of the subject.

"You paid them to pick me?"

My chest aches, and a relentless drumbeat sounds in my head. *I thought I was good enough. The study. The work. The late nights. The research. I tried so hard, and that internship made it all worth it. It was proof that I had chosen the right path. It was proof that my dad was wrong.*

Dad pulls his shoulders back, not a hint of remorse in his pale gray eyes. "You know, Rick Blanchard's daughter is the youngest partner at her firm, and Joe and Gina Peterson's son is already an associate professor."

"Is that really who you're comparing me to?" My voice shakes. "I'm nothing like them, Dad. For starters, Vickie Blanchard did so much coke in college that it's a wonder her nasal passage is intact. And do Gina and Joe know they have a grandchild in Scottsdale? Because Kyle sure likes to forget that he's a father."

Mom's hand flies to her mouth, and Dad stares at me with such fury that anyone would think I'd just driven his Porsche through the wall of the house.

"I don't know why I came here," I shout. "I don't know why I thought for a second that you'd be able to provide even a hint of comfort or understanding."

Dad is visibly seething, and Mom is craning her neck to ensure the curtain on the living room window is fully drawn.

"I think it's time you left, Spencer." Mom's tone is venomous.

"I was already leaving." I grab my bag and slam the door.

My feet are stinging from the pinch of my heels, and my skin is so hot, it feels like it's about to peel off in layers, but having the last word sends a rush of adrenaline through my system.

I hear Dad roar from the stoop as I walk off down the street and Mom's violent whispers as she drags him back into the house. She will blame me for this, and I'll have a text message to that effect before I make it home. Mom will demand an apology and wonder why she was cursed with such a disrespectful child. Dad will probably never speak to me again, and right now, that feels like a gift.

○

Three blocks later, my feet are screaming, and as I lean on a fence that faintly smells of fresh paint, headlights illuminate the path, and a car slows down, the electric window whirring as it lowers.

"Spencer? What are you doing?" a male voice calls out. I lean down to see a confused Doug Reilly staring back.

"Oh, hey, Doug." I shuffle over. "What are you doing here?"

He puts the car in park and presses a button on the console to unlock the door. "I dropped Judy and William home. Do you need a ride?"

"That would be great. Thank you," I say as I climb in, peeling my shoes off and dropping them into the footwell. When I lean back in the seat, I catch a glimpse of my smeared makeup in the side mirror.

"I saw you rush out of the gallery," he says, pulling away from the curb. "I'm sorry. I'm sure this is hard for you."

I fiddle with the gold clasp on my purse, the pain of the evening compounding as I stare at the illuminated dash. Doug and I, while close, have never broached the subject of my relationship with Alex. I buried the heartache, knowing that, like Gretchen, I wouldn't be the one to stick around. If Alex willed it, I wouldn't be part of the Reilly family anymore, and that's something I'd never recover from.

"It's hard to see him again," I whisper.

Doug shifts his body, wincing as he gets himself into a position that doesn't aggravate his long-standing lower back issue. "Can I let you in on something?"

I nod. "Of course."

"I know what I saw in the hall after your twenty-first birthday, and I knew it'd been going on for a while. He was listening to and writing love ballads twenty-four seven, and you were always finding excuses to sit near each other. Not to mention the way he looked at you. Like he thought we wouldn't notice. I don't know how Eve didn't see it." He sighs. "I didn't know how serious it was. I thought maybe you'd fallen into it because you spent most of your life at our place, and Alex happened to be there. But when he moved, and you said goodbye outside the house, I knew how serious it was. It was going to be tough, but it wasn't my place to say anything. Not that either of you would have listened."

I dig my nails into the soft leather of my purse. "No, we wouldn't have listened."

"I just don't want you thinking, for even a second, that he didn't love you. He made a huge mistake. And when he called me, crying about the mess he'd made, I was furious."

I wipe the stream of fresh tears with the back of my hand, spreading eyeliner across the cuff of my blazer. "He called you?"

"Yeah. He called me from your hotel room in Vegas. He knew he'd messed everything up, and there was no coming back from it."

"I didn't know what else to do, Doug," I say. "He surrounded himself with all the wrong people, and I couldn't compete with them. He was slipping away, but music was his dream. He'd never give it up."

Doug shakes his head. "Sometimes the dream isn't worth the damage."

There was so much damage.

"I don't agree with some of his choices, but I'm proud of my son," Doug says. "And I know you're the reason we didn't lose him completely. I can't thank you enough for that."

I suck in a breath, my chest filling with recycled air that's tinged with the pine tree air freshener hanging from the rearview mirror.

"He hurt me so much, Doug."

"You don't have to forgive him for any of it. There's no taking sides here."

I look over at him. There's honesty in his kind eyes. If I forgave Alex, it wouldn't be to absolve him of any wrongdoing. It would be to save myself. I want to move on. I want to let go of this hurt and anger because I'm tired. I don't want to feel an ache in my chest every time I hear one of his songs, or someone mentions his name. I want to think of him and smile. I want to remember everything that was good about us, not cry over everything that went wrong.

For the rest of the ride, Doug leaves me to my thoughts. In our companionable silence, I'm thankful Dad bought that house in Bristol Court, and Mom got to know our neighbors, even if it was to show off her enviable lifestyle. They inadvertently gave me all the love and support I needed in the form of Doug and Elaine Reilly. It's the only thing I'll ever thank them for.

As we pull up outside my building, I slip my shoes back on. When I look over at Doug, there are tears building in his eyes, and I can't help but match them. I lean over the console, wrap my arms around his neck, and cry into his shoulder.

"Thank you for understanding and for always looking out for me," I say as I return to the passenger's seat.

"You can talk to me about anything you'd like." He smiles. "You could even tell me why you're wandering away from your parents' house at this time of night?"

My head falls back against the headrest, and I let out an

exaggerated sigh. "Dad told me he paid someone at *The Sentinel* to select me for the internship program. All this time, I thought I was a good journalist, but no, Dad was trying to save himself the embarrassment of my inevitable failure."

"You are not a failure." Doug's tone is clipped. "If Don paid someone off, then I can guarantee he would have stepped in before they had a chance to see what you could really do."

"It didn't matter in the end, though, did it? Because I threw it all away."

"You made a choice, and you learned from it. Besides, you got the job at *TGP* all on your own." Doug takes my hands, clasping them between his own. "I'm so proud of you, Spencer. And if you ever doubt that for a second, then I'll show you the shoebox in my bookcase that contains a printout of every article you've ever written."

Warmth spreads through my chest as tears stream down my face. "Do you really have a shoebox of all my articles?"

He nods, and his eyes light up as he smiles at me. "And I have every issue of the *Bristol Court Bugle*."

CHAPTER TWENTY-ONE

Dear Alex,

    I knew what was happening when you called. I watched it unfold like a storm cloud rolling across an angry sea. The pitch of your voice was higher than usual. Fraught with nerves but bubbling with untold excitement. I was the one you wanted to share this joy with, even though I was the one who would be hurt by it.

    The time had come. You were leaving.

    I didn't mean to cry that much, and I didn't want you to feel bad, but I was in mourning for everything we were about to lose. My mind raced, and my heart ached when you held my hand. You said Miles was going too, and I sobbed harder because I was losing both of you.

    You told me I could see you in LA as you traced invisible lines on the back of my hand. We'd been lying on your bed for an hour, which was a scarce luxury. We were only afforded it because Eve was visiting her then-boyfriend in Tacoma. I'm glad you waited till we were alone to tell me, even though it sullied my enjoyment of being in that room with you. I used to love the softness of your sheets and how they smelled like you: the spicy scent of your deodorant mixed with the faint floral smell of laundry detergent. After that, I couldn't separate the safety from the pain.

You said Miles could be our cover when I came to visit. We shouldn't have needed a cover story, and hiding us from Eve wasn't just a pit in my stomach that grew every day. It was a fiery chasm, devouring me. Punishing me for being so calculating and deceitful.

I suggested we tell her, and you stopped drawing those slow circles on my hand.

I hated what we were doing. It cheapened something that was beautiful, making it a dark and terrible act that we should've been ashamed of. I wasn't ashamed of us. I was ashamed of myself for lying to Eve and forcing Miles to go along with it.

You said we'd made it this far.

I asked how much farther we had to go.

You joked we wouldn't be able to invite Eve to Thanksgiving in our LA mansion with our three kids because she might think something was going on.

I didn't laugh, and you were quiet for too long after.

I wondered if you were thinking the same thing I was. Were you picturing our happy life together? Not a mansion, but a modest home with a picket fence. Children with my hair and your eyes. Sweet kisses in the living room on Christmas morning. Growing old, hands clasped tight while watching the last of our sunsets together.

If you were imagining our future, I realize now it was vastly different from what I was picturing. You wanted the sprawling modern mansion in the hills with a studio and high ceilings. A home that populated the vision boards of design enthusiasts. You wanted non-stop flights on private jets to play shows all over the globe. You wanted tens of thousands of people screaming your name every night.

We were too young to make big plans, but I needed to hear you say that what we had wasn't temporary and this spectacular life was waiting for us. All we needed was each other, and we would have it all.

You rolled onto your side, hooked your hand behind my knee, and hitched it up over your leg. With our bodies intertwined, you said we'd tell Eve, and I'd come to LA with you. You said it so simply that it couldn't possibly be a question. My childish heart saw the plan as devotion, but it wasn't.

I couldn't go with you. I had the internship. I was on the cusp of something extraordinary, and moving seemed to cement the idea that your dream was more important than mine.

I told you I wasn't going with you and rested my head on your shoulder. You kissed my forehead, and I closed my eyes, thinking I could trap the feeling to call on it when you were miles away, and I needed to feel close to you again.

I pushed the doubt out of my mind as you leaned in, grazed my cheek with your calloused fingers, and tilted my chin so you could kiss me. It was sweet and lessened the uncertainty that held my mind hostage.

Then we pressed together. Our movements were muscle memory. We knew every part of each other. You touched me exactly where I needed you to, and the problems on the horizon melted away. It was just the two of us, and even though my heart was destined to break, I did it anyway.

Your hand raked across my stomach, under my t-shirt. You kissed the side of my neck and pressed your leg between my thighs. I laughed when you nipped at my ear. I couldn't hear what you were saying. It was a jumbled mess of sweet compliments and heated demands. We had to get closer. I couldn't be in my own skin anymore.

You caught my mouth in a desperate kiss, and it was clear you were worried too, though you'd never admit it. You liked to distract yourself, and I was happy to be that distraction. And a distraction I was. For hours, we laid together. Touching, exploring, laughing, and then panicking when the heel of my foot went through the drywall above your headboard.

CHAPTER TWENTY-TWO

It's been over a week since Fletcher's book launch, and I haven't said a word to my parents. Dad's revelation about my internship has rocked me to my core. I can't open my Florence Ritter article. It's not good enough, and I doubt it ever will be. I keep these thoughts to myself, though, instead opting to spend my lunch break tracking the rumors spreading through the building about me and Owen. Level four heard about the "date" and told eight that it's serious. Seven heard from twelve that I dated Alex Reilly, so seventeen got involved and insisted it's a love triangle. Twenty-seven said Owen found out about Alex's visit to *TGP* and apparent love confession over cold Earl Gray in the break room. Twenty-one told three and fourteen that this led to a fight in the parking garage, and now the lawyers on fifteen are offering to represent either party in the assault trial. Even the relationship counselors that moved to eleven want to help.

Owen and I laugh about this while I pick at my salad in the security office.

"Anyway, now the janitor from twenty-two thinks my

parents don't approve of you, and that's why our marriage has broken down," Owen explains as he eats the tomato I've picked out.

"That stands to reason. I mean, I did allegedly tell your mom her chicken was dry and made those comments about your dad's receding hairline at our rehearsal dinner."

Owen slaps his knee. "I forgot about that one. Did that come from the accountants on nineteen or the speech pathologist on twenty-five?"

"Neither. It was Luanne from the deli next door."

He shakes his head and sighs. "Great. The rumors have left the building."

"It was only a matter of time." I pierce a tomato slice with my plastic fork and hold it out to Owen as my phone vibrates across the metal desk. I lean over to see Ruby's name on the screen. She firmly believes in communication via text, and since this is the third time she has attempted to call, it must be something serious. I put down my lunch and tap the answer button.

"Hey, Ruby, what's up?"

"SPENCER!" she shouts, her breath escaping her in violent gasps. "He's not here. Why the FUCK is he not here?"

I pull the phone away from my ear. "What are you talking about?"

"Alex! Alex is not here," she hisses.

"Take a breath." I hand my salad to Owen. "I still don't know what you're talking about."

Ruby groans. "The photo shoot. I'm with Cass at the studio. Alex was meant to be here forty-five minutes ago, and we're still waiting. We only have a two-hour booking, and Cass has another shoot right after."

"Have you called him?"

"Of course I fucking called him! He isn't answering, and I don't know what to do."

"Alright. I'll call him."

I hang up, and Owen frowns. "What was that about?"

"Alex hasn't shown up for his photoshoot, and Ruby needs help to track him down." I sigh. "I really hope our marriage survives. I enjoy having lunch with you."

I pinch his chin, and a slight blush stains his cheeks.

"Of course, we'll make it work," he says, and with a smile, I step out of the security office.

I barely make it past the oversized monstera when Hazel comes tumbling out of the elevator, face flushed and her dark blonde ponytail swinging violently.

"Spencer! Thank god," she heaves. "Ruby's been trying to call you. She said everything is falling apart at the shoot."

"That's dramatic." I sigh. "I spoke to Ruby, and Alex is late. Not surprising since he's never been on time for anything press-related, but I'll head down and sort it out."

Hazel's breathing returns to normal, and I notice the small smear of mustard on the side of her hand and the crumbs on her peach-colored sweater.

"You can get back to your lunch, Haze."

She shakes her head. "No. I can't."

She tenses further, her shoulders bunching and a valley forming between her brows. Natalia's controlling her, so there's no way out of this deadlock.

"Alright, give me a sec." I take out my phone and call Alex. She frowns when it rings out, so I try again, to no avail. With each failed call, Hazel's face further drains of color.

"I'll fix it," I assure her. "Let Natalia know I'm headed to the studio."

Hazel drafts an email, hits send, and returns her phone to the pocket of her jeans before I can blink.

"Okay. Let's go," she says as she steers me out of the building.

It's a short walk to the studio, and since Seattle's weather is playing ball today, it's a gorgeous dash through the city. Hazel doesn't notice because she's busy responding to what I assume is an irate email from Natalia, and she almost rolls her ankle in a divot on the sidewalk. I'm not entirely sure this job is good for her. She's always exhausted, scattered, and racing from one place to the next. She takes pride in it, though. She's the first person in the office in the morning and the last to leave at night. She's nurturing, patient, and a comforting presence in the office, which takes the sting out of working for Natalia, who was particularly difficult to navigate when I first started at *TGP*. Hazel noticed right away, and for the first year of my employment, she left a Post-it on my keyboard every Friday, telling me I was doing a great job.

"I'm a big fan of his music. Especially his early stuff," Hazel says as we approach the photography studio. "I saw him play at The Palace when he was starting out, and I remember saying to my boyfriend that Alex was going to be big. You could just tell, you know? His music is poetry."

I'm glad she remembers him that way. It's how I wish I could remember him too. That young guy at The Palace, baring his soul on a stage that was far too big for him.

"Yes. He's very talented," I say as we stop at the recessed glass door of a two-story brick building. Hazel takes a breath, smooths her Betty Cooper ponytail, and gives me a nod to show she's all business.

When we step into the studio, Ruby is pacing the width of the exposed brick hallway, her foundation cracking thanks to the perpetual stress crease in her forehead.

"Did you call him?" She rushes over, gripping my shoulders. "Is he still coming?"

Her eyes are wild, and her breath smells of strong coffee and the fruit gum she's tried to mask it with.

"He didn't answer."

Ruby reels back, her eyes welling with tears. "Fuck. Fuck. Fuck!"

She paces again, and I watch Hazel's composure fray at the edges. Her deep brown eyes are wide and fixed on me.

"I'll see if we can reschedule." I pull out my phone and make another fruitless call to Alex as Cass Warren, our photographer, strides down the hallway.

She's the picture of elegance in her white button-down and tan, wide-legged trousers. Several thin gold chains hang around her neck, glinting under the soft pendant lights. At the sight of her, I do my absolute best to pretend the wheels haven't fallen off this entire project.

"Spencer." Cass beams. "Great to see you. Have we tracked down the talent?"

I hold up my phone. "Working on it now."

Cass inhales, her shoulders squared, and reassures Ruby with a friendly pat on the arm. I dial Alex's number again, listening to his entire voicemail message before I hang up and try again. With each failed call, Ruby's teeth grind harder.

"Have you been through the plan for the shoot?" I look at her. "If we give Cass the rundown on what we're looking for, we can get started as soon as Alex arrives."

Ruby clasps her shaking hands and follows Cass into the studio. Hazel hovers beside me in the hallway, biting her nail and glancing at the door.

"What is going on, Haze?" I press the call button on my phone but don't lift it to my ear. Alex's voicemail message acts as background noise.

"What do you mean?" she asks.

"If Alex doesn't show, we can reschedule and publish Ruby's piece in the next run."

"We can't." Hazel's words come out in a rush. "It has to be this month."

Her cheeks are flushed, and she shifts her weight from foot to ballet flat-clad foot.

I hang up the call and fold my arms. "Hazel. Tell me what's going on."

Her gaze shifts to a print on the wall of the Seattle Waterfront that Cass won three awards for.

"Natalia is going to lose her job," Hazel whispers.

"Over this?" I raise a brow. "It's just a celebrity profile."

Hazel shakes her head. "It's not about that. Readership has declined severely in the last six months. *TGP* is in a nose drive and Parkhurst is going to sell it for parts next quarter. There is nowhere for Natalia to go."

"And an interview with Alex is going to fix that?"

"Potentially," Hazel says. "Natalia's hoping we can leverage a readership spike into increased ad sales and buy some time to get *TGP* back on its feet."

I rub my forehead, an ache gaining pace behind my eyes. If TGP is in this much trouble, then I doubt a temporary bump in readership based on one article is going to save it. Natalia needs a better plan than that.

"I love my job, Spencer." Hazel's voice cracks. "And my boyfriend and I just bought an apartment."

Her pleading gaze is fixed on me like I'm the answer to this problem. I can't make Alex appear. I can't make him share personal details about his life to make Ruby's piece grittier and more interesting to the masses. I can't do anything to make this problem go away.

So, I unlock my phone and call him again. It rings once before he steps through the studio door.

I'm instantly reminded of all the times he stumbled through the door of our LA apartment when the sun was already up and a muscle ticks in my jaw. He's a mess, with sunken eyes and his hair looking like it hasn't seen a brush in years.

"Sorry I'm late. Traffic was bad," Alex says as he pushes his sunglasses up his nose. Hazel audibly exhales before rushing into the studio to tell Ruby.

"In there." I cock my head toward the door to the studio space. "They're waiting for you."

Alex goes on ahead, and I follow, settling against the back wall and trying not to let my frustration show.

Cass has set up the space perfectly. She's warmed up the exposed brick walls and dark hardwood floors with a long leather couch, potted plants, and soft furnishings in muted tones. There is a large, reclaimed timber coffee table in the center, and she's even provided an acoustic guitar, microphone stand, and stacks of sheet music.

"I'm Cass. I'll be running the shoot today." She holds her hand out to Alex, who shakes it and apologizes for his lateness.

Ruby brushes it off and directs him to the couch, her nervous giggle reverberating off the walls with a high-pitched sting. Alex drops onto the couch, his eyes barely open and his arms hanging limply at his sides. My hackles rise even further as I watch Cass struggle to get the lighting test done.

Hazel sidles up beside me and lowers her voice. "Is he okay? He looks… sick."

"Yeah, he does." I dig my teeth into my bottom lip so hard I almost draw blood. Sickness was always the go-to excuse. It garnered more understanding than "he's coming off a six-day bender and doesn't know what city he's in right now."

"I just need to make a couple of adjustments, and we can get started," Cass says to Alex, who barely registers that he's being spoken to. Ruby watches him closely, fake smile in place as she storms over to me.

"What is wrong with him?" she says through gritted teeth. "He's being really fucking embarrassing right now, Spencer."

I glance over at Cass. She and her assistant, Brent, are engaged in a quiet but heated discussion in the corner, and Hazel's panic has set in again. My cheeks heat with anger and embarrassment as I watch him slip down further on the couch, staring vacantly at the ceiling, his foot tapping against the leg of the coffee table.

"Give me a second." I step around Ruby, march over to the couch, and take Alex by the arm. He doesn't offer any resistance when I lead him out of the studio and into the hallway.

"What's wrong with you?" I hiss, and he tugs his arm away.

"What are you talking about?"

"Are you drinking again?"

His expression changes, confusion melting away as his nostrils flare and his jaw clenches. "No. Why would you think that?"

"Because you're almost an hour late, and you look like you haven't slept in days."

He leans against the wall and closes his eyes, his head falling back against the brickwork. "I'm fine."

His blasé attitude stokes the fire in my belly, and without thinking, I step forward, my nose an inch from his throat, and inhale deeply. I can't smell alcohol. In fact, he smells clean. Like oatmeal soap and mint toothpaste.

"I haven't been drinking, Spence," he says. "I swear."

"Then why were you lying on the couch and staring into space?"

"I'm tired."

I grumble as I step back. "You could have dressed up."

He pinches the front of his faded black t-shirt. "What's wrong with this? There aren't any holes in it."

"Congratulations on achieving the bare minimum, then." I clap my hands facetiously. "I'll have Ruby include that in the article."

"Spencer." He pinches the bridge of his nose and groans.

"That's if we even have an article. You've canceled the interview three times and can't be bothered to show up at the photoshoot."

"I've been busy."

"Busy doing what? Lying around Kit's apartment? Dropping your laundry off at Elaine's place? Sounds hectic."

He can't look at me and take a deep breath at the same time. Anger rolls off him in waves. The joy I feel at calling him out on his bullshit is like clean sheets and the sun on my face rolled into one.

"I flew in from New York last night. I was with the band," he says through gritted teeth.

"Well, you're not with the band now, so are you going to do this or not? Because you're wasting everyone's time, and God knows I've wasted enough of my time on you."

Alex's eyes snap to mine, and his chest deflates. Suddenly, that joy I felt evaporates, and when I see Hazel staring at me from the studio doorway, I realize how completely unprofessional I'm being.

I clear my throat. "You need to change. We can't have you wearing that for a feature."

"I didn't bring a change of clothes." He turns to walk back into the studio, and I halt him with a hand on his chest.

"Stay there. I'll fix this."

He exhales and places his hand over mine, pressing my palm against his racing heart. "Whatever you want, Pen."

CHAPTER TWENTY-THREE

Dear Alex,

The day you left was unfairly beautiful. Warm and with a cloudless sky. Seattle was showing you all the things she could be if you stayed. We could be as sunny and temperate as Los Angeles. I could wear a sundress, and we could walk down the street without the need to duck under the awnings of buildings to stay dry. Seattle tried her best but couldn't convince you to stay, and I couldn't bring myself to ask if you would.

You snuck over to my house around two in the morning. It was one of the rare times you'd set foot in my bedroom, and since my parents had jetted off on an impromptu trip to Miami the day before, there was no way I'd be sleeping alone.

We stayed in my bed for six hours, and I remember every second of it. We planned our entire future, genuinely believing it would come to fruition. I'd finish my year at *The Sentinel*, then apply at some news outlets based in LA. We'd tell everyone about this great opportunity I'd come across, and how lucky I was that my best friend's brother lived there. He could show me around. Help me settle in.

That was our game: stretching and warping the truth till it resembled something that helped us both sleep at night.

We'd been together for years at that point, and Eve still didn't know. The shame and guilt I felt was par for the course, but I often wondered if we were honest with ourselves and everyone else, would we have been stronger? What we had was so fragile. It wouldn't survive a year apart. You knew that as much as I did. That's why you held me so tight that night.

When you couldn't stay any longer, you dragged yourself out of my bed and got dressed. The way you kissed me then was chaste, like it wasn't our proper goodbye. Like you'd be seeing me later that day. I liked it that way. Unfinished.

I paced my room, watching your house across the street, waiting for you to leave. Doug appeared first, and he was carrying the duffle I bought you as a going-away present. He tossed it into the trunk of the car while you hugged Elaine on the threshold. Hugging her was the last thing you had to do before you left. The list was complete. Every item checked off.

It was happening. You were leaving, and the reality of that hit me like a tidal wave. It ripped my feet out from under me and spun my universe on its axis. It felt like my bones were collapsing. I didn't know how to be without you. How was it going to get better?

I was about to feel that way for a year.

I ran as fast as I could, not bothering to put on shoes, hurrying out onto the porch. You looked up, and the reassuring smile you wore every time we talked about you leaving disappeared. We weren't lying anymore. *We might not survive this.*

I was crying so hard that I didn't feel the sting of the asphalt as I ran across the street to wrap myself in you for the last time.

You whispered into my hair, telling me we were going to be okay.

I made you promise, and you did without hesitation. It didn't lessen the pain in my chest. And the gentle kiss you gave me only made it hurt more. You said you'd see me soon as you climbed into the passenger's seat. I nodded, wiping away more tears as Doug started the car. I'm sure you had some explaining to do on the drive to the airport.

I composed myself as best I could while walking back to my house and watched from the porch as you drove off down the street. You were embarking on this grand adventure, and you deserved it. It was selfish of me to want you to stay. But I would have given my soul for it.

The taillights waved goodbye as you rounded the corner, and I broke.

I sank down onto the step, my body heaving and my heart shattering. The world felt empty, and as I cried, the tiniest part of me thought, against all odds, that you'd come back around that corner, and we could carry on with our lives. No heartbreak and no separation.

I rubbed my eyes, tears streaming down my cheeks as I stared at the mouth of the street. You didn't come back, and when I looked over, Eve stood on the sidewalk, arms folded across her chest.

She knew.

And I lost you both.

CHAPTER TWENTY-FOUR

I lead Alex upstairs, through the studio's small office space, and into the room at the back. It's stacked with camera equipment and a few props from other shoots that are gathering dust. I scan the shelves, settling on a box with crumpled clothing, a trucker hat, and some tarnished costume jewelry. It's all we've got, so I sift through it and pull out a white t-shirt and red checked button-down.

"This'll do." I hold out the offering. Alex takes it, inspecting the shirts with a raised brow before pulling his own t-shirt over his head and handing it to me. I'm entirely unprepared for the familiarity of him changing in front of me, and look down at his shirt in my hands. The fabric is soft, and it smells like the old Alex. The way his hoodie used to smell before I used it all up.

I turn my head away, feigning interest in a precarious stack of SD cards. "We've got forty minutes left with Cass. Can you be professional for that long?"

Alex clutches the white shirt tightly and brings my eyes to his with a gentle tilt of my chin. Aside from the snack bar at the rink, the last time we were this close was in a tiny hotel room a street back from the Vegas Strip. I was buttoning up the shirt he was wearing to our wedding while he sang Carole King and moved my hips to the music.

"I am a professional," he says, throwing the shirt over his head and tugging it down his torso with such force that the seams groan. His face is pale, his eyes bruised, and there is a fear in them that draws me into the depths of his perpetually tortured soul.

"Alex, what is going on?"

He draws back, suppressing the anguish that's working its way to the surface. "It's nothing, Spencer. I'm fine, and I'm not going to fuck this up."

He takes the button-down, pushing his arms through the sleeves and rolling his shoulders to make it sit right before he attempts to button it with trembling fingers. He tries four times, but his thumbs are shaking too much to push the plastic button through the frayed buttonhole.

"Let me." My voice is soft, and I gently pull his hands away and place them at his sides. There's no space in the closet, and his body stiffens as I button the shirt, my hand hovering above his heart. He shifts his weight, his fingers flexing, and I notice the sheen of sweat on his brow.

"Alex?"

He tries to speak, but nothing comes out, and the room feels like it's halved in size. His eyes dart from shelf to shelf before settling on the clouded Edison bulb that crackles overhead. He takes a few breaths, but it sounds like no air is getting in.

"I've got a lot going on at the moment. This album is way overdue. The European leg of the tour is routed, but I can't think of a single thing to write." His words tumble out so fast that they're almost unintelligible. His shoulders cave in. He's so small and fragile.

"You have writer's block."

"It's not just that. Alfie got an offer from another artist and wants to take it. Ash is a talented singer, so it's a matter of time before she moves on, and Reuben is getting more into the production side of things." His breaths are short and shallow. "I'm losing my band. I think it's all ending."

No.

No, it's not ending. We went through too much for it to end.

"You're a solo artist. You'll find a new band."

He doesn't look at me. "I've got nothing for the next album."

"And that means you're giving up?"

"The label is going to drop me, Spencer."

My pulse quickens. *That can't be true.* Alex has been Summerland Records' cash cow since they signed him. A delayed album wouldn't have them tearing up his contract. Especially when he can still sell out an arena.

"Are you kidding?" I force a laugh. "You can't think of any lyrics, so you're giving up?"

"I'm not giving up." He smacks his temple with his palm. "There is nothing in here."

"Then dig deeper." I step closer. "You have the career thousands of people would kill for. You gave up everything for it. Don't let it go."

"I'm not ungrateful for what I have, Spencer."

"I didn't say you were ungrateful."

His eyes meet mine again. "Nothing I've written recently is good. It's nothing like my old stuff."

My voice catches in my throat as I look into his eyes. It's pain and panic, a vulnerability that makes him look so young. I can feel the chill of nights in the treehouse, my head on his chest, listening to his heartbeat, and the soft tambour of his voice as he sings to me.

For the first time in years, I wish he was still mine so I could fix this.

His fingers tremble as he grips the front of his shirt, trying to mask the panic that builds. It's useless; it's already careening toward him.

I reach for him, my hands on his shoulders as I lower us both to the floor. He's gasping for air, short, sharp breaths punishing his lungs as we sit side by side, backs against a rack of camera equipment. His body shakes, the panic rising further. We've been here before, a long time ago, when the weight of the world was too much, and the nasty voices in his head took over. They left him in a well of doubt and darkness with no way out. I can't tell him not to listen to them because they will scream louder. So, I do the only thing I can. I take his hand and cradle it in both of mine.

"We're okay," I say, rubbing my thumb over his knuckles. "It will be over soon."

His head falls back against the racking, and his fingertips dig mercilessly into his kneecap, leaving impressions in the denim.

"You're safe," I repeat as I gently squeeze his hand. He closes his eyes, lashes fluttering and his lips pressing together. I want to hold him until it passes, but that might not be a comfort anymore.

Instead, I settle beside him, our shoulders pressed together, bearing a little of his weight. It takes some time, but when his breathing steadies and his body relaxes, I feel like I can breathe again too.

"Do you want to talk about it?" I ask.

He slowly opens his eyes and stares at the overflowing shelves in front of us. Color slowly spreads across his cheeks, and he returns to the present with a tangible snap. "No. I want to get this shoot done."

He pulls his hand from mine and stands up, exiting the storage closet without looking back. I remain on the floor, thinking about the moments from our past that contain such rawness. They never ended with him storming out. They ended in each other's arms, with gentle words or beautiful songs.

I guess things really are different now.

The shoot goes better than expected. Ruby stops pacing the back of the studio, and Hazel and Brent discuss the best camera for Hazel to buy if she wants to get serious about her love of cityscape photography.

"These look incredible." Cass turns the camera to show me and Ruby the screen. "Look at the lighting on the side of his face."

I study the shot, admiring the sharp cut of his jaw and the way the light softens the ink-black strands of his hair. It's his eyes, though: unfathomably blue and bearing the weight of his every triumph and mistake.

"Can we try something a little more relaxed?" I ask as Alex adjusts his stance and looks at the prop guitar in his hands. "Something that shows more of the songwriter instead of the rockstar."

"Great idea." Cass nods as she taps her chin. "Do you want to set it up?"

Ruby leans forward, eyes wide and the vein in her forehead warning me that if I don't join Hazel at the back of the room and let her run the show, she'll wipe my hard drive. I ignore her because I know the exact shot this piece needs.

"Can you sit on the couch?" I say to Alex.

He sits down, sliding his butt back to settle into the aesthetically worn leather. It takes a moment, but his shoulders relax, and he crosses his ankle over his opposite knee.

"That's perfect." Ruby sweeps past Cass. "Put your elbow on the arm of the couch and rest your head against your hand."

He does as Ruby instructs, but she's off base entirely. I've watched him write songs for hours on end, and this isn't how he does it. This is pretend Alex. The star he's been told people want. Not the Alex overflowing with passion for his craft, desperate to get lyrics out of his head and onto the page.

"That's not it," I say. "Can you sit forward, on the edge, and lean over the coffee table?"

Ruby stares daggers again, but Alex does as I request and pulls the small table closer. I fetch a yellow legal pad from the desk in the corner, along with a pen, and sit them on the table in front of him. He realizes what I'm doing, and the corner of his mouth lifts.

"Can I move you? Is that okay?" I ask.

He nods. "Do what you've gotta do."

I take his arm, gently tugging him forward so his upper body is over the table. There is no resistance as I reposition his legs, pushing on the inside of his knees to widen them before handing him the pen. He rolls it between his fingers and looks at the page with longing in his eyes.

I lean closer, my lips a few inches from his ear. "Pretend you don't have writer's block."

I move away, but he wraps his hand around my wrist and looks into my eyes. "I don't have to pretend with you around."

There is a softness in his gaze, a truth that conveniently hides the way we destroyed each other for all the things he wanted.

"That looks great." Cass comes closer and takes a few test shots. "Let's go again."

I snap back to reality and move out of the shot so Cass can take over. She's seasoned and puts Alex at ease, carrying on a conversation while snapping pictures. She recounts the first time she saw him perform. He was opening for a pop group from The Netherlands in Portland. She tells him how much she loved his early stuff, echoing the sentiments that Hazel had on the way here. In this moment, I realize how often he gets that seemingly innocent compliment. From fans, old friends, and industry executives. They still love him. They always will, but something about his early work moved them.

And now he's lost the magic.

Alex has the same realization the moment I do. His breathing shallows, and he looks up, sweating profusely and unable to focus.

"Alex?" Cass raises a brow, but he says nothing. This draws the attention of Brent, Hazel, and Ruby, who cross the studio and assemble behind Cass.

"Is he okay?" Ruby cranes her head over Cass' shoulder. "Alex?"

He closes his eyes and grips the edge of the couch so tightly his knuckles turn white. His chest shudders. When he can get a word out, it's barely a whisper.

"Pen."

He draws more short, painful breaths in quick succession, his eyes searching as his face pales under the blistering studio lights. Cass, Hazel, and Brent take a step back, but Ruby doesn't register that space is needed. Instead, she stares at me, face pinched.

"I'm here." I move in and kneel beside him, ignoring the concerned chatter behind me.

"Pen," he says. "I can't move. I can't move."

I look up at Cass. Her dark eyes are wide. "Should I call a doctor?"

"No," I say. "But we need some space."

Alex stills, almost crushing my hand as his chest heaves.

"What is going on?" Ruby's voice transcends normal range to a high-pitched whine. "We need to get this done."

"We'll wait outside." Cass ushers everyone out of the room. When the door clicks shut, and Ruby's protests have faded, I take a deep breath and encourage Alex to do the same.

"Alex," I say again. "I'm here to help. Is there anything you need?"

"I want to get out of here," he forces out. "Can you take me back to Kit's place?"

"I can. Did you drive yourself here?"

He nods, his breathing still rapid and his muscles stiff.

"Okay." I stand up, gently guiding him to his feet. "Before we go, we're going to take some deep breaths."

I inhale deeply and watch as he does the same.

"That's good. Now we're going to keep doing that while we walk out to the car. Okay?"

He nods again and draws a deeper breath. "Thank you, Pen."

I look up at Ruby's flushed face through the glass panel in the door. She mouths something, which I ignore as I take Alex's arm and we step out into the hallway. Hazel pinches her bottom lip between her fingers, and Cass offers a reassuring smile as she rubs my upper arm.

"We still have a few minutes." Ruby looks from me to Cass. "Don't we?"

I shake my head. "No. We're done for today."

Alex's body relaxes a little when we exit the building. I hold his arm and encourage more deep breathing as the early afternoon sun warms my skin. Kit's car is parked a few blocks away, and Alex is silent for the duration of the walk, though he thanks me multiple times on the drive. I don't know what to say to make him feel better, but I assure him that everything is okay, and if he wants to talk, I'm willing to listen.

When we arrive at Kit's apartment, she isn't there, and the second I drop her car keys on the counter, Alex releases my arm and runs to the bathroom. I barely have time to register what's happening before I hear him vomiting into the toilet.

"Oh, shit." I hurry after him, turning on the light to see him heaving again. It sounds painful. Like he can barely breathe. I fetch a bottle of water from Kit's expertly organized fridge and hurry back to his side. He's done throwing up, and he downs the bottle of water in a few gulps while I rub his back.

"I'm sorry." His breathing is ragged as he slumps against the bathroom cabinet. "Fuck. This is embarrassing."

"It's fine. Cass is a professional. She'll work with what she's got."

"We can do another shoot. Just tell me when and where, and I'll be there."

I slide down beside him, and he leans into me, reaching out to touch my fingers. I look down at our hands, skin grazing as his breathing slows and he counts the wall tiles.

"Thank you for helping me today," he says. "It's been a while since...you know."

He runs his thumb over my knuckles like he's mapping every bump and line.

"Since you've had a panic attack?"

"Yeah." His shoulders drop, and his head tilts back against the cabinet.

"Do you want to talk about it?"

He shakes his head. "There isn't that much to say."

"I think there is. Your body doesn't do that over nothing."

His head rolls to the side, and he looks at me. He's exhausted. The circles under his eyes have darkened, and his skin is radiating heat.

"It's too much pressure," he finally says. "Sometimes, it feels like a stone is sitting on my chest. Nothing I have is enough, and I can't think of a single thing I have to look forward to. My career is a waste of time. My best years are behind me. I have no one because I either push them away or don't let them in at all. The people who do stay want me for what I can give them, and when I become irrelevant, they'll leave me too. My brain cycles through those thoughts on a loop, running over the worst possible outcome. And no matter what I do, I can't break the loop. It goes around and around, and I can't breathe or move or think. My head is just noise."

Alex's hand is still in mine, and I squeeze it gently. *What can I possibly say to someone who feels like their world is crumbling?* I don't get the chance because he rolls his shoulders back and blinks away the tears that well in his eyes.

"I'm fine, though," he says as he stands up and resets himself with a deep breath and a flex of his hands. It's exactly like that moment in the supply closet. A sharp return to reality before he gives himself the chance to address the problem.

"Can you stay for dinner? The least I can do is offer you a home-cooked meal made by Kit."

I eye him warily, again jarred by his sudden change in demeanor. "Sorry. I've got plans."

"Has Eve signed you up for a pottery class or something?"

I shake my head and pull myself up off the floor, using the sink as leverage. "No. It's movie night at Miles' place."

"Yeah. Right. I didn't know you guys still did movie night."

"We started doing it again when I moved back from LA."

There's a flicker in his expression and sadness in his eyes

before he forces a smile. It's been years, but I know him. He's lonely.

Should I feel victorious here? After all the heartbreak, is he realizing what could have been? Would we be on our way to Miles' apartment together? Hand in hand, ready to sit on the couch and watch some C-grade comedy while we drink beer and gossip about people we went to school with? Would we go home to our apartment? Would we wake up tomorrow, have coffee together, and make dinner plans?

I can never compete with Alex, though. Especially after I limped home from LA, broken-hearted and unable to face my parents. I camped on Miles' couch while Alex traveled all around the country and had people screaming his name night after night. It's clear I lost the breakup, but watching this loneliness brew inside him should feel like victory. It doesn't. It's a pain in my chest, a tender wound where our hearts are still connected.

In the short or long term, neither of us won. We kept on existing, tallying the mistakes and watching the light slowly die. How naïve to think we were the only two people to possess such magic.

CHAPTER TWENTY-FIVE

Dear Alex,

On my first day at *The Sentinel*, I was assigned to Veronica Cho, the paper's political editor. The consensus was that, of the three positions available, political journalism was the worst. The two other members of the program, Erica and Simon, were assigned to features and finance, respectively. Obviously, Erica scored big time, as she got to shadow three staff writers who were all chasing interesting stories. Even Simon was doing better than I was because a tech billionaire tweeted something about investments, and it wiped billions off the stock market.

The tide quickly changed, though, and on the fourth day of my second week, I was the object of their collective envy. A young woman came forward, claiming to be pregnant with the child of a mayoral candidate who was running on a pro-family platform. Veronica put me to work fact-checking everything the woman said, and before I knew it, I was happily working till all hours of the night, investigating every breadcrumb we could find. When the story broke, it was watertight, and I'll never forget the feeling when Veronica pulled me aside in the break room and told me I was born for this kind of work.

I wanted to tell Eve. I wanted to see her face light up with a mixture of pride for my achievement and thirst for the details of the mayoral scandal.

We hadn't spoken in weeks, and while I distracted myself with work, it was crushing to come home to an often empty house. The absence of you and Eve was overwhelming, and I wished more than anything that I'd told her about us years ago. We never gave her the chance to navigate the situation on her own. Instead, we blindsided her. Crushed her.

I could fix it, though. For both of us. Because you needed your sister as much as I needed my friend. That is what I told myself as I crossed the street and knocked on the door. Eve opened it, then slammed it in my face before I'd taken a breath.

I called you from my bed that night, but you didn't answer. Miles did, and he told me you were out with Howie, your new manager. He was making exciting promises, and I could tell from Miles' tone that LA was everything you'd hoped for, and you weren't coming back.

I'd never felt so small, and the vicious beast of doubt screamed louder as it clawed at my insides. You were doing things—big things, without me—and suddenly, my dreams didn't seem important. They didn't align with yours, and my parents didn't approve. What was the point of it all? Why would I fight so vehemently for something that disappointed everyone? Something that kept me from you?

It took hours, but you called me back. I pretended everything was fine and listened as you gave me the play-by-play of your evening. Howie got you a gig at a small bar on Sunset, and you'd written more songs in the last three months than ever before. You sang two of them, and by the time you'd finished, I was sobbing because I couldn't remember what it was like to hold you. In the time since you'd left, all the memories I'd promised to hold on to began to dissolve. I couldn't remember your smell and what your kisses felt like.

I continued to cry, tears landing on my pillow as you told me you were booking a flight. You were going to wait at LAX until you could get on a flight to Seattle. I told you that wasn't necessary, but six hours later, we met at arrivals, and you kissed me like you couldn't live without me. You held my hand all the way home. I told you we had the house to ourselves, and you insisted that we not tell anyone you were back.

You were in Seattle for thirteen hours, and we spent the entire time wrapped up in each other. You showed me photos of your neighborhood, talked about the people you'd met and the food you'd tried. You hastily wrote lyrics in your notes app as they came to you and thanked me for the inspiration every time. Having you back made me realize our new life wasn't sustainable. I still hold that night tightly in my memory, and over the years, whenever you let me down, I've remembered the man who bought a last-minute ticket and flew home because I needed him.

When you went back to LA, that crushing sadness hit all over again. It would always be like that. Every time you came back, you would leave, and I'd tumble back into that dark hole. I couldn't do it.

So, the next day, I gave my notice at *The Sentinel*.

CHAPTER TWENTY-SIX

Following the photoshoot, work carries on as usual with Natalia spitting venom and Ruby refreshing her email every three minutes to see if Cass has sent the photos. When her email dings, Ruby's whole body loosens. At first glance, the images look perfect. Alex looks worldly, contemplative, and handsome. Those are the adjectives Hazel uses when she looks at them over Ruby's shoulder. What they can't see is the panic that brews in his expression. He's smiling but doesn't show his teeth, and his fingers are digging into his knees in several shots. He's not okay, and when my workday ends, I message Kit to see if I can stop by.

"Your hair is really shiny and bouncy today," she says as I kick off my shoes inside the front door of her apartment. "Are you eating more vegetables?"

"I probably should, but no, Eve is just really into hair-oiling at the moment."

"Well, it's working," she says before digging through the fridge and producing an assortment of ingredients to make a charcuterie. It's almost dinnertime, and there is a crispy-skinned chicken roasting in the oven, but proper hosting rules still apply for Kit Reilly.

I watch her turn sliced salami into roses and make perfect pinwheels out of thin wedges of brie with a level of concentration that leaves no room to discuss her brother's panic attacks. "How is the rink going?"

"Great. Danny has stepped up and is managing the contractors well."

"How difficult has it been to let him do that?"

She sighs as she tears prosciutto into ribbons. "So hard. You have no idea. He doesn't use the spreadsheets I made. He just writes things on Post-its and sticks them all over the place. I found the contact information for the plumber stuck to the back of his jacket."

"Diabolical."

"I know." She throws her hands up. "So, I sat him down and told him that things need to change. We can't run this business together if he isn't following the procedures put in place to ensure smooth day-to-day operations."

I stifle a laugh. "And how did that go?"

She looks down at her cured meat and cheese masterpiece and chuckles. "He said he wants to lodge a complaint with human resources about it being a hostile work environment."

She grins, her cheeks flushing with true contentment. She's loved Danny for as long as I can remember, and seeing her this happy warms my heart. She's the closest thing I have to a little sister, and I wish I was half as strong as her. When Doug and Elaine announced their divorce, Kit took it the hardest. Eve and Elaine have never had a great relationship, so she withdrew. Alex was in New York and missed most of the fallout. And Bea moved to London. Still, Kit picked up the pieces and soldiered on. If anyone can help Alex now, it's her. Whether it's today or months from now. He will need someone, and she is rational and dependable.

We chat more about the rink while eating crackers with more seeds than I can count before Kit brings up her brother.

"Do you know how the article's going?" she asks. "He's been a little off lately, so I'm surprised he agreed to do it."

"What do you mean?" I ask.

She leans forward and lowers her voice like the walls might relay this back to him later. "When Bea moved, I stopped off in New York on my way to see her, and he didn't seem like himself. I asked if he was okay, and he brushed it off. I thought it might have something to do with Mom and Dad. Or maybe he was drinking again."

Her gaze softens with concern, and my heart feels heavy in my chest. I've lied to her and her family about Alex for years. I lied when he was at his worst, and I lied when I came back. I didn't want them to think less of him. I didn't want them to think less of me for not staying by his side when he needed me. I claimed my return to Seattle was because I wanted to be here. That was a lie too. I hated this miserable city for months. He wasn't even here, but he was everywhere.

"Kit. There's something I need to tell you." I fold my hands in my lap and straighten my shoulders. She looks up from the impractically small bowl of grapes in her lap.

"What is it?"

"It's about..." I hold in the words for a moment, and it's a moment too long.

There is a rattle of keys, and the front door opens. I'm hidden from view but feel exposed nonetheless when Kit calls out, knowing exactly who it is.

"Hey, Alex."

Her brother steps into the kitchen, and his eyes widen

when he sees me nestled amongst the throw cushions on his little sister's tastefully appointed couch.

"Spencer?" he says. "What are you doing here?"

"Talking to Kit." I stumble over my words, and she looks from Alex to me with a raised brow.

He drops the keys on the counter and doesn't take his eyes off me. He looks a lot better than he did a few days ago, hair brushed and clean-shaven. He's wearing a new henley and jeans, and I glimpse his song notebook poking out of the leather satchel he drops on the floor.

"How was the studio?" Kit asks.

"It was good." He doesn't look at his sister. Instead, he bumps one of his fists on top of the other like he's playing hot potato. "Pen, can I talk to you for a sec?"

A crease forms between Kit's brows, and she places the grapes back on the coffee table. "Is everything alright?"

"It's fine, Kit. I just need to talk to Spencer," Alex snaps.

There is a beat of silence, and Kit can't look at her brother. I've never heard him speak to her that way, and she's rattled.

"Kit." I reach for her hand, but she pulls it away.

"I'm good. I have to get to the rink anyway."

Alex has the good sense to look at the floor as Kit steps around him. I hear him whisper her name, but she doesn't respond, only grabbing her keys and leaving the apartment.

"Why would you snap at her like that?" I get up and take a few steps toward him, arms folded across my chest. He moves in, too, anger in his icy gaze.

"Were you about to tell Kit?" he whispers, though there is a touch of venom in his tone.

"Yes."

"Spencer, you have no right to do that. It's none of her business. Or yours."

"Alex, you're having panic attacks again. If Kit knows, she can help you."

"With what?" He rubs his temple. "She can't fix it, and she'll feel like a failure when she realizes that."

"She can support you."

His hands go to his hair, and he grips the black strands tightly. "I don't need support. I don't need anything."

I wring my hands as he paces the apartment that personifies his younger sisters. Everything is pastel-toned, lighter than air, and untouched since Bea left. The only hint that Alex has been staying here is the old duffle bag on Bea's bed and the tiny flecks of pleather that have fallen off its peeling handles.

"There's no shame in asking for help."

"I'm not ashamed."

"Then tell Kit."

"No." He raises his voice, and I step back, holding my hands up defensively. Something cracks in him then. All the hurt and anger dissipates, and his eyes grow heavy, apologetic, and genuinely sad.

"Why can't you tell her?" I whisper.

He doesn't answer right away, instead stepping closer. I'm rooted to the spot, mapping his softening features and knowing I can't walk away even if I want to. We're chest to chest, breathing ragged, staring at each other. We hold it for what feels like hours before he leans forward, his forehead pressing against mine, his hand tangling in my hair at the back of my neck. I lean into him, my hands on his waist, holding him to me.

"Because music is the only thing I have, and it cost me everything." His eyes close. "I love Kit, but I need some time to deal with this."

The confession deflates him. His shoulders drop, and he loosens in my arms.

"What's the plan, then?"

"I don't know. Let the band go. Accept my failure, tell my family that I'm sorry it didn't work out. Ask Kit if I can move in."

"That is a shitty plan," I say as he leans on me.

He exhales slowly. His body feels small in my arms. His disappointment is so tangible it makes my chest ache.

"Hey, do you remember that dive bar in Capitol Hill?"

His forehead wrinkles. "The one with the Polaroids all over the walls?"

"Yeah, that one." I nod. "Do you remember when you got booed off stage?"

"Yes. Thanks for bringing that up." He sighs. "You know how to kick me when I'm down."

I playfully push on his chest. "What I'm saying is that even after you got booed off that stage, did you quit? No. You played that place seven more times. When they downsized your venues on that first tour, did you give up? No. And two years later, you were selling out arenas."

He grins and taps me on the nose. "Stadiums, Pen. I sell out stadiums."

"My point is." I push his chest again, and he captures my hand in his, holding it to his heart. "We went through a lot together, and this isn't the first time you've thought it was ending. I've seen you at your worst, Alex. When you're utterly defeated. And we aren't there yet."

He pulls back and watches me for a long time, turning over my words. It feels like no time has passed. We're the same irresponsible kids with big dreams and no idea how to achieve them. The thrill of making plans is enough of a rush.

He pulls me to him, my hands finding his waist again, and I press my fingertips into the soft fabric of his shirt. His breathing is slow and even as his cheek rests against my temple.

"I need you," he utters. "I'm not the same without you."

My fingers flex at his waist, and as I let go, he catches my hand, our fingers intertwining. It's a comfort I forgot existed. It takes me back, reminding me of all the times I thought we were done, somehow knowing that was a lie.

We're never done.

"I want you to be okay," I whisper into his chest as tears build.

"Thank you," Alex says, his voice a low rumble. "Thank you for still caring. I know I don't deserve it."

"You used to deserve it. I would have done anything for you."

Alex leans in close, wiping a tear off my cheek as he exhales. My blood races through my veins, and my skin feels too tight. The tether between us strengthens, thread by thread, fiber by delicate fiber.

"Pen," he says.

I don't correct him. For the first time since we've been forced back into each other's lives, I want him to call me that. I tilt my chin up to look into his eyes. They're as beautiful as I remember, and I feel the current pulling me under again.

"I've missed you so much."

My confession is quiet but heavy, and I realize immediately that I shouldn't have said it. It's made everything too real. I should apologize, but I don't get the chance because he leans in hesitantly. I don't pull away, and a moment later, his lips touch mine. Gently at first, then with more purpose. It feels like home. Like taking a deep breath after holding it for too long.

I open up to him, moving my mouth against his.

"I've missed you too." He sighs as he kisses me again and again.

This is such a bad idea, but I can't stop myself. I just want him.

He slides his hands around my waist, pulling us closer. Our movements are completely in sync, and I run my hands over him like I'm following a memorized map. My mind is screaming, but when he holds my face, tilting my head back and kissing me deeply, it feels like it used to. Soft and sweet. That first kiss after we hadn't seen each other in a while.

Still, my brain won't switch off, and I think of what it would be like if it hadn't crashed and burned. *Would we be living in LA or New York? Would I still be at every one of his shows? Would he acknowledge me in interviews? Would he take me on tour? Would I be his wife?*

Or would he disappear for days at a time? Would he get so drunk and high that he couldn't remember my name? Would he forget to call me back when he saw my name flash on his phone?

I step back and press my fingers against my tender lips.

"We can't do this," I say. "Not again."

CHAPTER TWENTY-SEVEN

Dear Alex

Giving up my internship was the only way I would be happy. That's what I told myself on my last day when Erica and Simon said I was making a mistake. Veronica loved me, and I was getting noticed by the other editors. In six months, I'd have a permanent job at *The Sentinel* or have a good shot at another national publication.

But six months was an eternity, and when Dad found out that I'd quit, I couldn't be in that house anymore. I was walking on eggshells, either being berated or completely ignored. Mom tried, often acting as a mediator, but Dad refused to even look at me across the dinner table. He often left the room when I spoke. It eroded any semblance of a home life I had, making LA even more desirable.

I had to get there as soon as I could. Especially when photos of you on the Sunset Strip boozily rolling from club to club appeared. Every night, when I climbed into bed, I stumbled on all the photos you'd been tagged in the night before. Your arm was always around someone, and you smiled like you'd never known happiness until that exact moment in that club with that drink in your hand. I tried not to be angry because you still called often. You told me you missed me and you needed me. You said the nights out were a coping mechanism. You needed them to fill a void. You also needed to network and build relationships. Doing lines in a putrid club bathroom was apparently the best way to do that.

Still, you assured me you were nothing without me. Looking back, I'm not sure if that was romantic or sad. I told myself it was romantic, that soon we would be together and you wouldn't need to surround yourself with those people anymore. I would fill the void.

Dad yelled when I packed my suitcase. It was the first words he'd uttered in weeks. They were vile and hate-filled. I watched spit fly from his thin lips and land on the top of the designer hardshell suitcase Mom had bought me for our trip to London a few years earlier. The tidal wave of insults continued as I slid on my coat, and the cab pulled up outside the house. Mom, on the verge of tears, begged him to stop. But he didn't, because I had to hear him say I was a disappointment. A failure. A waste of time, space, and money.

I cried as the cab navigated the gray streets of Seattle. Through the tears, I mapped the city, trying endlessly to disconnect myself from my home. I wasn't coming back. I told my parents that. If there was one person my dad hated more than me, it was you. You were the one who led me astray. You were the reason everything I had wasn't enough. You brainwashed me. My small mind wasn't functioning, and not only was my career choice a mistake, I'd somehow made my college degree worthless.

When we pulled up at departures, I smiled because the plane ticket in my pocket felt like solid gold. It was the answer to all my problems. A clean slate and untold happiness.

I had no money and no job, but it was fine because I had you.

It was romantic.

I held onto that thought all the way to Los Angeles. At least, I tried to. Sometimes, all I could think about was Eve. I'd seen her through the dining room window as the cab pulled away. There was no anger in her expression. It was disbelief laced with disappointment, and it haunted me.

Then I saw you in the arrivals hall.

You smiled, and I swear, the world slowed. I couldn't get to you fast enough, and when we collided, you wrapped your arms around me and whispered into my hair that we would never be apart again.

I believed every word.

The drive to your apartment was surreal, watching palm trees whizz by and seeing the city lights ignite as day slipped into night. You pointed out the best restaurants, shops, and music venues with a lilt to your voice that sounded defensive. You needed me to like the city you called home, and I truly, deeply believed that I would. How could I not? You were there.

When we arrived at your apartment, I was still on the high of being with you. The place was perfect, though. There was a large bed in the corner of the single open space, right under the only window. The compact kitchen was robin's egg blue, and I pictured you on the leather couch, writing songs and humming a developing melody. I loved everything about that apartment. Even the bathroom door with the broken handle and the AC unit that hummed a tune. You said it wasn't much, but it was my new world.

You said you had something for me as you swept across the room and patted a small desk with pride. You'd sold your dining table and picked up a solid oak writing desk. You even had a small plaque engraved with my name on it and fixed to the top left corner. I took your hand, pulled myself against you, and rested my head on your chest. Your heart skipped for a moment before you wrapped your arms around me. If there was even a hint of doubt that I loved you, it evaporated at that moment. You made space for me. I belonged in the new life you'd created for yourself.

The days that followed were the best of my life. If we weren't curled up on the couch, we were in bed, making up for lost time. You ordered your favorite takeout to the apartment and switched off your phone. You took me to a flea market you'd stumbled upon, and we bought a pen cup for my desk that was shaped like an ear of corn. I unpacked. I settled in. And when the sun set each night, you played me the songs you'd been working on and wrote more lyrics while resting your head in my lap. You wrote about me, and I wrote about you. Journal entries that documented my every thought and feeling for the day. I needed to remember all of it. All of you, just the way you were. I wanted to remember the sunlight streaming through our window, tangling in your hair, and how much faster my heart beat when you held my hand.

I still have the journals. They're stacked in a box in the bottom of my closet. I get them out from time to time, and no matter how hard I try, I can never make it past the first page. I thought time would strip you from my memory, but as it turns out, I don't need those journals.

I remember everything, and it's a curse.

CHAPTER TWENTY-EIGHT

An hour ago, I typed the last word on my Florence Ritter story, and I've felt sick ever since. I got an email from Max Marlow's secretary last night to say he wants to see me. Naturally, on the walk to his office, all I can picture is my dad writing a check and sliding it across the table at *The Sentinel*. It makes me hate every word on the page in my hand.

"Spencer, what have you got for me?" Max's hands rest on his hips. He isn't wearing his suit jacket, his tie is loose, and there is a thin sheen of sweat on his forehead. If Natalia saw him like this, she might finally crack a smile.

"The Florence Ritter piece." I hand over the document with trembling fingers. The font is twelve-point, double-spaced, and it has optimistically narrow margins. In my delusional, sleep-deprived state, I thought Max would love it, but the harder his lips press together, the tighter the knot in my stomach gets. I should have researched more. I should have spoken to more members of the unsolved crime group on Reddit and looked over more public records.

"It's not bad." Max sits down and takes out a red pen.

With a flick of his thick wrist, he circles words, underlines sentences, and crosses out whole paragraphs. I watch every bleeding stroke of that pen, and my heart sinks deeper in my chest. I'm not ready for *The Herald*. I'm *TGP* stock and nothing more.

Max hands the article back, dripping with the evidence of my failure. There is a sharp sting behind my eyes, and my nerves fire with panic. *I can't cry. I need to focus and take in every crumb of his feedback. Live it. Breathe it. Or, at the very least, not have a breakdown in Max's office.*

"I understand the investigative intention, but it's surface level. You haven't given me a clear picture of who Florence is outside of being a murder victim."

I nod, perhaps too aggressively. "You're right."

Max leans back in his chair and taps the red pen on his bottom lip. "I need a new spin on it, Spencer. Your technical skill is great, but if you want a desk up here, I want to see more. Give me a timeline of Florence's life. Who was she? Who did she become? It's an unsolved case, so I don't expect a resolution, but I want theories. Something tantalizing and plausible enough to regain public interest. I want this piece to be required reading for up-and-coming internet sleuths who are looking into the case."

"I can do that." I hold the paper to my chest, embarrassed by its very existence.

"Good. You've got two weeks, but know I have several interviews lined up, and I won't hold the position for you."

"Yes. Of course. Two weeks is great. Thank you," I say before backing out of the office.

"What's the matter with you?" Eve snaps her fingers in front of my face because I've been pushing salad around a plate for the last few minutes.

"I'm fine. I'm good." I shovel the over-dressed greens into my mouth. "Totally fine. Fine."

"You've said 'fine' too many times for someone who's fine. What's going on?" She puts down her fork and stares at me.

I don't know where to begin. Should I start with my incredibly sub-par Herald *submission? Or fill her in on Alex's panic attack?* I could tell her about the kiss and watch her head explode all over the white tablecloth at this overpriced restaurant.

"Work is tense. That's all." I shrug. "My *Herald* article is nowhere near good enough to publish, and Max is interviewing other candidates for the job."

"Right," she says slowly.

"I mean, obviously, my suitability for the role hinges on this article, and who knows if I'm even capable of writing something Max Marlow likes? That thought runs through my mind roughly every ten seconds. Then I think about that mindfulness workshop we did and how I need to be kind to myself. I am trying, you know, just playing the long game. I have a huge number of writing credits, and I've done more in-depth content. I mean, obviously, there are fluff pieces out there with my name on them, but that is par for the course with a gossip site. And I'm trying not to worry about the rumors of more layoffs because my work is consistent. I don't provide a direct revenue stream for *TGP* like ad sales, but they need content, and I provide that. More than Ruby does, anyway. Natalia will fight to keep me. At least, I hope she will. Unless she gets fired."

"Now you're talking too much," Eve says, picking up her fork.

"I am," I say as I pick at my salad. "Anyway. Enough about

me. Has Darren backed off? He can't really be that attached to a floor rug."

She drops her fork again, takes a gulp of her green juice, and rolls her shoulders back. Eve's favorite topic of conversation is Eve, so switching gears is easy.

"He's being a bitch about it." She sighs. "I've already spilled wine on the upper left corner, so I don't know why he wants it. He always complained it was too big for the living room. Now, anyone would think he'll die without it."

"Sounds like he's having problems letting go," I muse.

"Of a rug." She rolls her eyes.

"It's probably more about what the rug represents."

"Wouldn't the engagement ring be more representative of our time together?"

"Are you giving that back?" I raise a brow.

"Never," she scoffs. "I'm going to be buried with it just to spite him."

"That seems healthy."

She wrinkles her nose and smiles through a mouthful of food as a way of acknowledging my sarcasm.

For the rest of lunch, I continue the conversation by covering topics like Kit and Danny's ice rink renovation and the later stages of Bea's pregnancy, and we round table some ideas to get Miles' pop culture-specific trivia nights off the ground. When I think I'm in the clear and our plates have been collected, Eve circles back to what's going on with me.

"Is Alex giving you hell or something? Kit said you guys had it out at her place the other night."

I shake my head, trying to dislodge the memory of kissing him. "No, no. He's been fine. The photoshoot didn't go as well as Ruby hoped, but we got what we needed."

I fiddle with the corner of the tablecloth, unable to meet Eve's wary gaze.

"Oh, fuck off," she says. "Something happened, didn't it? You're such a bad liar."

My stomach rolls. She may as well have me in a locked room with a spotlight on my face because I have the structural integrity of a soap bubble. *Surely, it's a positive thing that I can't lie to her as easily as I used to?*

"Nothing happened." My voice shakes. "I'm focusing on my piece for *The Herald*. That's it."

She leans back in her chair and crosses her long legs, her spike heels peeping out from the flared cuff of her royal blue pants. She looks me in the eye, and I swallow hard.

"Did you scream at him?"

I shake my head. "No."

"Kick him?"

"What? No."

"Pull his hair?"

I mean, a little, but it was more of a gentle tug while I pressed myself against him.

"No, Eve. We talked about his band. That's it."

Her eyes narrow. "Alright. I believe you, but I don't trust him."

For someone who believes me, the accusatory finger she holds out is hostile.

In the dying minutes of our respective lunch breaks, Eve drops the line of questioning about Alex, and I ask about her job. Her somber expression is enough to have me switching back to Darren's character assassination, which makes us both smile.

"How was lunch?" Owen asks as I step into the building.

"Company was great. Paying twenty-seven dollars for lawn clippings covered in olive oil has me morally affronted."

He reaches under the counter and pulls out a plastic container. "Will this make it better?"

I scurry over and plant my hands on the desk on either side of the container. "Oh, what is it?"

"Coconut cherry bars." His grin is so big. He looks a lot less threatening than his starched black security uniform implies.

"Stop it," I squeal. "I love it when you make those."

He pushes the container toward me, and I clutch it with both hands.

"They're all yours."

"You're too good to me." I'm already stuffing one in my mouth as I say it.

He shrugs casually. "You deserve it."

My smile slips a little. *I'm not entirely sure that's true.* He's sweet and kind and brings me baked goods. Aside from lunchtime company, I don't bring much to the friendship. I'm about to ask if there is anything I can do for him when the elevator doors open, and Ruby rushes out.

"Spencer!" she shouts, eyes wild. "Where have you been?"

My heart crawls into my throat, and the overpriced salad roils in my stomach. When the Parkhurst Media executive strolled into our office this morning, I figured something was about to go down. Still, they've already scraped *TGP* to the bone. There's no one left to fire and still be able to function as a publication.

"Lunch. What's going on?" My palms are slick, and I'm struggling to hold on to the coconut cherry bars.

"Natalia has been locked in her office with that guy from Parkhurst with the patchy mustache, and the marketing team is nervous," Ruby explains on the elevator ride to our floor. "We have so many staff writers. There is no way we're all going to stay. Not when half the sales team got fired."

"What? Sales got cut?"

She nods, her waves of blonde hair swishing. "Yep, about twenty minutes ago. This is so bad, Spence."

"What about freelance contracts?"

"I don't know. But freelancers will be cheaper, won't they? They're paid for content, not staff benefits and expenses."

When we arrive at the office, Natalia's door is closed. Ruby and I slip into our cubicle, and for the next two hours, my colleagues are called one by one into Natalia's office. At least half of them exit in tears. The rest look relieved as they scurry back to their cubicles. I keep my head down and come close to convincing myself that I don't need this job. I could move in with Miles to save on rent and learn to love ramen noodles and dented cans of beans. The atmosphere here isn't that good, and my office chair lacks lumbar support. The break room is small, and the view of the fountain in the park across the street isn't that nice. Three mornings a week, a homeless man bathes in it.

"Spencer." Hazel appears out of nowhere, and it makes me jump. "You're up."

Ruby turns away as if proximity to me will seal her fate. I say nothing and follow Hazel to Natalia's open office door. Thankfully, the Parkhurst exec has left all this unpleasantness to her alone.

"Take a seat," Natalia says as she dismisses Hazel with a glance.

I do as I'm told and fold my hands in my lap, worrying that the skirt I chose this morning shows too much leg and that I should have ironed my blouse better. I missed a part on the upper sleeve, and I know it's noticeable.

"Obviously, we're doing some restructuring," Natalia starts.

Hacking away every scrap of living flesh in this company would be a more accurate term for what this is.

"Our overheads are high, so we're condensing some of our departments," she continues. "This means there won't be a place for everyone. Since I'm handling the restructure, I've had to look at the function of each member and how they serve the larger team."

Maybe I am safe? All the crying people left a lot sooner than this. They had barely a minute in this office before Hazel was handing them a tissue and a sincere apology on the way out.

"How many staff writers are you keeping on?" I ask.

"Twenty percent will stay on to maintain general news coverage, and some will take on contract positions to provide the listicles and celebrity gossip content."

I take a deep breath and look down at my hands. *I don't like those odds.*

"Which category do I fall into?"

"I'm offering you a contract," she says, but from her inflection, I know it's not good. "The work will be sporadic, but you're welcome to submit content, and we can assess whether we'll run it."

Great. I have a job, but I'll be writing about celebrities grocery shopping or which director is banging his lead actress, and there's a slim chance they'll buy it anyway.

"So I'll be writing quizzes from now on?" I realize how petulant and ungrateful I sound, but I cannot bring myself to feign appreciation over this.

"No, you won't be." Natalia almost smirks, taking a long look at me before she sits down at her desk. We're eye to eye now. Equal.

"You know I hate that celebrity drivel, and I've always seen this magazine as a work in progress. Little by little, we splice that gossipy content with actual journalism. Before you know it, we're reputable. We've had a name change and a rebrand, and our journalists don't get laughed out of political summits.

That's my plan, and I need someone who sees that vision. Someone who can propel us into a different space."

Natalia looks more young and vibrant than I've ever seen her. The light in her eyes is almost tangible. Though her vision, while exciting, is not reality. This is about Max Marlow. She and Max have always butted heads, and his being selected over her to lead *The Herald* continues to be a bone of contention. Whatever she thinks she can do with *TGP* is another way for her to compete with him.

"When will I transition over to freelance?"

"At the end of the month."

The pressure of the *Herald* job is now a rope around my windpipe. I've got savings, but rent alone will burn through that fast if I don't find full-time work, and there is no way I'll ask my parents for help.

"What we really need is this Alex Reilly story to make waves. I know you've been helping Ruby, and I want that to continue. Your personal connection with him and his family is our way in."

"Into what?"

Natalia's cat-like eyes grow darker. "I want more, Spencer. I want a story that shows the seedy underbelly of his life in LA, and I want to know why his band is in New York and he's in Seattle. I want to know why he has a tour but no album release date."

"I think you're reading too much into it," I say. "And I'm not comfortable using him or his family for an article."

"Then why are you a journalist?"

"Because I want to write important stories about important people."

"Alex is an important person and a hard-hitting piece about a notoriously private musician is just what we need to keep this publication going. It could be our ticket to make a change around here. We're blending that gossip garbage with a deeper story about the private life of an elusive celebrity. If Alex is tight-lipped, he's hiding something. Ruby can get it out of him, but you can loosen him up first."

The thought of using him or the Reilly family makes me sick, and I don't want Kit or Bea to know anything about his past.

"I know Alex, and there is nothing to explore. He's talented, but he's focused. Don't hang your hopes of this being an explosive interview. That's not him."

Natalia taps her chin, clearly not buying what I'm selling. In fact, I doubt she's even listening.

"He hasn't released anything in four years, and Ruby said the label wants to drop him."

My blood heats, and I look toward my cubicle, even though Ruby is nowhere in sight. *Of course, she was listening outside the closet at the studio.*

Natalia sits up straight, arms folded across her chest. "I want to know about every woman he sleeps with and every line of coke he snorts when he thinks no one is watching. Get Ruby what she needs."

I open and close my mouth like a fish, realizing that Natalia operates on a whole different level. She's the very definition of "knowledge is power". And it's remiss of me to think she hasn't turned over every stone she can find with Alex. She will have scoured the archives to find every one of his publicized misgivings and every paparazzi photo with me in the background, attempting to shield my face.

"He was an alcoholic rock star for years. Surely, he impregnated a few starlets. What about the stints in rehab?"

"There were three."

"Three starlets or three stints in rehab."

"Rehab. Not starlets."

At least, there were three stints that I know of. When he cut ties with Howie Dawson, he went off the grid for a while. He checked in with his family so they wouldn't worry, but he made sure he was never photographed in public. There were rumors he was in a treatment facility. There were also rumors he was living in Europe on a yacht, followed by a trending hashtag about him being spotted waiting tables at a resort in Mexico. Eve debunked these of her own volition to save me the embarrassment of asking. She'd seamlessly slip into conversation that Kit had spoken to him the day before while he was in the studio in LA or that Bea was going to visit him for his birthday.

I stand to face Natalia, and she doesn't shrink back. Not that I expect her to, but what have I got to lose now? I'm going to be unemployed by the end of the month.

"I can't exploit my personal relationships for a story."

Natalia exhales deeply, and her head tips back a moment before she finds her composure. "I'll lay it out for you, Spencer. What Parkhurst is doing is only the beginning. They're trimming as much fat as possible to merge us with *Glamorize*. *TGP* will not survive this, but we can take what we have left and build something better."

She swallows hard, and there is a fleck of panic in her eyes. I've never seen her like this. She's almost vulnerable, but it passes quickly.

"If you want to make a name for yourself, then it's time to step up. You're a strong writer, and if we can pull this off, *TGP* doesn't have to die. We can leverage the influx of public engagement and site traffic to pivot."

"You're talking about selling someone out for a dream that might not happen. Why would Parkhurst hang onto and rebrand *TGP* when they have several other news publications that already have a loyal readership?"

"We have an opportunity here. Even if it crosses some lines." Her tone is too calm. Completely at odds with her violent stare.

I should go along with this to ensure my survival, but I don't care if *Glamorize* absorbs *TGP*. In fact, business-wise, it makes sense to merge a gossip website and beauty magazine. In my time at *TGP*, I've pitched several ideas about political scandals, police corruption, and environmental issues. And every time, they've been rebuffed for a story about a reality TV star's nip slip or a makeup mogul's messy divorce. *Why should I fight to save something that has never fought to keep me?*

"The answer is no." My words have a finality to them. Unfortunately, the delivery is like a child asking their irate mother for McDonald's when a home-cooked meal is on the table.

Natalia doesn't even blink. She is so impassive that it's impossible to know what is going through her head.

"Spencer, I like you. I do." Her deadpan expression begs to differ. "But if you aren't willing to help this team, then I don't know why we're still talking."

My whole body deflates as I take in Natalia's expression. There is conviction in her eyes. The self-satisfied glow of someone who believes their dream will be a reality. I won't be able to convince her otherwise, so I thank her for her time and return to my desk.

For the rest of the afternoon, I'm hunched over my keyboard, dissecting my Florence Ritter article and making no headway. It isn't until Ruby leaves that my mind wanders. I read over some early articles on Alex and pour through the sub-folder in my email with every message we sent to each other. It's a digital time capsule, our hearts gathering dust in the aether. There is too much of myself in those words, and I wish I could distance myself from the girl in the emails. She knows nothing but hopeless love. She wants nothing but him and the impossible life he's promising her.

I haven't changed, though. I still think about him. I still protect him. I still put him before myself and my job.

Maybe it's time for me to change instead of counting the ways he has. We won't ever be those kids in the treehouse again. The songs he sings about me don't hold real magic, and I am tired of romanticizing a time that held me back from the person I could have been. I fought for my parents' acceptance of my career choice. I worked hard at college to get my degree. Then, somewhere along the way, I faded. Burned out like a dying star.

That thought plays in my mind as I walk to my car. I continue to turn it over when I pull up at a stoplight and admire the gossamer curtains and neutral color palette of the hair salon six blocks from my apartment. Inside, a young woman wipes down the small wooden benches fixed to the wall in front of three white leather chairs. Behind the counter is a poster of a woman, her face half covered by a cascading wave of golden hair. It falls past her chin, her full lips visible and pouting as she grips the lapels of her gray suit. The car behind me honks its horn, and the car ahead disappears around the corner. As my foot shifts to the gas, a car pulls out of a space outside the salon. It takes all of a second for my mind to process the situation.

I take the newly vacated space, kill the engine, and hold my head high as I walk into the salon. The woman shows me to a chair, runs her fingers through my long, chestnut waves, and asks what I'm after today. I bring my hand up to my chin.

"Cut it to here."

CHAPTER TWENTY-NINE

Dear Alex,

    I was never a beach girl. I'm built for blustery winters and rainy summer days. My wardrobe has always been thick leggings, plaid skirts, turtleneck sweaters, and wool coats. I like boots and scarves, leather satchels, and that black beret Bea got me from Paris. Elaine always said I looked like the heroine of a romance novel whose love interest was a dapper English poet, and our meet-cute was dropped books on the green courtyard of an ancient university.

    My mother called it eclectic and suggested I swap the chocolate brown turtleneck for a white button-down.

    In LA, my Seattle style didn't translate when it was over eighty degrees and sunny. I swapped my skirts for cut-offs and my coats for band t-shirts. By the end of my first month, I had a selection of sundresses with thin straps that you liked to push down to kiss my bare shoulder. You said my skin tasted like summer days and sea air. I didn't know what that meant until we started spending lazy days in Malibu. We were so far from home, we could have been on a different planet, breathing different air, and living someone else's life. It didn't feel real. It was too good. Too perfect.

I started reading again, devouring crime novels like they were going out of print and growing a rather impressive collection of books courtesy of the second-hand bookstore two blocks from the apartment. You were writing too. Pages and pages of lyrics scribbled on sand-covered paper while we soaked up the California sun. You read me romantic lines as I drank in the sight of you in all your flawless beauty. The sun had bronzed your skin, and saltwater dripped from your hair. You had smile lines, and I kissed them whenever you were close enough because I believed this new life was the reason they were there.

We were sun-kissed, happy, and untouchable.

I'd cut myself off from everyone by then. I didn't answer when my mom called, and my friendships from college and the internship fell apart. I convinced myself that holding onto Seattle would tarnish LA. I wanted nothing but that life with you.

But that new life hadn't really started yet.

Howie was applying pressure to every contact he had to get you gigs. He'd introduced you to Reuben, and the next phase of the project was to hire a drummer, which you did when you and Miles stumbled across Stevie Costa at a dive bar in Venice.

You had your backing musicians, and Howie had a label willing to bite. Things in your professional life were golden, and that translated into our personal life as well.

You took me everywhere, never letting go of my hand as we navigated music venues, industry parties, and studio sessions. We came home to our little apartment, ate takeout from the Chinese restaurant on the corner, and got a buzz from that cheap wine I liked, even though you said it was too sweet.

We held each other for hours, bodies tangled and laughing at the jokes we made at our own expense. Adolescent drama didn't exist in California. That was Seattle business. How foolish it was to think that nothing would keep us apart.

I told you how much I loved watching the sunset in Malibu, and you vowed to take me there every Wednesday afternoon to watch the sun sink on another perfect day.

Those sunsets were everything to me. For those first three months, we didn't miss one. Even if you'd been in the studio for the better part of two days, you would race home on Wednesdays to take me to Malibu. It was our time and our place. Nothing could touch us there. We were perfect.

I remember one sunset in particular. It was colder than usual, but the stained glass sky was as spectacular as ever. You wrapped your arms around me, and as I cuddled into you, I asked how it was possible to be this happy and how everything could feel so right.

You said it was because we were soulmates, and soulmates were meant to be together. The universe wouldn't have it any other way.

By the time we got back to the apartment, you had the first verse of "Malibu Sunset" on the tip of your tongue. I fell asleep to the gentle pluck of guitar strings and the low hum of your voice as you sang about the freckles on the bridge of my nose.

If we were soulmates, right then, in that tiny apartment, I believed it.

CHAPTER THIRTY

My lungs burn, and my legs are jelly. I can't hold my weight, and my head feels like it's filled with helium.

"I...can't...do...this." I heave, and my breakfast of eggs and buttered toast threatens to resurface. Not even the early morning breeze off Puget Sound is enough to cool me down. "I'm gonna be sick."

"Spencer. We've barely cracked one mile." Kit jogs on the spot beside me and checks her smartwatch. She explained how her exercise tracker works before we embarked on this monumentally stupid idea to improve my cardiovascular fitness. She tracks her workouts in a spreadsheet that's more complex than an international corporation's tax filings.

I look up at her, gasping for breath. "I can see why Eve refuses to do this with you."

"This is low impact, Spence. Would you prefer to run drills with Danny at the rink? He's merciless."

I groan into the crisp air. "I'll stick with the running, thanks."

"We're jogging." Kit frowns. "Intermittently, I might add."

I stumble sideways, off the path, and collapse onto the grassy embankment that overlooks the water. The sun is barely up, but the pathway is packed with people who are just as diabolically enthusiastic about morning exercise as Kit.

"Even those old women are jogging faster than us," she says as she drops beside me and pauses the tracker on her watch. "And two of them are wearing weight vests."

"I just need five minutes," I lie as I fall back and inhale the salty sea air. Poor Kit doesn't know we'll be sitting here for at least twenty minutes, and her chances of having me walk home with pace are slipping away.

"I'm sorry about the other day, Kit," I say. "Alex shouldn't have snapped at you like that."

"He apologized and said he's under a bit of pressure." She looks down at me, her face bathed in golden sunlight and her mouth pressed into a line. "Hopefully, being back in LA helps."

I sit up to rest on my hands, the clipped blades of grass needling my palms. "He's back in LA?"

Kit's fine brows draw together. "Not yet. He leaves on Friday. Didn't he tell you?"

My blood heats, flooding my cheeks and sending wild, angry impulses to the rest of my limbs. He hasn't had his interview with Ruby *or* spoken to me since we kissed. *Was he going to let me know via text before he switched his cell to flight mode?*

"No, he didn't tell me," I grunt. "Because Alex only cares about Alex, and fuck everyone else, right?"

It might be the thousands of micro-tears in my underused muscles or the beeping of Kit's watch, but tears build, and my chest heaves. He should have told me he was going back to LA. He can't sweep in, do what he likes and jet off without a word. He made a commitment to *TGP*, and he forced his way back into my life. All the anger and hurt pushes to the surface, pressing against my ribs. I never vented about things ending with him. I didn't point out every one of his shortcomings over hard liquor or throw a tattered bath towel around my neck and paint my hair with drugstore bleach.

It was quiet, understated heartbreak.

"I know he's your brother, and you love him, but sometimes he's just a selfish prick."

Her gaze drifts to the shimmering water. "I know."

"I'm sorry, Kit. He's canceled on Ruby for the interview multiple times, and my boss is putting pressure on us to get this article done."

It shouldn't be my job, considering this article is the only reason Ruby didn't get moved to contract or let go completely. When she excitedly told me she was staying on, it took all my strength not to throw my laptop at the wall. To my obvious irritation, she tried to convince me contract work was better because I'd get paid more. Math isn't her strongest skill set, but apparently, delusion is.

Kit notices my breathing quicken. "Spencer?"

I can't stop the words that crawl up my throat, and I don't want to. I've bitten my tongue for so long, and it's exhausting.

"They want to know how far he fell, and I'm supposed to manipulate him into giving up that information." I raise my voice. "Natalia is promising me a future. An actual career. And all I have to do is stop protecting him. Maybe the world should know how difficult it was to love him."

Kit drops to the grass beside me. "Spence, no. Please don't do that. He's doing the best he can right now."

I meet her pleading gaze and think about how unfair it is that I couldn't grieve the death of our relationship because I didn't want her to know how unbelievably shitty his actions were. I'm tired of everyone looking at him like he hung the moon when all he did was drink himself into oblivion and break every promise he ever made.

At least the world got some good songs out of it.

"I told Natalia I wouldn't do it." I push myself off the grass and reach down to pull Kit up. "But I need to talk to your brother."

When we reach her apartment, my eyes are bulging with exhaustion because Kit insisted our workout continue.

"I know he wasn't good to you, and he doesn't deserve your forgiveness," she says as she uses the exterior wall of her building to stretch. "But thank you for looking out for him."

She hands me her keys before tapping her watch and taking off for a few laps of the block. It could be to give Alex and me privacy, but it's more likely because I didn't cut it as an exercise buddy.

I head up to the apartment and find him lying on the couch, his long legs stretched out while he mindlessly flips through TV channels. His old duffle, stuffed to bursting, sits innocuously on one of the dining chairs.

"Were you going to tell me you're going back to LA?" I ask as I drop Kit's apartment key on the dining table with a clang. "Or tell Ruby you aren't doing the interview?"

Alex springs to his feet and drags his hand through his mussed hair. A smile tugs at the corner of his lips, and it ignites a fire in my veins.

"You think this is funny?"

His mouth drops, and he holds his hands up defensively. "What? No."

I poke at the duffle, my finger leaving an impression on the worn pleather. "Then what's this?"

"I've got a meeting with the label, and Reuben, Alfie, and Ash will be in town. We're heading back to the studio because I think I've finally got something for the album." His gaze is intense, and color brushes his cheekbones. He reaches out, taking my hands and gripping them in his. "I've already called Ruby and arranged the interview for when I get back."

I look down at our hands, his long fingers encasing mine and the muscles in his forearms stretching as he brings the back of my hand to his lips. He holds it for a moment, our eyes locked before he presses a kiss to my knuckles. His breath is warm against my skin, and it sends my pulse skittering.

"Come with me?" he asks, my hand still resting against his lips. "I bought you a seat on the flight."

I yank my hands from his grasp and press them against my shaking thighs. "What are you talking about?"

"Wait. Let me explain," he says, taking in my shocked expression. "Your ticket is just for the weekend."

He turns and collects his phone from the coffee table, scrolling hastily with trembling fingers.

"Alex." I exhale, but before I can form an argument, he holds out his phone, directing my attention to an email on the screen.

I recognize the email address immediately. Nelson Cousland, author of three non-fiction works on Florence Ritter's murder and founder of The Golden Age, an online forum for people still actively investigating the case. I've read every post and used all of Nelson's research to track Florence's movements in the lead-up to her murder. Of course, it didn't take long for my curiosity to take over, and I started researching Nelson himself. He's married with five children and worked as a radio show host for most of his life. He retired a few years ago and ramped up his dedication to the relentless pursuit of finding out what happened to Florence. He's appeared on a stack of podcasts and is launching his own next month.

"What is this?" I take the phone and read over the email.

"He's agreed to meet you on Saturday morning. He's

going to take us on a tour of the city to all the places made famous by the case. You can ask him anything you like."

My mouth goes slack, and my hands are clammy. Nelson Cousland was the one who fought for years to have a judge unseal the case file. I've emailed him several times and never had a response. It's infuriating that one email from Alex has him agreeing to meet me.

"Why would you do this?" I look up from the phone.

Alex holds my gaze for a moment before taking my wrist and guiding me to a seat at Kit's tiny dining table. I say nothing, only watching as he sits down opposite me, his legs bracketing mine. My pulse quickens when he places his hands on his knees, his thumbs gently skimming my thighs. Every molecule of adrenaline has evaporated, and I'm left with the persistent ache of missing him. His hands slide across, resting higher on my thighs, and relief crests like a wave. We feel like puzzle pieces slotting into place all over again.

"Eve told me about the desk at *The Herald*," he says as he leans forward and rests his forehead against mine.

The connection is too much. I'm slipping under again, and when I try to draw on the memories of our ending, my mind clouds with the image of him writing emails to Nelson Cousland and arranging flights to get me closer to my dream. It's something the old Alex would do. And the old Spencer would fall a little more in love with him for it.

He lifts his hand and pinches the ends of my freshly cropped hair. "I like this, by the way. It suits you."

My eyes close, and I smile. I felt so brave when I had my hair hacked off—a decision I made without having to justify it to anyone else. It was me and a woman named Clara who upsold me on some shampoo and a conditioning mask I am yet to take out of the little bag that bears the salon's flora-themed logo.

"It was time for a change," I say.

Alex's fingers thread through my considerably shorter strands, his thumb brushing the shell of my ear as he tilts my face upward. Our lips are almost touching, and with this closeness, I map every freckle and feature on his ageless face. He's that kid backstage at The Palace, heart racing and breathing shallow. The world at his fingertips, but he's hesitating to take the leap.

It's dizzying to be this close to him again. Familiar and comforting, but reckless all the same.

"I'll come to LA." I pull my hands from his grip. "But it's for my article and nothing else."

"Understood," he says as he kisses my forehead.

I shamelessly lean into it, breathing deeply and hating myself a little more.

CHAPTER THIRTY-ONE

Dear Alex,

Those Malibu sunsets got me through a lot. When I received my eleventh job application rejection, I wondered if moving to LA was a mistake. I knew you wanted me, but it felt like Los Angeles didn't. I thought I could carve out a life for myself, but my only purpose was following you around. I thought I'd have more opportunities, but as three months turned into six, my self-imposed grace period was ending.

You were going from strength to strength, though, and Miles was enjoying the ride. I watched you both from the front row at bar gigs, and when you headlined your first show at that old music hall in Santa Monica, I got to stand backstage. You sang songs about us to crowded rooms and kissed me the second you walked off stage. Miles followed, sweeping me into a hug and saying, "We've made it" into my ear like I was part of your collective success. It didn't take long for momentum to build. The venues got bigger and the fans got louder. After that, it was all about money and contracts. That part was scary, but after every gig, you still held my hand when we left the venue.

You never let go of me. You held on tighter.

When I started freelancing, things got better. I had that purpose I was looking for, even if it was reviewing mid-range restaurants in the area and writing listicles for a travel blog. Slowly but surely, more and more projects trickled in. When I wasn't at the studio with you, I was at my little desk, writing copy for beauty companies and captions for corporate social media posts.

I loved weekends spent in our tiny apartment too. You were in contract negotiations, and since we didn't know how it would play out, we tried to be responsible with our money. We ate ramen so we could have the AC on, and instead of going to the movies or shopping, I watched you write songs and strum your guitar. The songs were still about me—all about me because my being in LA had unlocked something in your brain. You didn't sing about our present anymore. You wrote songs about our future. The children I would give you, and our house with a manicured lawn and pool for us to enjoy in the summer. I pictured it as you sang it to me, and my cheeks flushed with joy.

Those blissful days didn't last, though. You got busier, and concessions had to be made.

You were tired all the time. Run off your feet and pulled in a million different directions. Stevie wasn't happy with his cut from the ticket sales, and Howie was pushing you to overhaul the band. I knew you were struggling, and every night when you came home, I wrapped my arms around you and told you it would all be worth it in the end.

It was worth it, and I remember our drive to Malibu one Wednesday afternoon when "Girl Made of Stars" aired on the radio for the first time. You pulled off the PCH, sprinted to the opposite side of the car, and pulled me from the passenger's seat. I laughed as you held my body to yours, and we danced in a lopsided circle on the shoulder of the highway while you sang my song. We were a long way from the treehouse that day, and when the song ended, we continued onto Malibu and stayed long after the sunset. You held my hand as we walked from the beach back to the parking lot. When we reached the car, you gripped my hips and pulled our bodies together. I don't remember what you said, but I remember how much I needed you, and I remember the smile on your face when I pulled you into the back seat. Our kisses were frenzied at first, but you slowed me down. You savored me. Feeling every inch of my skin and telling me how beautiful I looked as I moved on top of you. There was another song in that, and when we drove home hand in hand, someone called the radio station and requested "Girl Made of Stars".

In the months that followed, your song received a record amount of airplay, and Howie capitalized on your newfound fame. The contract with Summerland Records was finalized, and you and the band were on the hook for an entire album. You reworked some of your other songs and wrote enough new ones for another album entirely. Everything about our life changed after that. You had fans. The venues were bigger. You weren't the support act anymore.

You were the main event.

And Miles was with you every step of the way.

That's when the dream became work, and you and the band spent days on end in the studio. Summerland moved up the deadline for the master, and you only came back to the apartment to sleep. It was taking its toll on Miles, too. Pressure from the label and exhaustion led to cracks in your friendship. There were lengthy talks about which songs to include on the album, and you and Miles had differing opinions. The label pulled rank and sided with you because you were the one on the album cover.

The fight that ensued is something I'll never get out of my head. Neither of you had the right to say the things you did. You were both out for blood, and it didn't matter whether the words were true. They just needed to do damage. And that is exactly what they did.

That was the first glimpse of what was to come, but I thought you would both come back from it. Sudden fame was a beast, but you and Miles could get through it. Together.

Your first full-length album was released the following year.

It broke my heart that Miles wasn't on it.

He wasn't even a line in the acknowledgments.

CHAPTER THIRTY-TWO

Both Eve and Miles are thoroughly confused when I explain my weekend trip to LA. I assure them it's for Florence Ritter research, but the wrinkled foreheads and tight frowns have me omitting the part about Alex paying for the flight. They still discuss it amongst themselves and decide that it's up to me, but they aren't supportive of the idea. I'm a child whose maturity is being tested. I tell them I'm going because this will help my *Herald* submission, and I get twin looks of disappointment and a warning from Eve not to touch her brother.

I make no promises because I haven't stopped thinking about touching him since I saw Nelson's email.

The flight to LA feels considerably longer than two hours and forty-five minutes. I show Alex the latest draft of my article, and he reads it twice over, chewing his thumbnail and nodding. He says he loves it and assures me Nelson will fill in the gaps. Then I stow my laptop, and our conversation turns to reminiscing about how we used to spend our weekends in LA. It cuts too close, and by the descent, we're both wearing headphones. He's listening to Bob Dylan's greatest hits, and

I'm listening to "Malibu Sunset" with the volume low so he doesn't recognize his own voice.

It's late when we exit LAX, and Alex navigates the sprawling LA streets with the ease of a local. By the time we reach Lincoln Boulevard, it feels like nothing has changed. I read the advertisements on the billboards lining the street and recognize several places. The yoga studio, whose offer for a two-week trial lived on our fridge for months, and the barbeque place where Miles ate too much mac and cheese and threw up in the parking lot. I remind Alex of that night, and he laughs as we turn off Lincoln toward our old neighborhood. At first, I think he is taking a detour for old times' sake, but when he clears his throat and grips the steering wheel tighter, I know where we're headed.

"It came up for sale last year, and since I spend so much time in New York now, it didn't make sense to spend money on a big house to sit empty." He speaks like he's read my every thought. Maybe he still can.

"Sure," I say, though I am wondering why he didn't move in with one of his bandmates or find a sublet closer to the recording studio.

"It's a good neighborhood too. Not that far from the airport, and it's quiet." He squeezes the steering wheel tighter. "And it's close to that Chinese takeout we like."

He speaks like we still get that takeout twice a week when he gets home from the studio and I don't feel like cooking. The familiarity of this place is a weight on my chest, made worse by the furrow in his brow and the way the passing street lights illuminate the sadness in his eyes. I wanted to see this vulnerability. This pain that mirrored mine, but it's not a win. If anything, it drags me further down.

Alex clears his throat again and shifts in his seat. "We can get dinner from there if you want to."

"That sounds great," I say, slinking back into my seat and watching my old life pass by through the freshly squeegeed window of the midsize rental car.

We don't talk on the drive to our old apartment. My focus is on balancing the flimsy takeout noodle boxes on my thigh. The heat sears my skin under the thin cotton of my lilac blouson dress, but the well-being of our dinner is a welcome distraction from the silent tension that builds between us.

"It hasn't changed," Alex says when he pulls up outside the aging three-story structure. He's right, and not only about the building. The neighborhood seems content to stay exactly the same, with its cracked sidewalks and neutral-toned sedans lining the narrow streets.

Memories ricochet through my mind. Leisurely Sunday walks to Venice. The way he kissed me as Reuben impatiently honked his car horn outside our window because they were late getting to the studio.

I loved everything about this building once. I adored the moss green facade, the neat hedges, and smooth stone steps leading up to the double glass doors. I wanted this place. I wanted to be a regular at the cafe nearby and buy all my clothes from the neighboring vintage boutique. I would be a changed woman here. I would exercise and drink water. I would wash my face morning and night with a specific combination of overpriced products that claimed to be a fountain of youth. I would thrive. We would thrive.

But now, the hedges are dry and patchy, and the planters that line the steps—once filled with colorful flowers—are blocks of baron dirt. Rust stains run like tears from the window frames, and it hurts to see that the once-vibrant colors of our universe have faded.

I step out of the car carefully so as not to drop the food while Alex collects our bags from the trunk. Together, we track the same path we have a hundred times before, through the sparse foyer with its checkerboard tiles and up the flight of concrete steps to the first floor. There are scrapes on the taupe walls from careless furniture removal, and the apartment at the top of the stairs is missing a number.

"If you're not comfortable with this, I can get you a hotel." Alex pauses with the key in the lock of our old apartment. "I thought it would be easier to stay here because Nelson lives in Ocean Park, and we won't be spending that much time here."

"It's fine. You still have a couch in there, don't you?"

"Yes. Which I will sleep on. You're taking the bed."

I can't help but smile at the conviction in his eyes. "Chivalry is not dead then."

Alex takes a breath and turns the key in the lock. When he pushes the door open, I expect to see the apartment completely changed, every piece of me scrubbed from existence, but that couldn't be farther from the truth. The cushions I picked out, though faded, are still on the couch. My first published article from the LA travel blog he'd printed out and framed still hangs on the wall beside the TV. And my collection of crime novels is stacked on the writing desk with the plaque bearing my name.

"You can put that on the coffee table." Alex nods at the takeout in my hand, and I follow his instruction, noticing the section of stripped varnish where I spilled nail polish remover.

I am everywhere, and that weight on my chest gets heavier.

"Are you okay, Pen?" His voice shakes a little as he places our bags on the end of the bed. "Because you really don't have to stay here. It's no troub—"

"It's fine," I cut him off. "It's just strange. Being back here."

I give the space another cursory glance, turning over the flood of memories that spread through my mind like ink on paper. I'm barely aware of what Alex is doing, but I hear the water running in the kitchen when he washes his hands and the rustle of clothing as he takes off his jacket and lays it over the back of the couch. It's so warm in here, and my breath catches as I suck in the stagnant air.

That's when I feel him behind me. He lifts his hand to my shoulders and slides my jacket off, tossing it over the couch with his own. With my eyes still closed, I lean against him, the back of my head resting against his chest. His voice rattles when he says we should eat before the food gets cold. It takes a second, but I blink back to reality and join him on the couch, where he hands me an open container of food.

"This is better than I remember," I say, savoring the salty taste of the tender strip of beef sitting on my tongue.

Alex's mouth is full of broccoli, and his hand lifts to catch the errant drip of sauce running down his chin. He doesn't catch it all, and a drop clings to his bottom lip. Without thinking, I lift my thumb to his face and collect the sauce before mindlessly bringing it to my mouth. He watches me, eyes never leaving mine, and in silence, he places his food back on the coffee table. I melt under his returned gaze, and with slightly parted lips, he wraps his fingers around my wrist and brings my hand to his mouth, kissing the pad of my thumb. A jolt runs through me—a surge I haven't felt in so long—and when he releases my hand, I ache at the loss of contact.

The interaction, while brief, rocks me, but there are no more suggestive glances throughout dinner, and when we're done, he cleans off the coffee table and performs the duties of a perfect host with a Kit-level of detail. There are fresh sheets on the bed, a clean towel in the bathroom, and bottles of cold water in the fridge. I thank him and explain that I have a *TGP* article to finish before bed. He hands me his state-of-the-art noise-canceling headphones and plugs my laptop charger into the outlet behind the nightstand before setting up the couch for himself. I watch his every move, trying not to think about this being the site of our worst fights or how much I loved to be wrapped in these sheets with him.

When my eyelids grow heavy, I close my laptop and slide down under the covers.

"Goodnight," I whisper, and he looks up from the couch, legal pad in hand and a pencil rhythmically tapping against his kneecap.

"Night, Pen." He smiles, and I fall asleep with the most perfect image of him in my head. It's midnight, and we are in the treehouse. We're about to kiss, and I'm certain it's the best thing that will ever happen to me.

CHAPTER THIRTY-THREE

Dear Alex,

Howie Dawson was the worst thing to happen to us. He was a smooth-talker wrapped in a polyester suit who overindulged in all the vices LA offered. He was making you a success. I could see that, but no one liked the way he was doing it. At the start, you were overworked and paid in promises. Even when you started getting paid in dollars, you still spent most nights in the studio or rubbing shoulders with industry people. So much so that your side of the bed went permanently cold.

By then, my freelance work was dwindling, and I told you I was worried I'd have no income. You saw this as a win. No job meant I could spend all my days in the studio with you. To your credit, you painted it beautifully. I was your muse, and that's all I needed to be because you could write a thousand songs about the beat of my heart and the curve of my body. All I had to do was sit in the corner, wanting for nothing and living every girl's dream.

What you didn't hear were the condescending comments

Howie muttered under his breath or his constant attempts to push me out of the picture. He wanted songs about me because they made money, but my existence was a stumbling block. According to Howie, the women who adored you saw themselves in your music. They cried at the sweet things you sang about, and giving this mysterious muse a face would negatively impact their perception of you. You had to be seen as available. When you winked at them from the stage, they had to believe they had a chance with you. They had to believe they were the one you were singing about.

I was damaging to your brand.

How did you not see what was happening? How did you not notice when I started spending your shows in the green room? Or did you see it all and choose to stay silent? You became quite adept at silence by the end.

You said nothing when Stevie's mom got really sick, and Howie said he had to choose between caring for his mother or being part of the band. Or when Howie replaced Miles with Harriet because he thought it would create some perceived sexual tension in the group. You said nothing when Miles got on that plane and flew back to Seattle. You'd been making music together since you were children, and you made him feel like he was a barnacle you couldn't scrape off. I still don't understand it. He wasn't a liability to your brand. He didn't stop women from fawning over you, and he was a better bassist than Harriet. You should have fought for him.

After Miles, the next phase of Howie's plan kicked into gear. Rumors began swirling around you and Harriet, and you assured me it was all just to keep your name in everyone's mouths. Give the fans what they wanted. Something sordid and exciting. You'd put your arm around her when you knew someone was watching. Left gigs together in the same black sedan with tinted windows. You even sang to her on stage.

But I was the one you came home to. I was the one you kissed. I was the one you slept with. I was the one you loved. All the songs you sang, plus the new ones you wrote, were all about me. Everything else was a performance because that's what you were: a performer. That's what I told myself while I was alone in our bed.

I ignored the wretched feeling in the pit of my stomach when she kissed your cheek on stage or wrapped her arms around you when leaving clubs with other celebrities. I pretended it was nothing, but it didn't stop my mind from wandering. It would be easy to slip up, especially with that much alcohol in your bloodstream. You could have kissed her in the back of that sedan or fallen into bed with her at one of those parties in the hills. I imagined those hands I knew so well, weaving through her waves of honey blonde hair. I pictured your lips on her skin and the sounds she'd make when you kissed her throat.

I never asked you about it. I never hinted that I thought you'd been unfaithful. This weak, coerced, and beaten down part of me believed that even if you were with Harriet, it was part of the job, and who was I to think that I could control you like that? It was my turn to be silent, or else I might lose everything.

I remained silent when Howie had me barred from the studio, and you disappeared for days at a time and came back like nothing was amiss. But it hurt. God, it hurt so much, and I tried to understand it. I was in pain, but all of your dreams were coming true, and how could I be sad when you were so happy? You had an album in the works. You had connections. You kept saying that all this pain was temporary, but it wasn't painful for you.

I tried to forget about it, and when Wednesday rolled around, I was sitting on our bed, wearing a cotton dress with thin straps, my hair braided and twisted around the crown of my head. I'd packed a picnic basket with your favorite snacks and walked to three different grocery stores before I found the right sea salt and rosemary crackers.

I waited, tapping my phone screen every few moments because it was getting closer and closer to sunset, and you hadn't texted to say you were leaving the studio.

The sky was stained pink and orange when you called and said you couldn't take me to Malibu. You promised we'd go next week. But we didn't.

We never watched another Malibu sunset.

CHAPTER THIRTY-FOUR

Nelson Cousland is fifteen minutes late to our meeting, and I believe him when he blames it on the LA traffic. He's shorter than I pictured, closer to my five-foot-seven than Alex's six-foot-one, and has a shock of white hair failing to be contained by his newsboy hat. His polo shirt is pressed, and he has an exciting amount of research under his slender arm when he arrives at the cafe Alex found on Google an hour ago.

"Thank you so much for meeting with me." I shake his hand and gesture to the vacant seat at the table.

"Alex tells me you work for an online magazine up in Washington," Nelson says. I don't miss the hint of disappointment in his voice. I'm quite used to disappointing old men with my career choice, but still feel the need to defend myself.

"I do. But my piece on Florence is for *The NorthWest Herald*."

This new information seems to put Nelson at ease, but I still straighten my posture, smooth the front of my high-necked blouse, and cross my legs at the ankles.

"Well, I have a few places to show you today. We'll start at the beauty salon she frequented. It's a tapas restaurant now, but you can get a feel for the neighborhood and what it would have been like in the forties. Then, onto the hotel where she was last seen on the night she was killed." He licks the tip of his index finger and uses it to flick through his stack of loose paper. "Then we'll finish up at the house where her body was found."

My fingers tingle with morbid excitement. I've researched all these places online, but seeing them in person will bring depth to the piece. I also appreciate Alex hanging on Nelson's every word as well. I'm sure he has better things to do than tour Los Angeles with a true crime podcaster who brings autopsy photos to a cafe meeting and offers to whip them out over scrambled eggs.

After breakfast, we drive through the neighborhood that Florence frequented before heading to The Bellegrave Hotel in Downtown. The Spanish Revival hotel is still magnificent, one hundred years on from when it was first opened. I can only imagine how impressive it would have been during the Golden Age of Hollywood. It had a reputation for being a playground for the rich and famous, and with Florence looking for her big break, it makes sense she would frequent the hotel's luxurious bar and lounges. I snap photos on my phone as Nelson maps out Florence's movements for the evening, as well as throwing out some theories about what happened. There are conflicting accounts in the police file, with some stating that Florence left alone around eight in the evening, and others saying she left with a handsome man in a trench coat and Homburg hat in the early hours of the morning.

"What do you think happened?" I ask Nelson as we settle on the couches that bracket the greenery-filled fountain in the two-story atrium.

"I think she was like any other beautiful starlet trying to

make it in Hollywood. She did what she had to do to survive. That meant courting rich and powerful men and being seen around town. She leveraged those relationships to secure auditions, and it was about to pay off. As for the night she disappeared, I don't think it was as simple as choosing the wrong man or being in the wrong place. She was hunted like prey."

"Do the unsealed police records support that theory?" I move closer and press the record button on my phone.

"Between you and me, those records are a mess. Crucial evidence is missing, and there was so much interest in the case that hundreds of false witnesses came forward. Along with several people confessing to the murder, none of whom could recount any facts of the case."

I continue to ask questions, and Nelson answers them in as much detail as he can. I record the entire conversation and take notes, listening intently when he delves into some facts about Florence's childhood. I'm even privy to the stack of research he brought while we wind our way up North Vermont Avenue in Los Feliz.

"You have a copy of the original deed to the house. And the renovation permits," I say as I sift through near-illegible photocopies. "Did any of this help?"

Nelson's hands relax on the steering wheel. "Not at first, but I sought some help with that."

"From who?" I ask.

"Walter Burkett's family."

I remember the name. He was initially interviewed as a suspect but was in Dallas at the time of the murder. He'd bought the house, but he didn't live there when Florence was found, making him a dead end.

"Walter Burkett was the head of Elton Northgate Pictures for decades," Nelson says. "He purchased the property in forty-six but never moved in because he was going to remodel it. It sat vacant until '47 when they found Florence. Burkett tried to sell it, but no legitimate buyer was willing to pay what Burkett had, thanks to the murder. In the end, it passed to his daughter, who traveled a lot and never spent much time there. It now belongs to Burkett's granddaughter. She's an architect and restored it instead of remodeling it, so it's exactly as it was when Burkett bought it."

Alex leans forward, his head appearing between the two front seats. "Even the bathroom?"

Nelson nods. "Even the bathroom."

I look over at Alex, whose face has paled at the thought. He didn't have the stomach to look at the crime scene photos, and when I told him the body was partially dismembered, he looked close to passing out. He has the same look about him when we round the corner, and the site of Florence Ritter's demise rises from the hill at the end of the street like a ghostly beacon.

There are no gardens around the main house, leaving the Spanish-style home's flat façade on eerie display. The smooth off-white stucco-clad walls and the terracotta tiled roof would have made it a grand estate in its day, and though it appears well cared for, there is something off-putting about its looming presence. I wonder if Florence came here willingly. *Would the sweeping stone steps or the Juliet balcony above the arched front door have impressed her? Or was she already fearing for her life?*

"Creepy," Alex breathes as he reaches forward and places his hand on my forearm. The slow strokes he makes with his thumb are an effort to calm himself. I place my hand on his as we crawl closer to the property. I recognize the sweep of the concrete drive and the curled iron fence from the photos of this house I've been pouring over for months. Seeing it in person is like a brush with fame.

Nelson parks on the street. Upon our approach, the large iron gate creaks open.

"She's expecting us," Nelson says as we make our way up the stone steps to the ornate front door.

The woman who greets us looks to be in her late sixties, with kind eyes and a welcoming smile. Nelson introduces her as Virginia Burkett, and her smile grows wider as she invites us into her home. Alex is pinned to my side, his eyes traveling up to the dark beams overhead, a small shudder running through him while I exchange pleasantries on his behalf.

"Shall we start the tour?" Virginia claps her hands together, and Alex jumps slightly.

We're shown all around the property, and I take photos as we wander through each perfectly preserved space, taking in the traditional Saltillo tiles, small arched windows, and heavy wooden furniture. None of the rooms look lived in, but there is not a speck of dust on any surface. Virginia spouts facts about its Spanish Colonial architecture and the history of this style of home in California. While it is interesting, I change track as soon as possible and ask about the collective obsession with Florence's murder by online sleuths all around the country.

For years, she's been bothered by people coming up to the house—hence the installation of the gate. However, her tone is almost chipper when she mentions that her home is part of one of LA's premier murder tours. This leads us to the purpose of our visit, and as we head toward the bathroom, Alex gently tugs on my arm and whispers in my ear that he'll be outside on the balcony.

The scene isn't how I imagined it, and I use logistical questions to distract myself from the horror these lovingly restored turquoise wall tiles have seen. The room is cramped and impractical for dismembering a body. Florence wasn't a tall woman, but she still couldn't lie completely flat in the recessed bathtub. Perhaps that's why the job was only half done. I can't stop myself from picturing the crime scene photos. Her blood soaking into the grout, and the vacant look in her deep brown eyes as she lay there, the desecration of her body covered by a blood-soaked bath towel.

She was there for days before someone found her, the passage of time stripping her of her dignity even further.

My stomach drops, and when I can't be in this room any longer, Virginia and Nelson escort me back to the living room. Alex rejoins us with slightly more color in his cheeks. We listen to them discuss theories, and the article takes shape in my mind. I map Florence's life on a mental corkboard. Her neglectful mother and absent father. The friends she made at the boarding house in McArthur Park. How she charmed everyone. She was tenacious and believed she would be a siren of the silver screen.

"But why this house?" I ask. "Walter knew her, but was immediately ruled out as a suspect."

Virginia and Nelson share a conspiratorial glance that has me shifting in my seat.

"Tell her." Nelson nods in my direction, his grin growing more unnerving.

"Well, you see, my grandfather bought the property from an investor, Paul Kershaw, who had several connections in Hollywood. Kershaw had properties all over the country, and this house sat empty most of the time. His wife wanted to keep it for their daughter, June, to move into when she married. Marriage didn't interest June. She was focused on using her father's connections to break into the film industry. Her career never really took off because she wasn't that talented and didn't have that Hollywood look about her," Virginia says. "That didn't stop June, though. She continued to attend parties hosted by her father's friends and ensured she was seen about town. Before long, she wanted to host her own parties in her own home. In this home, and for a moment, it looked like Paul Kershaw wasn't going to sell. June had spare keys cut for the property and hired contractors to make small repairs, believing she would inherit it. Shortly after, Kershaw ran into some unexpected government interest relating to his finances and quickly finalized the sale to my grandfather."

Virginia looks at Nelson again, a knowing smirk on her face as her story continues.

"June was livid. She didn't get her house, and the family's wealth was disappearing. To please his daughter, Kershaw used every connection he had and landed June the leading role in a movie called *The Last Song of Meadow White*. A few weeks after being given the role, a young Florence Ritter was spotted in the lounge at The Bellegrave Hotel by the film's director. In an interview for the Sunday paper, he said that, upon seeing Florence, he recognized her as the ideal choice for his upcoming picture. He was overheard calling her Meadow on the night they met. Soon after, he sent her flowers and personally asked her to audition for the role. After reading one line, Florence got the part. The studio notified June of the change, and she felt her father had let her down again."

"Poor Kershaw couldn't catch a break." Nelson pursed his lips and shook his head.

"And he was about to be arrested for tax evasion," Virginia continues. "June went into attack mode and spread rumors about Florence. All manner of lies, from her evening proclivities to her poor work ethic. Still, Florence had the look, and the director wanted her for the project."

My palms sweat, and my eyes stay locked on Virginia. I've seen photos of Florence, arm in arm with the director, twin smiles on their faces.

"We have little clarity on how it all came to pass, but our

theory is that June wasn't going down without a fight. So, she strutted into Elton Northgate Pictures and confronted my grandfather, who not only publicly backed Florence as Meadow White but took June's house as well. He had her removed from the lot immediately. Obviously, this was the last straw for June, and she now had an opportunity and motive to take down both Florence and Walter."

My chest flutters. "But Walter was out of town on the night of the murder, and Florence and June were never seen together."

"And that's where the trail runs cold." Nelson sighs. "We don't know how June got her to the house, and she was a slight woman. She couldn't drag an unconscious Florence up the stairs and into the bathtub."

"She had help," Alex chimes in.

Virginia shrugs. "From who?"

My soul deflates, and I'm stuck with the exact feeling I had as a curious fourteen-year-old when the documentary finished.

"What happened to June?"

"We don't know." Nelson exhales and twists his newsboy hat in his thick fingers. "She disappeared and was never heard from again."

CHAPTER THIRTY-FIVE

Dear Alex,

I wish I'd told you how much I hated Los Angeles. Everything about the city grated on me. It was hot, polluted, and the traffic was a nightmare. For a long time, I thought there was something wrong with me. LA was a dream for so many, and I wanted to leave. Facing my father and his relentless lectures on my failures would have been preferable to being locked in a tiny apartment, too scared to venture out. I was lonely, and you were playing bigger gigs and getting recognized, so it was difficult to go places without being photographed. Leaving a restaurant with a coat over my head became the new normal, but that was the price to exist in your turbulent life. If I wanted you, I had to share you with the world.

I needed an interesting life of my own. I wanted you, but I didn't have to slot into your world like a perfect puzzle piece. We could exist in the same space, doing what we loved, and come back to each other. Maybe LA held something for me? Maybe I just hadn't worked hard enough?

It didn't take long for that idea of independence to slip

away. Especially when I took my first bus ride to West Hollywood and interviewed for a periodical that peddled erectile dysfunction medication and the occasional story about youth crime. When I got yet another boilerplate email to say I was unsuccessful, I didn't cry. I was pissed off that it took me three buses and two hours to get to the basement storage closet they were calling an office.

I didn't tell you about the interview. Since you were at the studio for the next few days, I hastily applied for more jobs, hoping that when you came home, I would have some good news to share. I applied for staff writer jobs at six online magazines, two copywriter positions at ad agencies, and even tried to get a ghost-writing job for a bodice-ripping romance publisher. I was relieved when I didn't get that one. They would have fired me when they realized I couldn't write a romance novel.

Every time one of those rejection emails landed in my inbox, I grew more jealous of you.

You'd come home and tell me how electric the studio was or how you'd been invited to some A-list party. The disconnect between us was hard to ignore, and I could feel resentment spreading through me like poison. It was unfair that I gave up everything for this glamorous life, and you were the only one who got to live it.

Howie was at his worst by then, and every time we were photographed together, he became more passive-aggressive toward me. He worked overtime to make sure I wasn't included in any of your social engagements and you were being media-trained to keep your personal life a secret in interviews. On the increasingly rare occasion that I could attend a closed event, Howie would purposely take you away, saying it was business while I stayed in the corner nursing the warm scotch he handed me to keep me quiet. He wanted his cash cow untethered, and I was a weight around your neck—an unemployable weight with no prospects.

I'd never felt so small.

After another month of rejections and parties that had you stumbling home at sunrise, I came close to saying something. We were on the bed, your head resting on my stomach as I ran my fingers through your hair. It was soft but smelled of cigarette smoke and bourbon. You said you were glad I was with you as you slipped in and out of consciousness. You couldn't do any of this without me. You meant it to be kind, but the pressure your words applied was monumental. I had to be okay with my life because you needed me to be.

I cried so hard that night. Silent, painful sobs while you slept soundly beside me.

A few days later, when you got home from the studio at three in the morning, you were buzzing with barely contained excitement. You got a handshake or a fist bump from everyone involved after they signed off on the tracks for your album. They were planning on a summer release and discussing the prospect of a small tour.

I was tired, feeling like a wrung-out sponge with two new rejection emails sitting in my inbox. You asked if I was okay, and I gave you the answer you wanted. There was no sense in poisoning the dream you'd worked hard for. I said I was happy, and you kissed me so tenderly that I convinced myself that if I gave it more time, I would be.

Time wasn't the problem, though. You were.

CHAPTER THIRTY-SIX

It's dark when we get back to the apartment, and even though Florence's story still has no ending, I immediately get my laptop and start writing. I listen to my recordings over and over with Alex's headphones and transcribe pages and pages of notes. I pull out the copy of my article that Max tore apart and sit it beside me as motivation. For hours, my fingers dance across the keyboard, and I pour my heart and soul into Florence's story, flexing journalistic muscles I forgot I had. I tell it the way it was meant to be told. I include her childhood, her dreams, her relationship with the director, and introduce June, presenting her as a somewhat sympathetic figure before hinting at something sinister underneath.

I'm giddy with excitement when I research June and start fact-checking the information that Virginia provided. June's life and those of her parents are shrouded in mystery, thanks to her wealthy grandfather doing his best to conceal the family's shame. I determine she was an only child and appears to have no living relatives. I come across online newspaper archives containing information about her father's tax evasion and his prison record for the years he served on account of it. June herself disappeared, though. After Florence, she never appeared in a movie or in the society pages, and with her father's assets seized and sold off, I can't even determine where she lived. Maybe she got away with it. Took out her biggest rival, but reaped no reward.

"You should probably get some sleep." Alex drags me from my thoughts as he stands behind me at my old writing desk.

I look down at my phone and see that it's almost one in the morning.

"Sorry. I didn't mean to keep you up. I was on a roll."

"I'm not that tired, but I know how you get when you're working on something that fascinates you."

I close my laptop and stretch my arms over my head, still wired with all this new information. I doubt I'd have noticed if the sun was rising.

"I'll have a shower and go to bed."

I do exactly that, my mind whirring the entire time, attempting to connect dots that scores of people far smarter than me haven't been able to work out. If anything, it invites more questions, and I make a mental note to email Nelson to see if he knows anything about June's mother and where she fits into all this.

I'm still pondering June's mother as I exit the bathroom and find Alex on the couch, his feet hanging off the end and his neck at a horrible angle.

"Alex," I whisper as I crouch beside him, and he opens one azure blue eye.

"Pen?"

I gesture down the length of his body. "This looks uncomfortable."

He pulls the throw blanket tighter. "It is."

My eyes roam over his face. The face I loved for most of

my life. He didn't have to contact Nelson or pay to fly me down here to research my Florence article. He didn't have to accept the *TGP* interview either. So, in a moment of weakness, I push the pain of our past out of my mind and pull the blanket off him.

"Sleep in the bed," I say. "Before you destroy your back."

He stares at me, brows drawing together. "You're sure?"

"I'm sure." I stand up, walk to the bed, and pull back the covers. He follows, hovering behind me as I lay down on the mattress and shuffle over to my side. He waits for a moment before climbing in and laying on his back with his eyes trained on the yellow-tinged ceiling.

"Thank you," he says into the darkness.

"Thank you," I say back. "For bringing me here and helping with my article."

I shift onto my back, resting my hand at my side and listening to Alex's gentle breathing. It's almost musical, and as I close my eyes, his hand brushes against mine. It's featherlight, but unmistakably intentional contact. I turn my hand, palm facing up, and he drags the tip of his finger over it, tracing lines down each of my fingers and up my wrist. My skin heats, and my blood tingles in my veins as I concentrate on the agonizingly slow movement of his fingers. We've done a lot in this bed. It's the site of long conversations, heated arguments, and secrets shared with only each other. The threads that connect us seem to strengthen as he keeps tracing lines on my hand. Before long, my body aches.

He was my soulmate. My confidant. The person who knew me better than I knew myself.

He was my earthquake, and the aftershocks are still registering.

I roll onto my side, and he turns to look at me.

"I'm so sorry," he breathes into the stillness of the night.

Before he utters another word, I bring my hand to his face, gently brushing his cheek.

"Don't tell me you're sorry," I whisper. "Don't say anything."

I lean in, and his lips part slightly when they meet mine. It's slow and tender, but I feel the charge building immediately. It's almost blinding, and I have to remind myself to take it slow because I don't know what this means. All I know is that I want to feel him again. I want to be wrapped in his arms and think of nothing but how safe and loved he made me feel when we thought nothing could touch us.

His mouth moves against mine with more urgency, and it feels like every "Malibu Sunset" lyric and earth-shattering smile all rolled into one. Every shitty thing we did to each other and our collective loneliness no longer registers, thanks to this kiss. He pulls me to him, my thundering heart pressed against his bare chest as his hand slides down my thigh and pulls my leg over his hip.

"Are you sure about this?" he mutters against my mouth as his thigh presses between my legs.

My breathing is ragged, and I grip him tighter. "Yes. I'm sure."

He smiles, eyes darkening as he shifts to lie on top of me. I let out a whimper when his lips find my neck, and he peppers hungry kisses across my collarbone. We're both desperate, and I lift my arms so he can pull my t-shirt over my head. The rest of our clothes follow, and in the soft light from the sprawling city outside our only window, he sits back, looking at me and mapping every minor change in my body since the last time he saw it.

"Is everything okay?" I ask as I drag my finger down his chest and stomach.

"Yes." He leans down and kisses me deeply. "I wish I'd held you longer the last time I had you."

I press my hand to his heart. "You have me now."

He lifts my hand to kiss my palm, and I know exactly what he's thinking. Because I've been trying desperately to push it out of my mind. *We shouldn't do this because it's a minefield.*

I shift my hips and bring his face to mine, our noses grazing and our breathing sharp as he settles between my legs. He fits my every curve, and his weight is a familiar comfort that I've ached for since the last time we were together.

I've been angry. I've been heartbroken. I've been humiliated. But I can't remember what any of that feels like now that I'm surrounded by him, taking in the softness of his skin and the smell of his bergamot aftershave. He envelopes me, and I can't reason with myself. *We can have this one night. This one last time. We can be us again until the sun rises and the mistakes we keep making are brought back into the light.*

The world quiets, and our gazes lock as he moves. It isn't the desperate, ravenous tryst I was expecting. He knows me. He knows my body and exactly what to do with it. His hand slides to the back of my neck, and he presses his lips to my throat, smiling at how fast my pulse is racing.

"You missed me," he breathes, and I arch my back, my muscles tensing with every movement. *How have I lived without him for so long, and did I give it all up too easily?*

"You missed me more." I push against his chest, moving to a sitting position and straddling him. He groans when I sink onto him and roll my hips.

"Spencer," he murmurs, and it's almost too much when he buries his hand in my hair and pulls my head back. My whole body shakes as he drags his teeth down the column of my throat.

A moan escapes me, and I move faster, my body molding

to his. The sensation is intense. So exquisite that my limbs tingle and I remember all the times I felt this way. All the times it felt perfect.

But even at this moment, reality comes knocking, and I realize I'm doing the same thing I have a hundred times before, knowing he'll never truly be mine but loving him anyway.

CHAPTER THIRTY-SEVEN

Dear Alex,

It was three o'clock in the morning when I received the email. For the first time since I'd moved to LA, it wasn't a rejection for a job at a news outlet that pretended their single-room basement office was about sustainability or someone offering to pay me for blog posts with Amazon gift cards.

You woke up when my cell buzzed, and I scrambled over your bare chest to grab it off the nightstand. You locked your arms around me, kissed my neck, and demanded to know what all the fuss was about. I couldn't contain my excitement when I read the email. It was a real job. An investigative journalist position with a SoCal newspaper that still had a print edition. My eyes glazed over, and it felt like my brain had disconnected from its stem. It couldn't be real. The pixels had deceived me.

You smiled, your mouth pressed against my temple, and said if I aced the interview, it was mine.

I pulled back and took in your tousled hair and knowing smirk.

I accused you of having a hand in it, and it took three

seconds for you to cave and admit that you'd made some calls. My heart felt lighter when you listed all the ways I was perfect for this job. You were proud of me and believed in me. You knew it was what I wanted, and you did what you could to make it happen.

All that was tarnished, though, when I found out how you'd done it.

I hated Howie. You knew I hated Howie, and being indebted to him wasn't a position I wanted to find myself in.

You told me to be grateful. Howie had called in a favor to get me the interview, and any other journalist would kill for a meeting with Lance Gladwell. You were right, and I was grateful for the opportunity, but knowing Howie was involved took the shine off it.

Two days later, you drove me to my interview, and I mapped the route I would travel every day to get there. It was going to be a fifty-minute train ride with a five-minute walk at each end. I would have to get some new clothes. Lighter dresses for the summer and comfortable shoes that still looked professional. I was already spending my first paycheck before I'd even set foot in the Art déco-style building that sat proudly on its large city block in Downtown LA.

You wished me luck, told me I'd nail it, and that I looked beautiful. You also promised to take me to lunch afterward to celebrate. I got so caught up in the excitement and the assurance the job was already mine that my nerves were non-existent. I walked into that building with my head high, my most expensive heels clicking on the marble floor, and my freshly colored auburn hair falling down my back in smooth waves. I'd scrubbed my mind of Howie's involvement and decided that while he got me in the door, the rest was all me. And I could do it. I was a talented journalist, and Lance Gladwell was looking for that.

At least, I thought that's what he was looking for.

I couldn't have been more wrong, and the moment I stepped into his office, I knew Howie had done me no favors.

Lance was an imposing man. Tall and broad, with deep-set, dark eyes that demanded compliance. He shook my hand, holding it too long before he snapped the blinds shut on the window that overlooked the rest of the office.

It was cold in that room. The heavy furniture and lack of color made it small and suffocating. Lance guided me to the long sofa with his hand on the small of my back. He thanked me for coming, and when I sat on the farthest end of the couch, he sat down right beside me. His knee pressed against mine.

A lump formed in my throat, and I pulled the hem of my dress down as far as it could go without ripping a seam. His eyes traveled from my face to my hands, and I quickly folded them in my lap.

He asked me about myself. How long I'd lived in LA, and why I wanted to be a journalist. The conversation was polite and professional, but his body language was anything but.

He was too close. I could smell his oakmoss and patchouli cologne mixed with the linen spray that kept his starched white shirt wrinkle-free. My stomach rolled, but I focused on his words. The desk I would be assigned and the stories I'd be covering. Hoping that this closeness was a hallmark of his personality.

Then he put his hand on my arm and drew small circles with his thumb.

He said I'd cover high-profile criminal cases.

Then his hand moved to my leg.

He said I could choose the stories I wanted to cover.

Then he pressed his palm to the inside of my knee.

He said I'd have the best desk in the office. The one with the killer view.

Then his hand moved up, brushing the hem of my dress.

He said I'd be happy. I'd have everything I wanted.

Then his fingers inched higher, pressing into my thigh.

Would letting him do that allow me to have it all? Could I regain what I lost when I gave up my internship? Was Lance the same as everyone else scouting hungry, young journalists with something to prove?

My eyes stung, and my throat burned. I thought of you, waiting in the car, thinking about our lunch and how this job might make me happy to be in LA. Our life was about to start.

Was that how I wanted it to start, though? With Lance's nose against my neck and the smell of the whiskey he'd had for breakfast lingering in my hair?

The thought made me sick, and I wondered what Howie had said to make this man think I'd do this for a job. To think that it was okay to expect this of me.

I grabbed Lance's wrist, pulling it away from my leg, and leaned back. He paid no mind to my silent objection. In fact, he smiled, enjoying the game.

His hand slipped into my hair, gripping the strands at the root and pulling my face to his. I turned my head away, planted both my hands on his chest, and pushed as hard as I could. He reeled back, and I hurried to my feet, my heart hammering in my chest and my cheeks burning with anger and fear.

He stared at me, shock and confusion twisting his face in equal measure. He didn't understand what was happening, and it became apparent that we'd both been given the wrong impression from the outset.

As I yanked the door open, I noticed the photo on his desk of a beautiful woman with three children who shared his dark blonde hair and full bottom lip. Every place he'd touched me burned, and the shame of the encounter constricted my chest as I rushed through the building and out into the California heat.

You were waiting for me, leaning against the car with your arms folded. You dropped them to your sides as I approached, and your expression flipped from excitement to concern. You asked me what happened, and I told you to get in the car.

We were silent for six blocks before you asked me to say something.

I didn't know what to say, and your mind was already getting away from you.

You thought it was all about Howie. That I wasn't able to swallow my pride, and it was going to cost me a job. You said it didn't matter how I got it and that Howie had done so much for us. I should appreciate that he was helping me and how selfish and egotistical I was to throw it back in his face.

It really spiraled from there. I said nothing, and once again, you were defending the actions of a man who continuously drove a wedge between us. Our discussion escalated, and before long, we were pacing the apartment, shouting at each other and laying blame anywhere we could. By dinner, I was questioning everything. I felt complicit in the offense with Lance. I didn't immediately stop him from touching me, and I didn't say the word "no".

I should have said no.

The entire day was a heavy fog that settled over my rational brain. I'd considered that one transgression might be the price to get where I wanted to go.

I'd betrayed you.

I knew I'd never tell you what happened in that office. I would take it to my grave because even when we were fighting, you held me like a mirror. A perfect reflection of you. And I didn't want the cracks to show.

CHAPTER THIRTY-EIGHT

What happened in LA was a mistake, and it's going to bite me in the ass at any moment.

I've successfully avoided Miles and Eve for a week, but it's about to end because my mother has decided to break in the remodeled deck with a professionally catered cocktail party. The entire street is invited, which rarely prompts a strong turnout from the second generation, but Miles genuinely enjoys hanging with our neighbors. I tried to get out of attending, but Dad's scrubbing in on an emergency surgery, so I have to ensure the champagne flutes are brimming and no one uses the upstairs bathrooms.

"Oh, Spencer." Mom's mouth pulls down at the corner. "I asked you to wear sea foam. That dress is periwinkle, not to mention the uncovered shoulders."

She takes my purse from the entry table and stuffs it in the hall closet.

"I don't own anything sea foam." I tug at the gathered fabric at my hip. "I can throw on a jacket? I've got Eve's old bomber in the car."

She scowls. "Now is not the time for your silly little jokes, Spencer."

The stress of the evening has peaked early, but it's my fault for assuming that wearing a dress Mom bought for me would meet the dress code.

"I'll change." I sigh as I make for the stairs, but Mom stops me, saying nothing as she adjusts the molded cups of the fully boned corset dress so my tits aren't sitting so high.

"There's no time. The guests will be here any minute," she hisses and twists me around so she can fix the drape on the back of the dress. It doesn't need fluffing or adjusting, but I stand there like a model being primed for the biggest runway show of the season before Mom hurries off to the kitchen to check on the catering team.

As soon as she's out of sight, I pull my tits up and head for the backyard.

⊙

When the guests arrive, I'm tasked with receiving them like the lady of a nineteenth-century manor. I do this by the champagne station so I can throw back a flute and gauge whether our neighbors also consider the scale of this event ridiculous. There are no sizzling steaks on a grill or a circling cheese plate. Instead, the tablecloths are crisp white and freshly pressed, and the appetizers have at least ten ingredients each.

If our neighbors think this is a shameless display of disposable wealth, it doesn't show. They take the champagne I hand them and compliment Mom on her house, dress, jewelry, and the food. The ever-demure Gwen Caldwell collects these compliments and beams so brightly she's at risk of becoming a supernova.

The near-constant adoration distracts her. When everyone

has a crystal champagne flute in one hand and a spicy crab salad Crostini in the other, I retreat to the far corner of the deck, beside Dad's unused state-of-the-art outdoor kitchen, complete with a pizza oven. I gulp down another glass of champagne and watch Alex enter the party, flanked by Elaine, Kit, and Danny. He spots me immediately, his mouth lifting at the corner in a way that makes every part of me from the neck down clench.

Fuck.

His eyes move around the yard, searching for Eve. He doesn't have to worry because she has a work dinner tonight. Inviting her to this was like watching a bomb disposal tech trying to decide which wire to cut. The blue wire is an all-expenses paid seven-course restaurant dinner with the possibility of securing a decent listing. The red wire is bottomless champagne at my parents' expense. If there is one thing Eve loves more than free dinner, it's wasting my parents' money. She believes it to be penance for my abysmal childhood.

I wait patiently, and when an appropriate amount of time has passed, Alex strolls over and casually leans on the wall beside me.

"You look incredible," he whispers as his arm hangs at his side and his finger hooks around mine. He's staring straight ahead, and when he's sure no one is looking, he turns to block me from view and kisses the back of my hand. My skin is on fire, heat radiating from the center of my body. It's the same feeling I had years ago. Something illicit and dangerous.

The party is in full swing now. Smartly dressed servers circle the guests, who chatter and laugh over Dad's old jazz records playing through the outdoor speakers. Champagne fizzles on my tongue as Alex's hand leaves mine, only to have it return a second later. This time, he brushes my leg, and I shudder as his gentle touch travels up my thigh, under my dress.

I exhale. "Not here."

He leans down, his mouth on my neck, and I halt his wandering hand. It's a feat in itself because he smells good, and his touch is making my skin tingle.

Alex captures my mouth with his and pulls me around the corner of the house so we're out of sight. "Let's go somewhere."

We should not go somewhere. Especially not my old bedroom, with its lockable door and thick walls. Or my car, with its heavily tinted windows and spacious back seat.

His broad hands slide up either side of my waist, his thumbs pressing the corset bones like he's trying to squeeze me out of my criminally periwinkle dress.

My eyelids flutter when he presses his whole body against me, pinning me to the wall and snatching the breath from my lungs. "Oh my god."

Who cares if we slip again? We're practiced at not getting caught, and with the champagne flowing, no one will notice. We're already hovering on the edge. In the shadows. Invisible.

I grab his wrist and briefly press his hand between my legs. His lips part, and his eyes flash.

"Wait five minutes, then meet me upstairs." I step around him, brushing my hand across his stomach before I sneak back into the house.

It's the longest five minutes of my life.

I pace the landing above, chewing my freshly painted thumbnail and wondering if I should back out. I could go downstairs and avoid him for the rest of the night. Or I could text him from my room and tell him not to come up at all. I intentionally run over a step-by-step plan for every possible escape until it's too late. His voice travels up from below, wrapping around my chest and squeezing. I want that voice whispering sweet words across my skin. I want his mouth on my neck and his hands in my hair.

He brushes off one of Dad's golfing buddies and climbs the stairs, his footsteps light, and his body relaxed. I'm still pacing, but when he nears the top, he sees me, and we run to each other like it's our last second on earth.

He lifts me, pushing me back against the wall and kissing me fiercely. I'm outside my body, looking down on us in the hallway, desperate for each other, ignoring the ways it all went wrong, and thriving on the dopamine hit.

We stumble into my untouched bedroom, and I spin out of his arms to lock the door. His hand slides around my waist, and he pulls me back against him. Everything about him is so familiar, and I mold to him like we never stopped doing this. I don't think I ever wanted to stop. I just didn't want him to keep hurting me.

He isn't hurting me now. He's holding me. He can't get enough of me, and it's a rush.

"We don't have much time," I breathe as his hand slides into my hair and pulls my head back to press his mouth to my throat.

"Alright. Then we won't waste it." He spins me around, stepping me back until I'm pressed against the chest of drawers. The curved brass handle digs into my lower back, and when I wince, Alex lifts me and sits me on the edge of the drawers. He looks up, and in the soft glow from the lights of the street we grew up on, there is a flicker of something meaningful. The lust has faded, and he breathes me in the same way he used to when I was the safest place in the world for him.

"I still love you," he says. "I know I always will."

His mouth is on mine again, robbing me of the chance to answer his confession. I don't know what to say, but I do know

I want to savor this—savor him—before fresh waves of guilt wash over me again. I want to pretend we're back where we used to be. In the apartment, or his bedroom, or our treehouse. Some place where the outside world didn't matter, and we could have all of each other without worrying about what would happen or how it would end.

I reach for his jeans, undoing them with desperate and uncoordinated fingers. My frustrated grunt makes him laugh, but I can hardly breathe. I need him, and I'm spiraling. At any moment, Mom could twist that door handle, rattle it in confusion, and demand to know why I'm in here. We're on borrowed time, and my desperation spurs him on. He moves in closer, pushing my dress up my thighs and spreading my legs wider. The fabric has no give, and the seams groan.

"Let me take it off," he says, sliding his hands around my waist to my back in search of the zipper. It snags when he tries to slide it down, and when I press my lips to his jaw, a frustrated rumble crawls up his throat.

"Just fucking rip it," I say as my fingers thread through his hair.

The side seam of my periwinkle corset dress doesn't put up a fight, and he shoves the tattered remnants of my skirt up my thighs before his hands and mouth explore every inch of my flushed skin. The stuttering jazz music still plays, the lower level is swarming with people, and the window glows from a set of headlights.

With my legs wrapped around his waist, Alex carries me to the bed and lays me down. I move underneath him, lifting my hips and pulling his lips to mine. His movement slows, and he looks down at me, his eyes burdened with unspoken thoughts.

It's love.

The same love as before. It never left us.

He leans down and kisses me, parting my lips with his

tongue as he moves again. The dynamic has changed, though. Every movement is careful. Like I'm fragile.

Maybe I am.

He holds me for so long afterward, keeping me close to his side with my hand on his heart while he gazes at the beams overhead.

"Do you think we should talk about this?" I say.

He rolls onto his side to face me. "Do you want to?"

No. I don't because having him again will take its pound of flesh, and I have nothing left to give. Dissecting this lapse in judgment won't save me from being forever in love with him. Irrevocably tied to him in a million ways that matter and a million ways that don't. LA was a stumble, but this is a fall, and as soon as I hit the bottom, I'll decide what needs to be done. For now, I will bask in the glow of being wanted by him and forget that we still live separate lives.

"No," I say.

He lifts his hand and presses the pad of his thumb to my lips. "Then we won't say anything."

Alex kisses me again before standing up and collecting his clothes off the floor. He dresses in silence as a storm rolls in, darkening the room and sending a chill across my skin. I know what's happening. I've seen this distance before. His head isn't here, and the deep crease between his eyebrows sends threads of panic weaving through me.

Maybe this means nothing to him. Maybe I'm just a warm body.

"We should get back to the party," he says as he helps me off the bed and inspects the damage to my dress. "Sorry about that."

"I wasn't that attached to it, anyway." I awkwardly reach for the invisible zip in the back, but Alex turns me around and drags it down himself, trailing kisses along my spine until I shiver.

"I need to write," he says out of nowhere.

"Right now?" I hold my dress against my bare chest. "I'm naked."

"Yeah, I have an idea."

"Should I be concerned that this idea is striking while I'm naked?"

He laughs off my concern and digs his phone out of his pocket, fingers racing across the screen as he jots down his thoughts. I quietly throw on a pair of jeans and a T-shirt from my old closet while he slips away in thought.

His face is lit with possibility, and all the memories of our tiny LA apartment come flooding back, ending with our most recent one. My blood runs cold, and I can't shake the thought that my only purpose was a means to get over his writer's block.

"Are all your songs about me?" I ask as I twist the hem of my t-shirt.

He answers immediately. "Yes."

"Why?"

"Because I have a lot of things to say, and this is how I say them." He lifts his shoulders, his concentration still fixed on his phone. "And I don't want to sing about anything else."

I cross the room and stand before him, lifting his chin with my index finger to look into his stunning blue eyes. "Then why wasn't I enough?"

"You were always enough." He stands, his phone landing on my crumpled comforter and his hands holding my face. "I'm sorry I made you feel like you weren't."

But you did. And I can't shake this feeling that if it wasn't for the uncertainty of his future, we wouldn't be here right now.

Am I the spark to jump-start his creative process, or the consolation prize if his time is up? My heart rattles in my chest.

"You buried me in your songs, but I didn't want to be hidden. I wanted to hear my name in the same breath as you saying how much you needed me."

Alex pulls my mouth to his. It's as desperate as before. "I do want you. I've always wanted you."

I open my mouth to speak, but a thunderous knock at the door shatters our moment. Our time is up, and Mom will be ready to scold.

I unlock the door and swing it open, but it isn't Mom. It's Miles. And he knows exactly what I've done.

CHAPTER THIRTY-NINE

Dear Alex,

It didn't take long for the cracks to spread, branching off in different directions until we really splintered. You'd forgiven me for not "taking" the job Howie had so graciously arranged, but you'd stopped making me coffee in the morning. And when you kissed me goodbye, it was rushed. I wanted to tell you the truth, and I was close to doing it until Howie cornered me backstage at a gig and berated me. I was reckless and stupid, and I'd get nowhere by biting the hand that fed me. He told me that sometimes I needed to shut my mouth and do what I was told.

If that was his advice, then I wondered what you had done. What lines you'd crossed to be standing there under those blistering stage lights.

I thought about it until I frayed at the edges. I thought about it so much that I made myself sick. Paranoia crippled me, crawling over my skin and dissolving all rational thought. I considered things I never had before, like reading your texts or following you to see if you were actually going to the studio. For weeks, these diabolical and intrusive thoughts plagued me.

Still, I held on tight and reminded myself that of all the people who came and went in your life, I was constant.

Unfortunately, so was Howie Dawson, and he was getting results. You were getting more famous and cashing bigger checks. You felt indebted, so you wouldn't speak out against him, and you vehemently defended him when I did.

It all came to a head when you went to Palm Springs to play a festival. You offered me a seat on the bus, which you thought was a kind gesture, but for me, it meant hours of standing in the punishing heat with little chance of seeing you. I declined and told you to have fun and call me after your set. You did, but nothing prepared us for the content of that conversation.

I'd cleaned the apartment while waiting for the call. It was covered in loose-leaf paper and legal pads with the bones of songs scrawled on them. You jotted down anything that popped into your head. There were photos of us, moments captured on film that you insisted on having developed so you could paper the walls with inspiration. From time to time, I wish I'd kept some of those photos. There was one of me lying on the couch, pencil between my teeth, and your songbook on my chest. I liked the way my hair framed my face. I looked youthful and happy, not yet ravaged by the ordeal that was loving you.

I placed those photos in a shoe box, stacked the legal pads on the coffee table, and found a plastic folder for your musings. But amongst the mess, I found other documents, contracts outlining your fee, and the cut each member of the band got. There were notices of payments into an account I didn't recognize, and the cogs in my brain started turning. Had you not looked at any of it? Had you not seen that Howie's cut was so much more than a manager would usually get? Did you not realize that the account your money was being paid into wasn't controlled by us?

You were tired when you finally called. I could hear it in your voice. I asked about the contracts and payment notices, and you said you didn't deal with that side of things. You said Howie's accountant took care of everything, and your cut was paid into your account at the end of each month. So much was amiss, though. These statements showed exorbitant fees collected by Howie and his agency. He was pilfering thousands, and you didn't even question it.

You told me not to worry, and I felt like a broken record. This wasn't about our difference of opinion on Howie. He was robbing you.

You asked why I was so concerned about the money. You insinuated I was only with you for the promise of a lifestyle that I didn't have to work for. Did you forget I was with you before that fame and promised fortune? That I supported your move to LA and did everything I could to earn an income to help with rent and bills? It killed me when you paid for things because I couldn't afford it. You called me money-hungry and selfish, but all I heard were Howie's words tumbling from your beautiful mouth.

Nobody around you seemed to see what I saw. No one noticed the hold Howie had over you. I wondered if I was the problem.

We argued for over an hour, our conversation a spiteful circle of raised voices that ended with you telling me your career wasn't my business.

I never brought it up again. When I read an article about you taking him to court over it years later, the vindication I felt was like sunshine, chocolate, sex, and a warm bed all rolled into one.

I particularly enjoyed seeing the footage of Howie leaving court with sweat soaking the collar of his shirt and his eyes searching the sea of journalists for a familiar face. I wasn't there, of course. But I ensured Natalia splashed his name over the *TGP* website, and everyone knew what a snake the man you worshiped truly was.

CHAPTER FORTY

I'm waiting for a call from Eve. She's at a conference in San Francisco for a few days, but when Miles stormed out of my parents' house, I knew it would be a matter of hours before I'd hear from her. I imagine she's seeing red and primed to tear strips off me. Honestly, I want her to because what I've done is stupid, and in my first act of redemption, I told Alex not to call me. I need space and time to think, and I can't do that when his presence seems to rattle every rational thought from my head. I can't change him or fix what's broken. He will always want his music, and I will always want him to want me more. Loving him is like touching a plate you've been told is hot. You know it's going to hurt, but you want to see how much.

It's been three days, and while trying to ignore the noise in my head, I've thrown myself into Florence and June's last days. The article is done. I've read over it more times than I can count. I'm not just happy with it; I'm proud of it. I've never written something so powerful, and I only hope that Max sees it too.

I'm on my couch, wine in hand when I press send on the email. I expect an onslaught of panic. My gut to churn or my heart to race. But nothing happens. The most important piece I have ever written is whisked off into the aether, and I'm still on my couch, listening to my upstairs neighbor dance to nineties classics while she makes dinner. It's anticlimactic.

I sit my laptop and glass on the coffee table and reach for my phone. I ignored the message that came through while I was tensely typing Max's email address into the send bar, but with that off my plate, I'm ready for Eve's wrath.

But it isn't from Eve. It's from Owen.

> **OWEN**
> Are you busy this weekend?

> **SPENCER**
> No plans. What do you have in mind?

> **OWEN**
> I'm painting the guest bedroom and I need some help with colors.

> **SPENCER**
> So we're going to the hardware store and you're making me dinner to thank me for my valued opinion on which shade of white will match your hardwood floors?

> **OWEN**
> Yes

> **SPENCER**
> Say less. I'm in.

I put the phone down, cheeks flushed and a grin on my face as a knock sounds on my front door. I pad across the apartment and swing it open to find Alex standing on the

Fairview Office Supplies welcome mat Eve stole from outside her old apartment while Darren was at work. She called it scorned fiancé justice, and apparently, stepping on it every morning when she leaves for work powers her up like a video game character.

"I think we should talk to Miles," Alex says.

"I think we should too. But I've called him six times, and he won't answer."

Alex presses his lips into a line, and I hate that I'm watching his mouth.

"Can we go to his place together? See if he'll listen?"

"You saw the look on his face. I think he might actually kill you."

"It's worth a try, though, isn't it?" His eyes droop.

I try to call Miles on the drive to his apartment, but it goes unanswered. Not speaking to him first feels like an ambush, so I send him a text to let him know we want to talk. He reads it, and my heart seizes in my chest as the dots dance. He must think better of responding because nothing comes through.

"Let me talk first," I say to Alex as I knock on Miles' door.

He nods and takes a step behind me. "Can do."

Miles makes us wait, eventually opening the door but offering no greeting. Instead, he walks back across the apartment and flops down on his secondhand couch, leaving us on the threshold.

"Miles." I step inside, dragging Alex behind me.

"I don't really want to see either of you," he grunts, leaning back into the couch cushion that can no longer be flipped to hide its stains.

Miles isn't one for finery. His shoebox apartment is sparsely furnished with pieces he picked up from roadside collections and classified sellers. His kitchen is decoration at this point, and the bathroom door fell off its hinges three months ago, so the only privacy guests are afforded is a bedsheet thumbtacked to the doorframe. Alex gives it a once over and Miles scowls at the look of concern on his former best friend's face.

"Miles," I say, sitting on the stack of weather-worn pallets he uses as a coffee table. "Please talk to us."

He relaxes onto the couch, one ankle hooked over the opposite knee. "You can talk, but I think you're wasting your time."

"Come on, man," Alex says. "We don't have to make this a big deal."

It's the exact wrong thing to say because Miles sits up, his jaw tightening. "It is a big deal. Why would you drag her back down? You're a piece of shit, man."

"Okay, okay." I hold up my hands between them. "Let's be civil."

Miles shifts his attention back to me, some of the fire leaving his eyes. "You promised me, Spence. You promised."

Alex's forehead wrinkles. "Promised what?"

"I know what I said, Miles, but there is a lot of history here, and it's more difficult than I realized."

"What did you promise?" Alex's eyes dart from me to Miles and back again like he's at Wimbledon.

"I know there is a lot of history. I'm a part of it," Miles barks. "So is Eve, and she is going to kill both of you when she finds out."

Alex steps forward so he's positioned beside me. "Hold on a minute. Eve doesn't have to know."

Miles lets out a sarcastic laugh. "Are you serious? You're going to get back together and not tell Eve? She's going to notice when you quit your job and move to New York or LA or wherever the fuck Alex lives now."

"I'm not moving anywhere," I say.

"I can talk to Eve when she gets back from her conference," Alex says, shoulders bunched and hands balled into fists. "Not that it's her business. Or yours."

Miles is up in a flash, stepping toward Alex. I watch on, openmouthed as the tiny apartment erupts with viciously thrown insults. It starts with name-calling before Miles pokes Alex in the chest, and Alex shoves him back.

"Stop! We're not doing this," I shout over them. "Now, sit down. Both of you."

I take them both by the arm, depositing them side by side on the couch, which looks like it's halved in size since their shoulders are touching. Miles pushes against Alex, who pushes back before they spit venom at each other under their breaths.

"Stop shoving each other," I scold, and they both fold their arms over their chests like petulant children. "Can you act like grown men for a second?"

They can't because the apartment erupts once more. They talk over each other, yelling defenses at the other's accusations until they're shouting at me.

"Enough!" I boom as I grab the TV remote off the coffee table and hold it up. "If you're going to act like children, I'll treat you like children. This is the talking remote. If you're holding it, you can talk. If you're not, shut up."

Miles gives Alex another shove before snatching the remote from my hand.

"Alright. Miles can start," I sigh. "Is there anything you want to say to Alex?"

Miles' dark eyes sweep slowly from me to the intruder on his couch before landing on the remote in his hand. "You're a dick."

"Oh, come on." Alex throws his hands up. "That's just rude."

"Hey!" Miles holds up the remote in his face. "You don't have the talking remote, you dick."

"You can't use the talking remote to call someone a dick," Alex fires back.

"I can say whatever I want if I'm holding the remote." Miles tightens his grip. "That includes calling you a dick."

Alex looks at me. "Spencer, tell him he can't call me a dick just because he's holding the remote."

"Spencer, tell him he can't talk unless he's holding the remote. And also that he's an asshole."

"Can we ease up on the name-calling?" I groan.

Miles shakes his head. "No, and I don't know why you aren't on my side."

"What side?" I pinch the bridge of my nose. "If anything, I'm on my side and exercising my right to do what I want."

"Spencer, are you serious?" Miles scoffs. "You weren't good for each other. Why are you starting this again?"

"Just stop, okay?" I drag my nails down my thighs. "We haven't talked about it. We just… I don't know… we slipped."

I intentionally do not look at Alex.

"What does that even mean?" Miles' jaw tightens as he looks at me with confusion. "I don't understand. How can you do the same thing over and over and expect a different result?"

"It's not the same," Alex interjects. Miles waves the remote again.

"No talking remote means no talking."

Alex looks at me for support, but my head is nothing but TV static. "What do you want me to do? That is the rules of the talking remote, and at least he's stopped calling you a dick."

"You're still a dick, though." Miles slinks back into the couch, the remote firmly grasped in his hand while he stares at the floor. Alex reaches for the remote, but Miles turns away. "I'm not done."

I put my hand on Alex's shoulder. His body loosens a little.

I should have come here alone. It's apparently too soon for reconciliation, and Alex and I aren't ready to have the conversation we need to. Still, we wait patiently, and when Miles speaks again, there is no malice in his tone. No name-calling. Just deep sadness, and I remember there is more on the table than what Alex did to me.

"I didn't want it as much as you did, but it still hurt when you didn't talk them out of dropping me." Miles exhales as he holds out the remote. Alex takes it, gripping it in both hands as he looks at his oldest friend.

"I tried. I swear to God, I tried, but they were going to drop me too. The label needed someone who'd do what they wanted. If I said yes, I could make the music I wanted to." Alex squeezes the remote. "I didn't know what to do. Spence had given up her internship to be in LA with me. I had to make it work. I had to."

Miles stares at his hands, pinching the skin on his palm. "You didn't give a shit about any of us, Alex, and you could have walked away. You would have been okay without Howie. You had connections by then."

"I should have walked, and I'm so fucking sorry that I didn't. I was weak and not thinking clearly."

Miles takes a deep, chest-rattling breath. "I wanted this for you. I wanted you to be successful because that's what friends do. But you didn't even say goodbye. You just did everything Howie told you to do. You fucked it all up, and you're going to fuck it up again."

"I wasn't good then. I'm better now." Alex's breathing accelerates, the tips of his fingers digging mercilessly into the armrest of Miles' couch. *He is different now, but that doesn't mean he's better.*

Miles is silent as he and Alex share a look. It's an entire conversation that I'm not privy to.

"I want to talk." I take the remote from Alex's hand. "I want to know the truth."

The attention of both men snaps back to me, and Alex arches a brow. "The truth about what?"

"Why did you ask me to marry you?"

"Because I loved you."

I shake my head. "If you loved me, we would be married. Now tell me the truth. Why did you ask me to marry you?"

He scratches the back of his head, his eyes unable to meet mine, and I already feel the heartbreak building. My chest is ready to crack.

"Alex."

"Spencer."

"Tell me why you asked me," I whisper. "And tell me why you didn't go through with it. Was it something Howie said?"

"It wasn't Howie."

"Who was it then?"

He shifts uncomfortably, his lips parting but no words coming out.

"It was me," Miles says, his voice low and even. "I told him not to marry you."

Alex's hands are shaking, and a muscle ticks in his jaw. "Don't bring that up, man. It won't help anyone."

The warning in his tone has my heart crawling into my throat. "Miles, what are you talking about?"

Both men go quiet, nostrils flared as they stare at each other. It's a deadlock punctuated by the gentle hum of the muted television and a car alarm several blocks over.

Alex breaks first, regret painting his face and his posture loosening.

"Alex?" I ask. My pulse is in my ears, and my skin is heating. "What is he talking about?"

Miles drags his chewed nails down his thigh. He can't look

at me, but I need one of them to tell me what is going on because my head makes it so much worse.

"Miles," I whisper, and he finally looks up.

"Spence, I'm so sorry."

"What are you sorry for?"

He looks at Alex, who provides no support or comfort. "I called Alex and tried to talk him out of the wedding. But he said he was going through with it no matter what I said."

I remember standing outside the chapel, blinded by tears and my chest heaving as I fell into the deepest, darkest hole imaginable.

"What does that mean?" My words are a shuddering whisper. "Miles, what did you do?"

His eyes close on a deep exhale. "I called Howie, and I told him every instinct he had about you was true. I told him you were convincing Alex to give up music and you'd been asking questions about money." His confession is barely a whisper, but it slices through me like a freshly sharpened blade.

My muscles seize, and a steady drumbeat rumbles behind my temples. "Why?"

I scramble to recall every phone conversation I had with Miles while I was in LA. All the things I told him about Howie and Alex and how badly I wanted it all to be over. He handed everything I told him in confidence to the person I hated most. The person who had more influence over Alex than I did and would not hesitate to exercise that power.

"And you listened to Howie?" I look at the once great love of my life, my heart sinking like a stone, plummeting through my body and cracking every bone on its way down.

Alex deflates, his shoulders slumping and his chest caving in as he looks into my eyes. I don't know what I expect him to say, but I don't expect it to hurt as much as it does.

"It was wrong of Miles to get involved, but I'm glad he did

because Howie said a lot of things I needed to hear." Alex sucks in a shallow breath. "I wanted my career, and I wanted you, but I didn't know how to have both. I was never going to make you happy, and I knew that. I just kept telling myself I could."

"Then why did you ask me to marry you?" I can't stop the tears. "What did you think would happen?"

"I didn't know what would happen. All I knew was that I loved you, but I could feel you slipping away. I couldn't lose you."

"You'd already lost me!" I shout. "But I was weak, and I trusted you. I lost Eve, my parents, and my job. I had to start my life from scratch."

Pain and anger distorts my vision as tears pour down my cheeks. I remember the feeling of warmth that spread through my body when he asked me to be his forever. *How could I have been so blind?*

"Spencer, I am so sorry. Truly, I am. I fucked up so badly, and I know how much it hurt you."

"No, you don't," I sob. "Because I never told you how much you hurt me."

"Then tell me now." His eyes are pleading. "Tell me how horrible I was and every single thing I did that upset you. I want to apologize for it all."

"I shouldn't have to tell you all the ways you hurt me. You should have seen it, and you should have fixed it back then. It's too late now."

The wind goes out of him once more, and his red-rimmed eyes are locked on mine. "You're right. I should have seen it. But I was selfish."

He was, but to see him now, so defeated, my brain conjures memories from when it wasn't all about him. I think of the succulents that lined the windowsill in the old apartment. I over-watered them because I thought LA was too hot, and when they died, he replaced them without telling me. He didn't want me to be upset that I'd failed them but had to come clean when I noticed one of them no longer had the pink hue on its leaves.

I take a deep breath, wipe my tears, and pull my jacket tighter. "I can't look at either of you."

I leave the apartment with my head high, but Alex is on my heels, shouting my name down the stairwell and bursting out into the alley behind me.

"Pen, please talk to me."

I round on him, wiping the tears from my cheeks. "I don't want to talk to you. Going to LA with you was a mistake. Sleeping with you again was a mistake."

He swallows hard, and his arms hang loose at his sides. He can't deny the truth. We have no future together because there are mistakes I won't make again and things he'll never give up.

"It's over, Alex," I breathe into the crisp night air. "It has to be."

CHAPTER FORTY-ONE

Dear Alex,

    When the music world opened completely, it swallowed you whole. You tried to keep us normal, but every day, we got further and further from it. When you were in the apartment, you were fielding calls from Howie, your new publicist, Ingrid, and media outlets. Everyone wanted a piece of you, and you wouldn't say no. I could see that it was wearing you down. Before long, those nights in the studio were replaced with nights on the Sunset Strip. And when you came home, you smelled of cigarette smoke, alcohol, and a spectrum of designer perfumes. I asked where you'd been, and you were always honest. I knew you were honest because I'd been following your movements online via gossip channels. There were never photos of you behaving inappropriately with other women, though I'm sure Howie had been advocating for it. You were staying relevant, and as a star on the rise, you had certain obligations. It makes me sick to think of it now. That bar was low: don't cheat, and we'll be fine. I conveniently forgot about the other obligations of a healthy, functioning relationship.

It didn't stop my stomach from roiling when I smelled your nights out on your clothes as I washed them.

At first, you didn't seem to like the partying. You'd rather be writing songs or hanging out with the band. Then you loosened up. You started drinking, and it didn't take long for your industry friends to be slipping bags of coke into your pockets on the cab ride to whatever exclusive club you were headed to.

I remember one night, you came home so drunk that you couldn't string a sentence together. You fell into bed, and I removed your jacket. In the pocket was three hundred dollars, a business card for a different record label, and a napkin with song lyrics on it. Black ink ran all the way around the edges, spiraling into the center.

I read every word.

It was about opportunities, having it all, and being happy. It was about how much you loved this new life and what it would cost you. I wanted to screw it up and throw it away, hoping that you'd never remember it. Because how could you love something that was so obviously bad for you? Bad for your body. Bad for your mind. Bad for us.

The next morning, you threw up three times, and my knuckles were white as I anxiously drove to In-N-Out to get you a burger.

That was the first time since I'd moved to LA that I blamed you for how unhappy I was. I still didn't have a full-time job, and it brought the colossal mistake of giving up my internship into harsh focus. I had never felt so alone, and to make it worse, I chose that life over Eve. I burned my most important bridge to spend my days in that apartment, nursing you through a hangover.

You made space for me, but it wasn't mine. I wanted you,

but felt like I hovered in your life. I was an outsider. An inconvenience. Existing when you needed me for one of your songs, but an ultimately useless appendage. For so long, I convinced myself that being the object of your songs was romantic. I refused to acknowledge how much it broke my heart to hear you sing about me to a room full of strangers when I wasn't allowed to be seen in public with you.

We scrambled to hold on for so long. You drank more, and I pretended it wasn't an issue. You were making mistakes, and I was always saying sorry.

Then, I started having a bottle of wine with my microwave dinner. That way, when you got home, I'd have enough fight in me to tell you how angry I was that you left me alone all night for the millionth time. You'd tell me it was your job, and I had to be patient. I yelled and blamed you for everything I gave up.

We screamed, then cried. Then we held each other until your eyes closed. You slept soundly, and I tried to cry as quietly as possible.

The next night, it would start over again.

Then it stopped because you didn't come home. Instead, I got a call from a nurse at Cedars-Sinai Medical Center.

I rushed through the LA traffic to get to you, and when I made it to the emergency department, it took forever for them to let me see you. Because I wasn't your next of kin. Howie was.

He reluctantly collected me from the waiting room and told me you had a concussion, split lip, broken nose, severely bruised eye socket, and three cracked ribs. He said you held your own as he patted you on the back. His grin was so wide, and I wanted to split his lip.

A bar fight. You'd gotten into a fucking bar fight, and there were photos of it.

For the next few days, those photos were all over the internet. You still had bruises when you played your next show, and I listened from backstage as you joked with the audience about it. Three nights later, I had to call an ambulance when I found you unconscious in a pool of your own vomit in a luxury hotel suite Howie had rented for your next bender. That was yet another night spent in the emergency department for hours, crying while waiting to hear if you'd lost brain function.

You weren't just killing us. You were killing yourself and the career that you were apparently doing it all for.

I'd reached my limit. I didn't know you anymore. All I knew was that it was time to end this cycle of destructive behavior, so with the minuscule amount of strength I had left in me, I typed the address of an alcohol treatment facility into the navigation app on my phone, and we drove there together in complete silence.

CHAPTER FORTY-TWO

When Saturday arrives, I do my best to be good company for Owen. I'm now ignoring Miles' phone calls, and Eve is asking questions. I told her I've got a lot on my plate at work, which is a lie because I'm about to switch to my contract arrangement and have no assignments. I've also been frantically refreshing my email at every opportunity to see if Max has responded. After every check of my empty inbox, I remind myself that he's a busy man and my Florence Ritter article doesn't mean as much to him as it does to me. If this job is meant to be mine, it will happen in due course.

I repeat that three times in the mirror every morning and night when I brush my teeth.

It doesn't make me feel better, but I do it again when I'm washing my hands in Owen's remodeled half bath and appreciating his textured subway tiles.

After lunch, we head to the hardware store and spend over an hour looking at a wall of color samples and commenting on the outlandish names. It soon becomes a competition to see how many color names we can use in a sentence, with the winner choosing the color for Owen's guest bedroom.

I didn't realize he had such a competitive streak, and in the end, we walk out with three gallons of Snow Dragon's Archipelago and a fresh set of brushes that the sales assistant says we need for painting around light switches.

"What's an archipelago?" Owen asks as he peels open the lid of the can, exposing the satiny gray surface of the paint.

"It's a chain of islands."

"What has that got to do with dragons?"

"Snow dragons."

"Sorry. What's it got to do with snow dragons?"

I place two small buckets beside the can and hand Owen the little cup that came in our brush kit for paint transfer. "Nothing. Because it's a paint color."

"I kinda like it, though. It's mysterious."

"No, Mysterious was purple, remember?"

"Oh, yeah, it was." His brow furrows. "That's a bold choice."

"Bold Choice was too yellow, and Subtly was too blue."

"I hated Subtly. I liked Blueberry Whisper, though."

"Yeah, because Blueberry Whisper was gray. Much like Snow Dragon's Archipelago."

"Swiss Melody was nice too."

I take the paint-filled bucket Owen holds out. "It was too close to Brandy Mushroom, and you said you wanted gray gray, not brown gray."

He picks up a small brush and inspects the primed walls of his guest bedroom. "I'm glad we went with this, though. Wyvern's Private Island will make the room look bigger."

"Snow Dragon's Archipelago," I correct him.

"Is there a difference?"

I nod, stifling a laugh. "A dragon has four legs and wings.

A wyvern's wings are part of the front legs. Also, it's an island chain, not a singular island. Don't sell the snow dragon short. He probably worked hard for that archipelago."

"Stop saying archipelago."

"Archipelago."

"The word is losing all meaning."

"Which word? Archipelago?"

"Yes."

"It's such a great word, though." I grin. "Archipelago. Archipelago. Archipelago."

"You started to lose it on the third one. Go for five in a row."

"Archipelago. Archipelago. Archipelago. Archipelago. Archipelago. Archipelago. There. I even gave you a bonus one."

"Are you going to gloat, or are we going to paint these walls?" He holds the paint-tipped brush a little too close to my nose and I step out of the way.

"Gloat for a while, I guess."

"Alright then." He puts the paint down and faces me, hands on his hips. "Let's see who can say it for the longest."

"Oh, you are on." I rub my hands together.

We both start repeating "archipelago," our voices rising until they are nothing but unintelligible noise bouncing off the unpainted walls. I break first, dissolving in a fit of giggles while he keeps repeating some word that sounds nothing like "archipelago".

"Alright, alright. You win." I put my hand over his mouth, feeling his lips move under my palm. The warmth of his breath makes my skin tingle, and when he stops speaking, he wraps his fingers around my wrist and lowers my hand.

"I want to kiss you," he says, his eyes locked on mine.

The air becomes thick, and it's so quiet that I'm certain he can hear my heartbeat. "Because you want me to stop saying archipelago?"

"Because you mean the world to me." He says it so frankly, like he's been sitting on the response for years. I am speechless, watching as he takes my hand, running the tips of his fingers over my knuckles. I know I'm not going to let go because there is so much about him that fits me perfectly. I'm not scared to be myself or show vulnerability. I trust him.

He gently traces every fine bone in my hand before moving to my wrist and feeling my accelerated pulse with the pad of his thumb. A small smile parts his lips, and the hammering grows stronger. I lace my trembling fingers through his and press them to my heart. "Then kiss me."

Without hesitation, he leans down and presses his mouth to mine. It's slow and tender, a gentle exploration of the moment that will change our friendship. I release his hand and sink into him as he wraps his arms around me. He tastes like the hazelnut coffee I bought him, and the clean, sun-drenched smell of his skin is at odds with the sting of Snow Dragon's Archipelago.

Everything about him, including his kiss, is sweet. It's not a desperate, fiery desire or a meaningless search to feel something other than sadness. This kiss is its own entity. It's all-new, and in the wake of it, my heart feels a little less splintered.

Unfortunately, it's this realization that has me pulling back. A thunderhead of guilt passes over our moment. A week ago, Alex was in my bed, and even though it's over, it's unfair to pretend the dust has settled. Owen isn't a Band-Aid or a distraction. He's so much more, and he deserves so much more.

"Owen." I place my hands on his chest, his heart racing underneath his t-shirt.

"Is everything okay?"

"Yeah." My voice is small and strained. "I just need a little time."

I'm cursed with the expectation that he'll be frustrated or irritated with me, but he couldn't be further from it. His brows knit with concern, and he looks at me like I'm battle-worn and broken. In need of a friend.

"I'm sorry if I made it weird."

I shake my head. "No. You didn't make it weird. I'm not in a good headspace, and it's not fair to drag you into it."

He steps back, arms at his sides and affection in his eyes. "You don't have to explain yourself."

For a moment, I want to explain myself. I want to tell him all about Alex and every painful thing he did. I want to tell him how angry I am at Miles, and how disappointed I am with myself that I broke another promise to Eve. I slipped at the first opportunity because with Alex, I am so blind and broken that I forget we didn't work.

Owen lifts his hand to my cheek, brushing away the tear that falls.

"You don't have to stay," he says.

I look down at the small buckets of decanted paint and the packet of brushes. The entire time we were at the hardware store, I didn't think about Alex. LA never crossed my mind, and neither did Howie Dawson or Summerland Records. There were no songs about me playing in the back of my mind, and I was laughing so hard that my sides hurt. On the drive home, I noticed that Owen's hair has gotten lighter since we've had a week of sun, and that being in this empty, unpainted room is the most comforting place I've been in a long time.

"I want to stay," I say as I reach down and pick up the paint buckets, handing one to Owen.

He takes it with a gentle smile, and together, we approach

the window and start painting around the taped window frame. We glance at each other, and I feel like a teenager with the kind of earth-shattering crush that has all my nerves fluttering. I haven't felt like this in so long. It feels like it's come out of nowhere, but I want to revel in it. I want to be honest about it.

"Owen," I say, and he turns to face me, sunlight tangling in his hair. "I like you, and even though I'm a bit spacey right now, I'm glad you kissed me."

He rests the paint container on the windowsill. "I'm glad you let me. I've been wanting to do it pretty much since I met you."

"Why didn't you say something?"

He shrugs. "Because the third time we had lunch together, you told me how much you valued my friendship and how good it was to have someone in the building you could have fun with. You told me about Ruby and how challenging Natalia was, and I didn't want to be the guy you opened up to who hits on you at the first opportunity."

"So you decided to play the long game?"

He reaches for my hand, letting it rest gently in his. "Yeah. I figured if I stuck around long enough and baked for you, I'd get my guest room painted for free."

"That's a solid strategy."

"Well, it was, but my guest room still isn't painted, and your work ethic is compromised because you're thinking about kissing me."

My cheeks are flushed, and he's living for it. "I'm still capable of painting four walls."

"Good. Because I won't make you dinner otherwise."

"At least I'm getting paid for my labor."

"The quality is based on performance, and so far, you aren't doing great."

I look at my work and notice that, in my haste, I've accidentally brushed some Snow Dragon's Archipelago on the Whisper White window frame.

"I can fix that." I wipe the spot with the sleeve of my hoodie and make it infinitely worse. Owen watches on, laughing at the paint that is now smeared across the glass and pointing out that I've somehow stripped some paint off the wall.

"Okay, Rembrant, that's enough," he says. "I'll make you whatever you want for dinner so long as you don't paint anything else."

I place my paint bucket on the floor and roll up my sleeves, feeling the paint smear my forearm. "That was easy."

Owen's brow wrinkles. "What was?"

"I got out of painting, and I still get dinner."

"Alright. Game recognizes game. But I bet you're still thinking about the kiss."

"Of course I am, and it's got me thinking that if you're playing the long game, where does it end?"

His lip curls as he retrieves the finest brush from the kit and dips it into the paint can. With a new level of concentration, he lifts my hand and draws a band in Snow Dragon's Archipelago on the fourth finger of my left hand.

"Hopefully here," he says.

CHAPTER FORTY-THREE

Dear Alex,

Two days after you were admitted, I got a job at a little breakfast place a few blocks away. I went out for coffee, saw the handwritten help wanted sign in the window, and took a chance. The next morning, I was waiting tables and trying desperately not to think about you not being around. I built a little life for myself while you were away. I got to know the regulars, and after my shift each day, I'd walk a different path home to explore our neighborhood. I bought groceries instead of takeout and listened to your old vinyls while cooking dinner using recipes your mom had emailed me. It was the first time since I'd moved to LA that I didn't feel this crushing weight on my chest. It was the first time I felt like I'd made the right decision.

That was until Howie Dawson came knocking on our door. When I opened it, he stormed in, swinging it back so hard the handle left a dent in the wall. He demanded to know where you were because he'd been trying to contact you for weeks and heard nothing. You'd missed several studio sessions and a meeting with the label. I asked why he didn't come knocking before now, and he said he assumed you were on another one of your benders. I also learned that when you said you were staying at the studio, you were actually passed out in various hotel rooms and celebrity homes around LA.

I told Howie that I'd taken you to rehab, and the look in his eyes was both scary and gratifying. There wasn't a damn thing he could do. I was your next of kin now, and you were only going to be released into my care at the end of your treatment. He screamed at me for twenty minutes, telling me I'd tanked your career, the label was going to drop you, and you'd never recover. Then, he changed track and said if I loved you, I would want what's best for you. I didn't have the energy to explain the irony in that.

When he left, I went back to eating my home-cooked Tuscan chicken pasta with garlic bread and watched three episodes of a hospital drama before going to bed and sleeping like a baby.

You were a different person when you finished your treatment. It was like watching you discover the world for a second time. You'd come back to me—finally—and everything was going to be better.

I truly believe you thought that too.

You were six months sober when Howie slithered his way back into our lives. He'd secured your first big tour. You weren't the support act anymore. You were the headliner, and you were going all over the country. Chicago, Boston, New York, Nashville, and Las Vegas, just to name a few. Your excitement was on another level. You came through the door, dropped your guitar on the floor with a clunk, and pulled me up off the couch in one swift movement. You could barely catch your breath enough to get the words out. I had to hold your head steady, and when you told me, my first thought was, "No." I couldn't let you go. I'd just gotten you back.

But I smiled, and you kissed me before rapidly listing the tour stops and talking about set lists and money. You were electric, and the excitement was infectious. So, I reasoned with myself. I had a job and was doing better. Maybe I'd be okay. You sensed my hesitation, though. You knew I didn't want you to go, but you would never offer to stay.

So, we stopped talking and kissed before going to bed. You took your time, removing each item of my clothing, then your own. You laid me down and kissed the hollow of my throat, followed by the rest of my body. You wound me so tight, and I wanted you so badly. I momentarily forgot that it was an apology. Everything seemed right with the world, and when we finished, you laid down beside me and took my hand in yours.

You said I was coming on tour with you with such finality that I didn't know how to respond.

We stayed in bed for hours, tangled up in each other and making promises our future selves would never keep. If it wasn't for our matching rose-colored glasses, we would have realized we didn't want the same things. You would always want music, and I would always want you to want me more. It was selfish to silently wish for a limit to your success, and there was a time when being next to you was enough. That time was gone, and I realized we'd both changed but forgot to tell each other.

My head was on your chest, and we watched the sunrise through our tiny window. I was about to tell you I didn't want to go on tour when you said you wanted to marry me.

I asked if you were serious, stumbling over my words as my heart thrummed.

The first stop was Vegas. We would do it there.

I sat up to look at you. Your smile was intoxicating, and your eyes glistened before a brief panic took hold. You said it was an idea. We didn't have to do it in Vegas. You just wanted to marry me.

I genuinely thought it would solve all our problems. The insecurities I felt about Howie trying to push me out evaporated because I was going to be your wife. He couldn't hide that.

I would marry you in Vegas, and I murmured it against your mouth.

As soon as you left for the studio, I called Miles. I'd been talking to him a lot, but I could tell he wasn't happy about this news. I told him you'd changed, and the two of you could mend fences. He said that ship had sailed, and I was a fool to think that a Band-Aid marriage would fix the problems we had.

I'd never hung up on him before, and when he called back to apologize, he promised to stay out of our business. I realize now I should have held him to that.

A few weeks after the proposal, I found my wedding dress. It was at this vintage boutique a few streets from the apartment. I hadn't planned on walking that way. Usually, I got milk from the convenience store on the corner, but that particular Wednesday, I went to the market instead. As I strolled past the boutique window, mostly stocked with motel art in tarnished frames, a floor-length, v-neck, ivory lace gown caught my eye. The lining underneath was champagne, and while the butterfly sleeves weren't usually my thing, I fell in love with its ethereal look. It was the dress I would marry you in.

A few minutes later, I stepped out of the narrow, curtained booth and inspected myself in the full-length mirror that was crammed between a bookshelf of old records and a floral-patterned china display. I tried not to imagine Eve, Kit, Bea, and Elaine sitting on the little sofa and drinking champagne, mouths agape when they saw my dress for the first time. Instead, Tonya, the shop owner, offered to take a photo with my phone before continuing to price the uranium glass.

I declined Tonya's offer and walked home with my wedding dress in a recycled paper bag along with a pristine vinyl of *Tapestry* because you always said we could never have too many copies.

Weeks later, we drove to Vegas on the tour bus. We shared a bunk. Literally living on top of each other. And every hour, you told me you couldn't wait to marry me. When we arrived at the venue—a casino hotel one street back from The Strip—we checked in, and I helped you put on your suit before you hurried off to catch up with Howie. He'd been blowing up your phone since we arrived, desperate for a meeting.

I found a chapel while I waited. There was one a block from that hotel that had availability. I texted you the address and went back to pinning the flower crown on my head. It was made of white roses, and it was the closest I could find to the one Eve made me for your first show at The Palace.

We were supposed to meet at nine, but I was so excited I arrived at the chapel at eight-thirty and had to wait at the bar next door.

I called you at nine-fifteen, and you said you were on your way.

I called you again at nine forty-five, and it went to voicemail.

At ten-twenty, the call connected, but there was loud music and muffled voices before the line went dead.

At eleven-fifteen, a gossip website posted a photo of you leaving Caesar's. Howie was beside you, cigarette pinched in his veneers. You were still wearing your wedding suit. Navy blue with no tie. You looked handsome, but your eyes were bloodshot, and liquor stained your white shirt.

By midnight, I'd stopped crying.

By two-thirty in the morning, I was waiting at the airport for a flight to Seattle.

CHAPTER FORTY-FOUR

What if it's still not good enough? What if the June theory isn't that interesting, or I missed a typo?

I drag my hands through my hair and take my first even breath since I passed Max in the lobby, and he didn't mention my submission. He dipped his head, said "Spencer," and kept walking. *Why was he leaving the building, anyway?* He never leaves the building in the middle of the day. He should be at his desk, reading submissions and putting possible staff writers out of their misery.

That unproductive thought continues to circle while I scour real estate sites, looking for a more affordable apartment. I send a suspiciously cheap one-bedroom to Eve to see if the previous tenant died before heading down to the lobby to see what Owen is up to.

"Aren't you a sight for sore eyes?" he muses as he leans back in his chair, his hands folded on his stomach.

"I love how you talk like a middle-aged dad sometimes." I lean on the security desk and grin. "If we went to dinner, I'd expect you to say 'What's the damage?' when you got the check."

"Restaurant dinner? Do you think I'm made of money?"

His grin is spectacular, and his eyes shine like he's smuggling stars inside his body. I can't deny the crush I have on him, especially when his dumb dad jokes give me butterflies.

"I swear to God, if the next words out of your mouth are 'let's rock and roll', I'm never having lunch with you again." I point an accusatory finger. "Except for right now because I'm hungry."

"Pleased to meet you, hungry. I'm Owen."

I close my eyes, sucking in a deep, audible breath. "You've gotta stop this, hey."

"Hay is for horses."

"I'm no longer engaging in this conversation."

He laughs as he produces a container of chocolate chip cookies from under the desk and shakes it. "Guess I'll keep these for myself, then."

"You've had cookies this entire time?"

He stands up from his chair and leans over the desk, his eyes fixed on mine as he opens the container. "It's how I lure you down here every day."

I grab a cookie and take a bite. "Works every time."

For a few moments, we share the cookies and building gossip. There's currently an issue on the seventh floor with fridges being raided after hours, and whoever it is dodges all the security cameras. Owen thinks it's an inside job, and the time he's put into the investigation proves nothing of note happens in this building, and the night shifts are taking their toll.

"Are you going to tell me what's happening on your floor?"

I raise a brow. "What do you mean?"

"I mean, why did most of your staff hand back their security passes and parking garage access keys?"

"Right. That." I snap the lid back on the cookie container and round the security desk to sit beside him. "*TGP* laid off eighty percent of its staff."

Owen chokes on some cookie crumbs and pounds his chest to dislodge them. I spring forward and slap my palm against his back while simultaneously passing him a water bottle with his company logo on the side.

"Eighty percent," he coughs after chugging some water. "Why?"

"Restructure. And they're merging with another publication."

His eyes are watery and wide. "You're safe, though, aren't you?"

I look down at the desk and the slight orange tinge on the cookie container from the spaghetti and meatballs Owen made for lunch last week. He'd brought extra for us to share, but with Natalia out of the office, I wanted to work on my Florence article. He still brought me the food, heating it up in our break room and placing the plate on my desk with a note telling me not to work too hard.

"No." I shake my head. "I finish next week."

The slight amount of color that returned to his face after the cookie incident drains away again, and his mouth goes slack. "Spence. No."

"They're going to contract me instead, so I might pop in from time to time."

He shakes his head. "No. I don't like that. You have to stay. I'll talk to them. I'll talk to Natalia. I returned her keys once after she dropped them in the elevator, so she owes me."

I smile at the light in his eyes and the conviction in his voice, but there's really nothing he can do.

"Thank you, Owen. But I promise, I'm fine. I didn't like working at *TGP* that much. I wasn't writing the stories I wanted to write."

"You still have a shot at *The Herald*, right?"

I nod. "My submission is in Max Marlow's inbox as we speak."

Owen reaches for my hand. "You'll get it. I know you will. And we can still split turkey sandwiches for lunch, and I'll make those red velvet cupcakes all the time."

There is so much hope in his eyes and enough conviction to almost convince me that everything will work out. He releases my hand and stands up to pull me into a comforting hug. I take a deep breath and relax into his chest as his chin rests on my head. I feel like liquid in his arms. Completely at ease.

"Thank you for being so kind to me," I say into the starchy fabric of his uniform shirt. "Seeing you is always the best part of my day."

"Is it because I feed you?"

Tears salt my cheeks. "It's because you care about me."

His arms tighten. "Oh, Spence."

We stay like this for a while, tears rolling down my cheeks as he presses his lips to the crown of my head. My thoughts spiral. *What if none of this works out? What if I don't get the* Herald *job?* I can't be thirty and have nothing to show for it except an empty idea that whatever is on the horizon is exactly what I've been waiting for.

These thoughts swirl, and before long, the voice in my head isn't my own. It's Dad's, and I'm a child who has disappointed him all over again.

"Everything is going to be okay," Owen says, wiping the tears from my cheek with the backs of his fingers. "And if it's not, then you'll try again."

"What would you know? You're twenty-five." I smirk through tears.

He clutches his chest and groans. "Oh, direct hit. I know nothing about life because I'm so young. Even though I have a mortgage and a job and can change the oil in my car."

"You know how to do that? Because I've never done that, and I probably should."

He takes my hand again, pulling me against him. "I'll teach you."

His other hand is on my waist, and it's far too intimate for the lobby of the building where he still works. I can't step away, though, and when my eyes fall to his lips, he breathes deeper, and a little crease forms between his eyebrows. I want to smooth it away because he should never look this concerned, and I certainly don't want to be the reason for it. I roll onto my toes and place a gentle kiss on his cheek, feeling his muscles move as he smiles. When I pull away, I notice a few flecks of Snow Dragon's Archipelago in his hair, and my heart flutters.

"I don't want to not see you every day," he says before the oversized glass door swings open and his hand falls from my waist. I take a step back too, flushed and grinning, as I look up to see Alex on the threshold.

"Hi, Pen." His voice is low, melodic, and too familiar.

"What are you doing here?" The words are scarcely out of my mouth before Ruby strides out of the elevator, bouncy-haired and crimson-lipped.

"Alex. Right on time," she says. "Are you ready?"

"As I'll ever be." He gives Ruby his megawatt, paparazzi smile and follows her back to the elevator. When the doors close, Owen runs his hand down my arm and links his index finger around mine.

"Are you okay?"

I shrug as the cold, suffocating air ripples across my skin. "Yeah. He's here to do the interview, I guess."

I wait with Owen for another few minutes until I'm certain Ruby and Alex are settled in the conference room. When I get back to my floor, I see the door is closed, but Alex's presence has captured the interest of the remaining twenty percent of *TGP*'s staff. Heads periodically pop up over cubicle walls, and there is chatter rolling through the vacant space. Ruby's senses will tingle at all the attention—probably to where she isn't listening to a word Alex is saying—and she'll rely on Hazel to help her transcribe it from the recording later.

I return to my apartment search and painfully empty inbox. Still nothing from Max. And as fifteen minutes turns into forty-five, I wonder how much Alex really has to say. Maybe Ruby is getting exactly what Natalia wanted.

It's well over an hour when the conference room door opens, and Ruby walks Alex back toward the elevator. He steps closer to her, whispers something, and she returns to her desk. As soon as her ass hits the seat, her fingers dance over the keyboard like she's playing Beethoven's Moonlight Sonata. Alex is standing at my cubicle.

"Pen, have you got time to talk?" he says, leaning over the partition. "I can take you to lunch."

We haven't so much as texted since that night at Miles' place, and I am thankful for it. That small amount of distance allowed me to focus on the article for Max. To my credit, I only had one breakdown where I cried in the shower, bought overpriced sweatpants online, and contemplated calling Dad to berate him for bribing the internship panel. That revelation is still a festering wound, and my imposter syndrome is feasting on it. Still, I pressed on and finished the article. Now, it's time to take care of another pressing matter in my life.

"Lunch sounds great," I say.

In the elevator, he tells me he's already booked a table at what used to be our favorite Italian restaurant in the hope I'd agree to lunch. He doesn't say much else but continuously runs his hands through his hair on the walk to the eatery.

When we arrive, we're shown to a private dining room at the back of the restaurant. It's been at least eight years since I've walked past this place, let alone stepped inside. It's had an upgrade in that time. The old gingham tablecloths are now crisp, white, and professionally starched. The silverware is heavy, and the menu is only one page. The hostess places a wine list on the table and promises our server will be right along.

Alex doesn't even glance at the menu before he pushes it aside and rests his forearms on the table. His eyes are sharp, and his jaw is set. We're getting into this straight away.

"I should have seen how miserable you were in LA, and I shouldn't have put pressure on you to move. I didn't think about what you'd be giving up."

I can't count the number of times I've wondered where I would be if it weren't for him. I might have my own office at *The Sentinel*. I'd probably own a house, maybe even be married with children. I might not wake up every day and wonder where my life is going.

"We can't change any of it now," I say.

"I know, but I need you to know how deeply sorry I am for how I acted. I was not good to you, and I should have been at the chapel because you deserved a better goodbye."

A better goodbye? How about a goodbye at all? Whether it was good or bad. It would have been better than sitting in a gutter, drafting a mental list of all the things I did wrong to make him skip out on our wedding. I cried until my ribs ached, and I had nothing left. Rehashing and dissecting every moment of our time together, and the apologies and explanations given too late.

"I spoke to Eve," Alex says, picking at his nails.

My heart surges into my throat. "Why? What did you tell her?"

"The truth, finally. I told her all the fucked up things I did and how terrible I was to you. Then I let her yell at me until her voice was hoarse. Then she whipped me with the scarf I got her for Christmas two years ago and called me a selfish dog. That kept her busy for a while. But then she got tired, and we could have a rational conversation."

"Sounds painful. Is that what I have to look forward to?"

"Depends on what you got her for Christmas."

I drag my hand down my face. "A stoneware frying pan."

Alex winces. "Yeah. Make sure you duck when she swings."

Our conversation is interrupted by the server we were promised. She's a slight woman with large brown eyes and a constellation tattoo above her eyebrow that's still visible under lashings of concealer. She recognizes Alex and speaks so fast that I barely catch a word of it, but he smiles and leans back in his chair, taking it all in. He thanks her for the stream of what I'm assuming are compliments and signs her notebook before she remembers to take our order.

"Did you tell Eve about...what happened when we went back to LA?" I ask when the waitress extricates herself from the table.

"Yes. I told her everything," he says. "I told her about the early days. How I let Howie lead me around and chastised you when you questioned him. I told her about asking you to marry me and how I fucked all that up. I told her about the night I kissed you in the treehouse, and that I've loved you since I was old enough to know what love was. I told her that I only dated Gretchen because I couldn't have you, and I didn't care that it cost their friendship. I agreed that I'm selfish and my career is the most important thing to me. And promised not to drag you down a second time because I want you to have everything you can possibly dream of, even if I can't give it to you."

My nose tingles, and I have to close my eyes to take in everything he's said. Turning it over and feeling a few old wounds stitch together.

"I told her you were the one who got me into music in the first place and how grateful I am for it."

"I didn't get you into music," I say, my forehead wrinkling.

He smiles. "Remember when Dad gave me a guitar he found at a yard sale? I was twelve, sitting on my bed, pretending I knew what I was doing, and you walked past my room. It was when Eve was really into making jewelry, so you were dripping with strings of beads. You looked uncomfortable, and you had your arms bent at the elbows so all the bracelets wouldn't fall off. I said you looked like a T-Rex, and you told me I wasn't good at playing the guitar."

I fight hard against the smile that tugs at my lips. I remember that moment with unnatural clarity.

"You kept going down the hall," he continues. "Then you ran back and told me to keep practicing, and I'd be good one day."

He looks up at me, and there is a tugging sensation in my chest.

"That's what "Good One Day" is about." I nod slowly as the lyrics of his song click together.

He nods. "Yeah."

Alex released that song after we broke up, and I hated how much I loved it. I added it to obscure and lengthy playlists.

Never searching for it, but listening to it a second time when the shuffle feature worked in my favor.

"You're telling me that this whole thing?" I wave my arm around. "Your entire career is based on some off-the-cuff remark I made as a ten-year-old?"

"Yes."

"Alex, that's...like...I don't know, your second most popular song? And it's about me, wearing five pounds of plastic beads like a straight jacket and insulting you."

He treats me to that familiar and still dazzling smile. "But you came back and told me I'd be good one day. So, technically, you were motivating me."

I fold my hands in my lap to keep them from reaching for his.

"I was right, though. You are good."

There is a beat of silence, and we stare at each other. I'm proud of him. Though he was selfish and sometimes misguided, he worked hard and is learning from the mistakes he made along the way. I hope he doesn't lose sight of himself again, and I hope he remembers everyone he hurt. Not just me, but Miles and his family. He overindulged in every vice that came with such a weighty opportunity, and he listened to people who knew nothing about him.

I hope he remembers London and the time the tabloids caught him leaving a club with an Instagram model and some suspicious white powder under his nose. I hope he remembers the photos that were splashed all over the news with his gaunt features and the stains on his designer clothes. I hope he remembers how Elaine cried for three days and the pain in Kit's voice when she called him for an explanation. They'd be devastated if they knew the number of times he was treated in hotel rooms by a doctor who traded wads of cash for silence.

And I hope he remembers what I did for him and how much I loved him. Because I'll never forget.

"Can I ask you to do something for me?" Alex asks.

"I think that depends on the request."

The corner of his mouth lifts for a second before he corrects it. "Can you go easy on Miles? You have every right to be mad about what went down in Vegas, but would you have been happy if you'd married me?"

I can unequivocally say that I would not be happy if I was married to Alex. In the years since we broke up, his life hasn't gotten easier. His fame skyrocketed. He got bigger deals, more money, and longer tours. Where would I have fit? I wouldn't want to spend months on the road or be left alone in our apartment, waiting for him to call me from a different time zone to tell me he loves me but that he's beat and needs to sleep before his flight leaves. That's if he even called me at all. Who knows what temptation he would succumb to on tour?

"No. I wouldn't have been happy," I admit.

He pauses as the scrape of silverware and chatter of patrons punctuates our seemingly endless moment.

"I loved you," he breathes. "Please tell me you knew that."

I look into his eyes—a deep, endless blue that doesn't hold the power over me it used to—because at this moment, in this place, I have a crystallizing thought.

Being loved and feeling loved are two different things.

And for a long time, he didn't make me feel loved.

"I loved you too," I say. "And I am thankful for every wonderful moment we shared, but I never felt like I was enough for you. Every song you wrote was about me, and then you and everyone else in your life worked hard to make sure I didn't exist. Were you all so scared that this empire you'd built would crumble if I was named in your acknowledgments or if you held my hand when you left a gig?"

His lips press together, and I brace for more apologetic words that carry no culpability for all the ways he failed me. I spent years convincing myself that he did what he had to do, but what if that was never the case? What if I wasn't a problem? What if he just wasn't willing to fight?

"I don't know what to say to you, Spencer. I know sorry isn't enough, so tell me what I can do."

"I think we should stop trying to fix something that can't be fixed," I say. "I wanted to be enough for you, but it didn't work that way, so now, I want to move on. I want to be free."

He doesn't get the chance to respond because the server arrives and makes more small talk with Alex. I let it play out, digging into my food and thinking about this moment for her. She'll never see him again, but this encounter is something she'll tell her friends about at every opportunity. She'll tell them how handsome he is and that he's polite. She'll tell them he ordered rigatoni with red sauce and that she still has the glass he drank out of with his lip print on the side.

This moment is everything to her and nothing to him. I'm sure there are many people out there holding onto moments with Alex Reilly that he never thinks twice about.

So, I let her have her moment, and when she is called away, he smiles, looks her in the eye, and thanks her for her hospitality. Her cheeks flush, and I remember all too well what it's like to be on the receiving end of his devastating smile. I also recognize that it doesn't have the power over me that it used to.

After lunch, we hover on the sidewalk for a beat before Alex wraps his arms around me and presses a kiss to my temple. I'm sure I'll see him from time to time at family gatherings, but I know, in the very marrow of my bones, that this is the last time he'll hold me.

"I wanted it to be you," he whispers into my hair. "I really did."

When we break apart, I feel the last thread that's kept us tethered for all these years snap. It's over now. As I watch him walk down the street, hands in his pockets and the early afternoon sun tangled in his hair, I think of Malibu and my old writing desk. I don't regret any of it, and I don't regret him. Because our end doesn't devalue our journey, and it was a hell of a journey.

CHAPTER FORTY-FIVE

Dear Alex,

 I've never broken a bone, so I can't be certain of the pain, but the entire flight back to Seattle felt like every one of my ribs had cracked. Every bump had those shards of bone knocking together, making it hard to breathe. I was exhausted and desperate for sleep, but every time I thought of you, I started crying all over again.

 I felt like an idiot, the seatbelt crumpling my wedding dress and sobbing while wearing airline-issued headphones.

 When I landed, I went straight to Miles' apartment. He gave me a change of clothes, made terrible pancakes, and we watched Jurassic Park until I stopped crying and fell asleep. I stayed on that couch for four days.

 I could feel the world moving around me, watching the clouds roll in and dissipate in what felt like seconds. Miles came and went, working long shifts at the bar and calling to check up on me all the time. I'd blocked your number, but you tried to contact me every way you knew how. That was when I deactivated my social media and blocked your email as well. I didn't want to know you anymore. In my bleak, new reality, you didn't need to exist.

I couldn't escape you, though, because even without me, your world didn't stop. I wondered what time you got back to the hotel in Vegas and didn't find me there. Did you go to the chapel expecting me to be waiting? Did you assume I was back at the hotel and you could stumble in, armed with an apology, and we could do it all again the next night after you played the show?

I read the rave reviews on that Vegas show, by the way. It hurt knowing that while I was in a heap on Miles' couch, you played a sold-out theater and smiled while everyone cheered for you.

I hated you then, and I'd never been more sure of it.

After that, you went to Chicago and onto New York. Night after night, you got up on that stage and sang about how much you loved me.

Did it hurt? Even a little? Those songs should have tasted like ash in your mouth, but you smiled through them. Closing your eyes, swaying peacefully as you sang about how you'd do anything for me. I wanted you to choke on the microphone because I was forced to remember everything you had the luxury of forgetting.

It wasn't until the Miami show that I saw the cracks. You were photographed outside a club. You had a bottle blonde under your arm, and you looked so strung out that you didn't know where you were. It made me feel a little better, knowing that you felt enough to not want to feel anything at all.

Did you really think, when Howie pushed that first glass of bourbon into your hand at Caesar's, that you'd stop at just one? You had an addiction, and that was always going to be a part of you. You were a sober alcoholic, but still an alcoholic. At least you went back to the treatment facility after the

European tour. You were a real mess by then. Maybe we have that to thank for you finally turning your life around.

Returning to LA for that one day to get my stuff was harder on me than I ever imagined. You were still on tour, and Miles offered to join me, but I felt like I needed to do it on my own. Mostly because I knew I'd spend way too long lying on our bed, our smells mixed on the sheets I bought for us with my first paycheck from a travel article I wrote.

I still can't accurately explain how it felt to be in that space without you. I expected it to feel empty, but it was the opposite. It was oppressive. Like the expectation of our future was left to rot in the small space, and the apartment itself knew we weren't coming back together. The succulents on the windowsill were already wilting, and a layer of dust had accumulated on the nightstand.

It didn't look the same to me. Just how you didn't look the same to me.

You weren't this polished, impressive, talented musician or that kid on stage at The Palace. You were someone else entirely. Some disappointing anomaly wearing your skin and singing so beautifully, no one could tell the difference.

I was one of them for far too long.

I cried on the drive to LAX. I called Miles and told him I wanted to be home. I wanted my old life and my family.

I wanted Eve.

I wanted to tell her how sorry I was that I lied and that she was right when she said you would always do what you wanted, regardless of the casualties.

I felt stupid for thinking that I would be different.

I felt stupid for thinking I could change or fix you.

It was never my job to fix you, even though it felt like I had when I took you to that rehab center. I wasn't your moral compass. I wasn't in your life to ground you when you felt reckless, and you shouldn't have made me sit on the sidelines, waiting for you.

In the years after, I went through so many phases. Making mistakes with unavailable men to feel whole again. Seeking validation that I was worth something, even though it meant nothing.

I took the job at The Gossip Project to make my degree worth more than the paper it was written on.

I committed to Sunday night dinners and endless lectures to make my parents call me their daughter again.

I started over, and when I landed back in Seattle, eyes stinging from tears and remnants of my former life in suitcases, I wasn't sure I could do it.

That was until I saw Eve waiting for me in the arrivals hall, arms open, promising that I would be okay.

CHAPTER FORTY-SIX

I can do this.

I am ready.

Worst-case scenario, I throw the wine at her and run.

Best-case scenario: we drink the wine, I tell her about lunch with Alex, and she says she's proud of me for finally untangling myself from her brother.

She's heard me coming because my key is in the lock when the door swings open, and Eve is standing there in sweatpants and an old t-shirt. It may as well be battle armor because my stomach is already fizzing in anticipation of the worst-case scenario.

It doesn't happen, though. There's no shouting. No rage. No flared nostrils or red ears. Instead, her face crumples, her eyes welling with tears as she grabs me and pulls me into a hug.

"Spencer," she sobs, and I pat her back, not entirely sure what's going on.

"Eve, are you okay?"

She steps out of the way, taking my arm and leading me through the apartment to the couch.

"You could have told me," she says as we sit down. "You could have told me about everything. I would have understood."

Bless her for believing that's true. Eve has always been a shoot-first and ask-questions-later kind of girl. It's part of her charm, but after Gretchen and how much losing that friendship upset her, there was no way she'd handle Alex and me together.

"I'm sorry I didn't tell you," I say. "I just didn't want you to look at me the way you did when he left."

Her cheeks are flushed, and tears build in her bright blue eyes. "I'm sorry if I made you feel you couldn't confide in me. I didn't want us to not be friends because of him, and it happened anyway. We missed out on so much time because I was mad. It was stupid. I could have come to LA with you."

"LA wasn't good, Eve," I say, wondering if it would have been better with her there. She would have seen right through Howie from the start. She could have helped her brother. She could have helped me.

"I can't believe he left you at the altar!"

"It wasn't so much an altar as a small step with a carpet square on it."

Eve pouts. "But you had a dress and everything."

"I still do. It's in the back of my closet."

She's quiet for a moment, staring at the rug we stole from Darren and pressing her teeth into her bottom lip. "I really want to say I told you Alex was a bad idea, but I think you've been through enough."

I laugh. "Yes, I have."

"And he's done with the interview now, so you won't have to worry about seeing him at the office."

"That's not really a concern, considering I won't be at the office."

Eve's face pales. "What?"

"Parkhurst cut eighty percent of the full-time writing staff at *TGP*. Natalia moved me to a contract position. I finish at the office next week."

"What do you mean by contract? That's still a job, right?"

"Freelance. I'll only get paid for what they publish."

"Spence," Eve sighs. "Why didn't you tell me this is why you wanted to get a cheaper place?"

"Because I was hoping Max would give me a shot, and then it wouldn't matter, but I haven't heard from him yet. Every day, I worry *The Herald* is a pipe dream as well."

Eve reaches for me, enveloping me in a hug. "You're going to get the *Herald* job. Trust me."

My eyes mist, and I hold on to her as tight as I can. She rubs my back, and I realize I should have told her because she would have listened even if she didn't understand.

"I'm still going to have to move." I wipe my face. "I can't afford this place without a full-time job."

Eve pats my hand, and her eyes light with suspicious optimism. "That's okay. I got a place today, so you can live with me."

"What do you mean, you got a place?"

"I mean, Miles is letting me take the apartment above the bar. The rent is next to nothing, which is dumb because it's a good neighborhood, and the place has lots of natural light."

Eve moving into the compact one-bedroom above Whiskey Double makes perfect sense. It's become the temporary accommodation of choice for anyone nursing a broken heart. Miles's older brother, Fletcher, moved in after his divorce, and when he vacated, Doug took it over. Now that Doug has found his own place, it's sitting empty. I'm sure Eve will do wonders with it. Or, at the very least, all the furniture will match, and she can use the built-in bookcases to display her designer shoe and handbag collection. She might even get an Ektorp of her own.

We sit on the couch for a few hours, sipping the peace offering wine I bought home, and talking over everything from start to finish. She's patient and listens to every kind and sometimes spiteful word I have to say about her brother. Sometimes, she defends him, and other times, she curses his name. We talk about Gretchen, her job, her parents' divorce, and how hard it's going to be to get the rug up to her new apartment. After all of it, when my eyes are closing, and the weight feels like it's lifted off me, there is a knock on the door.

"You can get that. I need a shower." Eve pulls herself off the couch and saunters into the bathroom.

I hurry to the door and swing it open to find Miles on the threshold.

"Please don't slam the door in my face before I say what I need to." He holds his hands up. "I don't regret telling Howie about you and Alex. I'd do it again because it was never going to work, and you knew that. We spent hours on the phone, Spence, and you were so miserable. You and Alex were both idiots to think that getting married was going to make it better. He wouldn't stop doing what the label wanted, and Howie was never going to treat you with respect. You deserve so much better, and it killed me when you said you were fine with a Vegas wedding. You had that scrapbook of your perfect wedding. It wasn't some shitty off-the-strip chapel with a drunk as your witness."

He sucks in a deep breath and rolls his shoulders back.

"Okay. You can slam the door now."

His whiskey brown eyes soften, and he swallows hard. I can't bring myself to be angry because he's saved me so many times and in so many ways. He kept Alex and me a secret when we asked. He supported me in LA and always answered when I called to cry about how much I was struggling. He let me live on his couch after the breakup and let me vent about everything. He's never been cruel or selfish or dismissive. He's been there even when it felt like I was completely alone. I love him for that, and I love him for doing what I couldn't—leaving Alex when I needed to.

I reach out, grab the lapel of his coat, and pull him forward, wrapping my arms around him. "Thank you."

His arms are loose at his sides, and his body tightens as I hang off his neck. "What's happening?"

"Thank you for looking out for me and helping me when it all went to shit."

Miles is silent for a beat, sucking in a breath before he wraps his arms around me and holds me so tight my ribs ache. "You deserve the best, Spence. I want you to be happy."

"I will be, Miles," I say into his shoulder. "Because it doesn't hurt anymore."

The end of my tenure at *The Gossip Project* is bittersweet. Natalia pays for a cake and grants us fifteen minutes to eat it. Ruby gifts me a travel coffee cup with my initials stamped on the side before she moves her things to the desk I used to occupy. At five on the dot, Owen comes up to the office to help carry my things to the car. We quickly realize it looks like I'm being escorted out of the building, and I ask him to keep me posted on what the rumor mill prints for that.

"Are you still going to be my date for Whitney's wedding?" he asks as he closes the trunk of my car with a hearty thump.

"Of course. I'm looking forward to it."

His face relaxes, and a sigh escapes him.

"Wait, did you think I was going to bail on you?"

"I wasn't sure." He scuffs the toe of his boot on the concrete. "I asked you a while ago, and a lot has happened since then. You missed a few of our lunch dates."

He's right, and I'm needled with guilt at the thought of him sitting in that security office, waiting for me.

"I'm sorry, Owen, but let me make it up to you," I say. "I can bring you lunch on Monday. Or help you with your wedding speech. Or paint your living room."

He laughs. "You don't have to do all that. But some help with the speech would be great."

I clap my hands together in triumph. "I can do that, and I swear it will be the best wedding speech ever written. There won't be a dry eye in the house."

"It's a garden wedding, so it's a marquee."

"There won't be a dry eye in the marquee," I amend. "I'll call you later tonight, and we can brainstorm."

"Thanks, Spence." He leans down and drops a light kiss on my cheek. "Also, since you're no longer employed by a company operating out of this building, I'm going to have to ask you to leave the premises."

The smirk on his face earns him a weak little punch to the arm. "I'm going, I'm going."

As I drive out of the garage with Owen waving from my empty parking space, I say an internal goodbye to *TGP* and cross my fingers that I'll be getting a new parking pass soon with *The Herald* logo on that sliver of laminated plastic.

CHAPTER FORTY-SEVEN

Alex's explosive interview with Ruby is up on *TGP*'s website and garnering the exact amount of interest Natalia was hoping for. He refers to me—not by name—and tells the story of growing up in Seattle and making it big in LA. I can't bring myself to read all of it, but send Ruby a message to congratulate her.

"Why is my bar the dumping ground for the unemployed or recently single?" Miles sighs as he slips into the booth beside me.

It's after closing, and I've been occupying this table for hours.

"Technically, I'm contracted by *TGP*, but I am looking for a job," I explain. "And maybe you're the most stable out of all of us, so that's why we gravitate toward you."

"I'm trying to run a business."

I pinch his cheek. "And you're doing amazing, sweetie."

He slaps my hand away and takes a sip from the glass of wine I've been nursing for the last hour. He won't like it, but he swallows it painfully and screws up his face as the sweetness coats his tongue.

"Are you planning on staying here all night? Because the apartment upstairs is taken."

Eve had a guest tonight, but I don't know who it was. Miles said someone keeps dropping by, staying for an hour, and then disappearing into the night. It's creating such a mystery that even Danny and Kit are becoming invested. I texted them before when I saw the guy leave, and Kit suggested that next time, she and Danny stake out the alley to see if we recognize him.

"I'll go home," I say. "But thank you for letting me take up space."

He puts his arm over my shoulder and presses our heads together. "You're welcome."

Miles slips out of the booth, and as I'm about to close my laptop, it dings with an email alert.

To: Spencer Caldwell <spencer.caldwell@inknet.com>

From: Max Marlow <max.marlow@parkhurstmediagroup.com>

> *Read your submission. Stop by my office tomorrow at 9am to discuss.*
> *Max*

My breath catches in my throat as I reread the email over and over, separating every word and turning it over in my head until it makes no sense. I forget I'm in an empty bar on a Wednesday night.

"Why do you look like you've been slapped?" Miles asks as he flips the last chair and sits it on a nearby table.

I turn the laptop to face him, and he hurries over to skim the email.

"Are his emails usually that direct?" His nose wrinkles. "Is this a good thing?"

"I don't know, but if I didn't get the job, wouldn't he say that?"

I pull my laptop back over and read the email again. With every passing day, I've been losing hope. I started wondering if he never received my email or if he hated the piece so much that it would be an embarrassment to even discuss it with me.

"I guess you'll find out at nine tomorrow," Miles says as he claps his hand on my shoulder.

⬤

As predicted, I don't get a wink of sleep. I recall every word of my article in my head. I even get up and fact-check every claim and verify every source. It's undoubtedly my best work, but the fear of it not being good enough surges inside me until I can't keep my breakfast of dry toast down.

At eight-thirty, I enter the building to find Owen at the desk. His face lights up when he sees me but quickly falls when he sees the panic in my eyes.

"It's bad, isn't it?" I hold out my phone with Max's email on the screen. Owen scans it quickly.

"No, I don't think so."

"You're a terrible liar."

"He's a man of few words."

"There are practically no words. There is nothing about the article other than he got it. There's no 'well done' or 'it was great'. There isn't even a 'try again'. This email tells me nothing."

Owen hands my phone back. "I mean, it tells you to meet him at nine."

I roll my eyes. "Yes. I got that."

For twenty minutes, I pace the security office, occasionally breathing into a paper bag that Owen brought his lunch in. I want this job so much, and the possibility this dream will die within the hour has my brain folding in on itself. The only reason I could make peace with the *TGP* restructure was because I thought I had a real shot at this. *What if I never had the shot? What if this is the end of my career in journalism?*

Owen walks me to the elevator, tucks the paper bag in my coat pocket just in case, and pats my shoulder like a proud father sending his eldest boy to war.

"You've got this," he says as the elevator doors close.

I recite Owen's affirmation several times under my breath, but as soon as I step through the door of Max's office, I realize I don't have this. His desk is clear save for his laptop and a small, leather-wrapped tray at the top corner. He hasn't even printed out my article to tear to shreds this time.

"Take a seat, Spencer."

My stomach lurches into my throat as he watches me keenly, his hands clasped together, seemingly at ease. I swallow hard to dislodge the mass that blocks my windpipe.

"The piece was great. You took my instruction and ran with it. Unfortunately, we've filled the spot."

There's no emotion in his voice. No remorse or empathy. This is just a Thursday for him. Nothing of note. Not even a dot point on the rundown of his day.

"I see." It's all I can manage, and even then, my voice shakes.

"I know you've been moved over to a contract for *TGP*, and I'll take a look at anything you have to submit, should we be looking for a contributor."

My cheeks are hot, and I'm on the verge of tears, but I nod and stand up from my chair. "Thank you for reading my submission."

Max dismisses me, and when I step into the hall, I'm consumed by this harsh reality. I didn't get the job. After all that, I didn't get it. It didn't matter how many hours I spent researching or how I meticulously chose every word. Someone else will sit at that spare desk on Monday morning.

The trip back to the lobby is a drawn-out affair. It stops on several floors, and every person who gets in doesn't understand the concept of personal space or being quiet. When we reach the first floor and some space is freed up, I suck in a deep breath. All I can picture is Max's indifferent expression and my chest heaves.

By the time we hit the ground, tears are pouring down my cheeks.

"Spencer?" Owen rushes over from the desk. "What happened?"

"I... I... " I can't string the words together. Even though there was a chance this was coming, I'm not prepared for it to hurt this much. "I... I... didn't get it."

"Shit," Owen grunts as he collects me in his arms, holding me against his chest while I sob. "It's okay, though. Everything is going to be okay."

He holds me, gently swaying from side to side in the middle of the lobby while workers flow in and out of the building. They skirt around us, some on their phones and others grumbling that we're in the way.

I pull back, wipe my eyes, and look at him. "Sorry. I know this seems like an overreaction. I just really wanted that job."

"Don't be sorry." He pats my shoulder. "You're allowed to be sad. You can scream if you want to. Security won't escort you from the building."

I blink at him. "Can I really?"

"Yeah." He smiles. "You can shout or cry. Unleash hell if you want."

I roll my shoulders, and Owen takes a step back. "Maybe in the security office."

He puts an arm around my shoulder and guides me to the office, closing the door behind us.

"Okay. Let's go. Tell me exactly what's on your mind."

I wipe the drip from under my nose and suck in a breath. "Well… I'm… I'm frustrated."

Owen folds his arms. "You can do better than that."

"Like, really frustrated. I've been pitching these great articles to *TGP* for years, and they constantly knocked them back. We could have been something so much better, and I did a great job on the pieces I did write. Even that listicle on what your favorite ice-cream flavor and star sign says about you."

"I read that one." Owen grins. "I'm choc-chip cookie dough and a Taurus rising. Which makes me laid back but grounded and at risk of developing diabetes in later life."

I frown. "I would have taken you for a mint choc chip man?"

Owen scoffs. "Absolutely not. But we're going off on a tangent. Keep letting it out."

I roll my shoulders back and take another breath. "And I'm angry with myself for making dumb decisions because I'm always worried about what other people think. I should have told Eve I loved Alex when I realized it myself because I'm not Gretchen, and I would not let it get in the way of our friendship. And I should have stood up for Miles. He didn't deserve to get kicked out of the band. He had the right to be there. The same goes for Stevie. He shouldn't have had to choose between his career and caring for his mother. I should have stood up to Howie, too. I shouldn't have let him lead

Alex astray, and I should have told him all the stuff with Harriet made me uncomfortable. Instead, I faded into the background because I was too fucking scared to use my voice."

"I don't know who most of these people are, but I'm loving this energy," Owen says.

"I shouldn't have given up my internship. I should have put my career first because I've spent my entire life defending my decision to be a journalist, and then I let it go without a second thought."

My pulse is racing, and the tears are long gone.

"And I shouldn't have agreed to marry him. It would never have solved our problems, and I was an idiot for thinking it would."

Owen's face falls. "You were going to marry Alex?"

"Yes, but he left me at the altar."

Owen frowns. "Oh, God. I'm so sorry. Are you okay?"

"It was years ago, but no, I'm not really okay. I have this deep-seated fear that whoever I end up with is going to care about someone or something else more. It's maddening because I want to be happy. I want to have a career I'm passionate about. I want to get married and have kids. I want a life. A real one."

The sound of the bell on the security desk rings, and Owen pulls open the door to see who it is.

"It's the building manager." He sighs, his conflicted gaze falling back to me.

"That's okay." I reach out and squeeze his arm. "You should go."

He looks at me like the fate of the world rests on his shoulders, and he doesn't know which wire to cut.

"But then I'm leaving you, and I don't care about the building manager more than you."

I let out a soft laugh. "Owen, it's okay. I'm okay. I'll catch up with you later."

As we exit the security office, Ginny, *The Herald* receptionist, steps out of the elevator. She scans the lobby, and when she catches sight of me, she exhales.

"Great, you're still here," she says. "Have you got a second? Max wants to talk to you."

Owen gives me an encouraging wink, and I follow Ginny up to Max's office again.

My palms are sweating on the approach, and I remind myself that he can't not give me a job for a second time today. The damage is done. My ego is bruised.

This relaxes me enough to stop my hands from shaking as I enter his office. The atmosphere has taken a turn now. Max's jacket is off, and he's leaning on the side of his desk. He must be done eviscerating people's dreams for today.

"Spencer, glad I caught you." He looks up from his phone. "I was speaking with a colleague. Told him you're good. He has a position for you."

The shards of my career appear slightly less splintered, and nervous energy crackles in my blood. "What kind of position?"

"Beat reporter for the *New England Tribune*. Parkhurst acquired them two hours ago."

My heart hammers against my ribs, and my mind scatters. "New England?"

"Yes. You'll be based out of Boston, reporting to the city editor. It's a good job. Worth the move."

Boston? I'd be a beat reporter in Boston?

After LA, I couldn't picture myself ever leaving Seattle. This is my home. I have Eve and her family. I have an apartment here and a grocery store that does the best crispy potatoes with sour cream dip. I have sunsets over the sound and confidence that I can drive myself to the airport if the need arises. I'm safe in Seattle. And Owen is here, too.

Max gives me a further twenty seconds of consideration before he looks poised to withdraw the offer.

"Spencer?" His glacial eyes narrow, and I feel the opportunity melting like snow in the desert.

"I'll take it," I say. "Just tell me where to sign."

CHAPTER FORTY-EIGHT

In the lead-up to the wedding, I fulfil my promise of helping Owen with his speech. In the end, he finds the perfect words himself, so I coach him on some public speaking techniques I picked up from debate club in high school. He stands tall and recites his speech as he paces his living room, pausing in the places we agreed to allow for the best flow. When he muddles a line, we move on, and he brings it back around for another perfect read-through. Watching his forehead wrinkle with concern and his hands shake with nerves would be endearing if I wasn't constantly thinking about how to tell him about Boston.

On the day of Whitney's wedding, Owen arrives five minutes before the agreed time, and his mouth falls open when he steps out of the car.

"Spencer, you always look incredible, but this is next level." He beams. "Give me a spin?"

I smooth the sides of my corseted wrap dress and turn around, displaying every inch of the silky, bordeaux-colored fabric. I bought it two years ago, and the first time I wore it was to have dinner with my parents. Mom said it was too busty and inappropriate to wear in public. It made me love it all the more. Owen appreciates it too because when he comes over for a closer inspection, his brain and mouth have disconnected.

"Are you okay?" I laugh.

Owen shakes his head and snaps his mouth shut. "No. I'm not."

"Well, you don't look too bad either." A blush floods my cheeks, turning my face the same color as my dress. He looks handsome in his classic tuxedo that's been tailored to fit him like a glove, and his blond hair is smoothed back and neatly trimmed at the sides.

"This old thing." He inspects his jacket. "My mom chose it."

I laugh as I pick up my overnight bag and step toward the car. Owen's brain catches up, and he takes the bag and hurries ahead of me to open the door. When he grips my hand to guide me into the passenger's seat, I notice his palm is warm, slightly clammy, and his fingers are trembling. I keep hold of it and pull him closer.

"Don't be nervous about tonight. Your speech is beautiful. The perfect balance of humor and heart. There won't be a dry eye in the marquee, remember?"

He leans forward, bringing my hand to his mouth and brushing the back of it with a gentle kiss.

"I'm more nervous about standing on your toes when we dance."

He releases my hand and closes the door. My head and heart are buzzing as I watch him rush around to the driver's side with a grin on his handsome face.

Owen practices his speech a few more times on the two-hour drive to the private estate belonging to Whitney's fiancé's family.

He tells me all about it, but it doesn't prepare me for the grandeur of the stunning neoclassical mansion. The three-story property is surrounded by manicured lawns, and a huge marquee is set up on one side of the main house. On the other side, a white arch dotted with baby pink and white hydrangeas stands before rows and rows of gold Tiffany chairs. Event staff are ferrying supplies from the house to the marquee, and one of them rushes over to direct us down a gravel driveway to the designated parking area.

"Simple garden wedding, hey?" My face is glued to the window as I take in the back half of the mansion.

"It's a bit more than Whitney expected, too, but Dale's family wanted to give them a memorable day."

Memorable? I don't think any building I step into from now to eternity will compare to this place. This might be the best day of my life by association.

Owen parks the car at the end of the row and helps me out. I offer to take my bag, but he playfully swats my hand away before we cross the lawn to the house.

We're greeted at the front door by a tall woman with a pinched face and badge that identifies her as the event coordinator. She walks us through the cavernous home to the guest wing and tells me to be down on the lawn in exactly two hours. She then informs Owen that she will collect him shortly, as he is to join the rest of the groomsmen in Dale's room. Her severe expression sends a chill up my spine. Owen bows when she says goodbye, clearly confused and crumbling under the pressure.

"What are you doing?" I laugh as I grip his shoulder and pull him upright.

"I panicked," he whispers. "I've never been in a house with wings."

We both look ahead to the white door with a temporary

sign fixed to the front that reads 'Owen Delaney and Spencer Caldwell'.

"I think this is beyond a house. We're getting into hotel territory."

"Do you think we get a mini bar?" His face lights up.

"Let's find out." I slide the key into the lock and turn the handle.

We're immediately hit with the scent of fresh linen and the honey-sweet hydrangeas that have been artfully arranged in a glass vase on the writing desk by the window.

"Holy shit," Owen breathes as he drops our bags on the cream carpet.

"This is..." I trail off.

The room is decorated with every shade of cream perceptible to the human eye. There are two queen-sized beds stacked with cushions of varying sizes and textures, a freestanding wardrobe, bench seats at the end of each bed, and nightstands that have bottled water and eye masks. Even the adjoining bathroom has an array of travel-sized skincare on its gleaming marble vanity.

"No mini bar," Owen huffs as he picks up the bags and deposits one on each of the benches. I stick my head through the bathroom door to get a better look at how utterly ridiculous this suite is.

"No mini bar, but you can fit like six people in this bathtub."

Owen steps behind me, his hand landing on my waist as he looks over my head at the wall-to-wall marble bathroom. I try not to focus on the contact, but my back brushes his chest, and I feel my cheeks heat.

"How many people are we inviting to the bathtub?"

I turn to face him, and his hand doesn't leave my midsection.

"I wasn't planning on inviting anyone, but it's nice to have the option."

His fingers flex at my waist, and he leans closer. "I'd prefer it if it were just us."

There is a knock on the door, and his hand falls away. It leaves me cold and guilt-ridden. *I have to tell him about Boston.*

"That will be that scary organizer lady again." Owen sighs. "I'll see you at the ceremony, I guess."

"I'll be there in exactly two hours." I smile, and he leans down, kissing me on the cheek.

"Thank you for coming with me. I love that you're here."

"Happy to help," I say. "Now go because that organizer lady's forehead vein is probably on the brink right now."

His face splits with a grin, and he winks before hurrying from the room.

One hour and forty minutes later, I make my way down to the lawn. Wedding guests are being ushered into seats by a stocky man with a headset whose fuse looks to be even shorter than the event coordinator's. I avoid eye contact with him and slide onto a vacant chair in the last row on Whitney's side. Her third-grade teacher is seated beside me, and I pass the time talking about the favorable weather before Dale, Owen, and the rest of the groomsman arrive. They line up beside the hydrangea-covered arch. Dale takes several deep breaths and closes his eyes. Owen pats him on the shoulder before stepping out of his place and leaning down to a blonde woman in the front row. He kisses her on the cheek, and she straightens his tie. His mother, I assume.

Before stepping back behind Dale, Owen looks up and scans the crowd. When his sights land on me, I give him a small wave. He grins and hurries down the aisle, dropping to his knee beside my chair and taking my hand.

"Are you good?"

"Yes. I'm fine." I give him a reassuring smile. "Now, get back up there before you get in trouble."

He pats my hand, and as I watch him return to his post, I notice his mom has turned around, and she's looking at me. She's flawless with her early nineties Princess Diana hair and lilac coat dress. She offers a tight yet curious smile before returning her attention to her son.

Whitney arrives soon after, and the wedding is romantic and heartfelt, considering I don't know the couple. I watch Owen the whole time, and my heart skips when he wipes away a tear at the sight of his sister walking down the aisle. Whitney and Dale exchange vows, rings, and a kiss before the bridal party and immediate family are corralled to a separate section of the lawn to have their photos taken.

I stay in my seat, watching the world move around me, the sun starting its descent and the breeze rustling the gossamer fabric wrapped around the guest chairs. It's peaceful, and for a brief moment, I wonder what it would be like to be in Whitney's satin block heels. This perfect day and this beautiful family, all present to celebrate the love she and Dale have for each other.

It's a long way from a Vegas chapel with a red carpet that was too short for the aisle and the next three couples waiting in the back row.

An hour later, the guests move to the marquee, and everyone has a glass of champagne in their hand. When I track down my assigned seat, I realize it's the singles table, though my table mates are welcoming, around my age, and looking to have a good time. I swap my beef for Whitney's hairdresser's chicken, and Dale's doorman tells me his idea for a kind of robot vacuum that cleans windows on skyscrapers. I tell him I'd invest if I had the capital, but he's barking up the wrong tree.

He keeps going, though, and I have to politely shush him when Owen steps up to the small lectern beside the bridal table. He pulls a familiar sheet of paper from his pocket and clears his throat before he taps the microphone with a shaking finger.

He smoothly opens with a joke about the cake being in tiers that sends a ripple of laughter through the marquee. From there, he's off to the races, reciting every line perfectly and bringing tears to his sister's eyes. Between the laughter and coos, he raises his glass to his sister and her husband, gulping down his champagne in a manner that gives away his nerves.

After the rest of the speeches, Owen hightails it over to my table. He's taken off his jacket and sweat beads on his forehead.

"You did amazing." I clap my hands together as he drops down beside my chair.

"I stuffed up the third line." He frowns. "I missed the bit about Whitney falling in the pool before prom, so the bit about her makeup didn't make as much sense."

"It was great, Owen, I promise. Not a dry eye in the marquee."

He stands up, reaches for my hand, and pulls me to my feet. "Thank God it's done now because I want to introduce you to my family."

He links my arm with his as he guides me through the wedding guests to the corner of the marquee. His mother spots us immediately and gives me a warm smile.

"Mom, Dad, this is Spencer." Owen releases my arm and steps behind me. "These are my parents, Jill and Grant."

I shake both their hands. "Nice to meet you."

"Likewise." Jill's mauve-painted lips split into another demure smile. "Owen has told us so much about you."

I raise a brow. "He has?"

Grant gently bumps his shoulder into Jill's. "He told us about the Florence Ritter story you wrote. We've watched a documentary or three about that case."

Jill laughs as she places her hand on her husband's arm. "Alright, Grant. How about we bend Spencer's ear about that over breakfast tomorrow? I don't think Whit would be happy to hear us discussing a brutal murder at her wedding."

"It was brutal, wasn't it?" Grant contemplates as he swirls the amber liquid in his glass.

Jill shushes her husband before they are swept off into another conversation with a man wearing an actual monocle. This prompts a rather lengthy discussion about the possibility of Owen being able to pull off the Monopoly man look, and we both agree he can't.

Through monocle jokes and champagne giggles, Owen leads me back to the dance floor, only we're stopped frequently by people wanting to chat with him. To every smiling face, I'm introduced as his date. He proudly tells them I'm a journalist and lists my limited achievements with beaming pride and a blush in his cheeks. I hold onto him, hoping physical contact will prolong this feeling of adequacy. This feeling that I'm someone or something to be proud of.

When we dance, he holds me gently, smiles, and keeps his eyes on mine. It makes me feel like I'm the most important person in the room and that his friends and family should be indebted to him for having met me.

By the time we're ready to exit the dance floor, I've met all of Owen's aunts and uncles, several of his cousins, a few second cousins, and his best friend, Jack—who raises his thick eyebrows at Owen when he thinks I'm not looking. I dance with Jack for a couple of songs, reveling in stories he tells of him and Owen growing up. Owen tried his hand at baseball, hockey, basketball, and football, while Jack preferred video games and mystery novels.

Jack and I are digging deep into their high school experience when Owen returns from the bathroom and steers me away.

"That's not fair," I huff. "Jack was about to tell me about your prom afterparty."

"You don't need to know about that." Owen spins me across the temporary parquet dance floor before pulling me against him with a flourish. My head falls back, and I laugh as he turns me around to the uptempo pop music.

A few hours and many blisters later, Whitney and Dale leave the marquee, and the other guests disperse soon after. Owen throws his jacket around my shoulders, and we walk arm-in-arm back to the main house. It's even more grandiose at night with its high ceilings, neoclassical columns, and ornate archways, all bathed in golden light from the sconces that line each hallway.

"They even dropped off champagne," Owen points out as we step into our room.

I look over at the writing desk under the window, where a bottle sits in the silver bucket of ice, flanked by crystal champagne flutes.

"This place is absurd." I shake my head. "I don't think I can afford to breathe the air here."

"You and me both." Owen drops onto the bench at the end of his bed and takes off his shoes before laying back and letting out an exhausted sigh.

I slide his jacket off my shoulders and hang it over the chair as I slip off my heels. My feet ache, and I let out a pleasurable moan when my toes sink into the high pile carpet.

Owen sits up and looks at me, the near-permanent grin falling from his face as he takes me in.

"Thank you for coming with me. I appreciate it."

"No need to thank me. I had a great time."

He stands up, his bare feet crossing the carpet to stand in front of me. His mouth is pressed into a line, and worry wrinkles his brow. He smells like aged whiskey, clove cologne, and sweet hydrangeas. His eyes are bright, wild, and fixed on me so intently that my heart skips.

He adores me. I know he does, but I don't know what I've done to deserve such adoration. It forces Boston to the forefront of my mind again.

"Why did you introduce me to all those people tonight?" I ask.

His hand brushes my waist. "Because I want everyone in my life to know you."

"But I'm just a girl who worked in your building?"

His fingers press into me, causing my pulse to spike. "You're much more than that. You're smart, charismatic, caring, beautiful, funny, strong, and a tenacious journalist. You're so impressive that I don't deserve to stand beside you, let alone have you as my date to a wedding."

A comforting warmth spreads through my whole body as I look at him. I don't know how to respond because it's not what I expected him to say, and it moves something inside me. My heart, once so bruised, doesn't feel quite so damaged.

"Can I kiss you again?" Owen asks as he leans down and gently presses his forehead to mine. The air between us is charged, and my blood pulses. "Please?"

He's made me feel included in this place where I should feel like an outsider. He made me feel like I'm good enough. He made me feel loved.

"Yes," I whisper, and his hand moves up, resting on my neck with his thumb under my chin, tilting it up.

I close my eyes, and his lips meet mine. It's soft, tender, and I taste the champagne he sipped before we left the marquee. Sweet and crisp. I need more, but Owen breaks the kiss, his heavy breathing matching my own.

"Turn around," he says.

I do as instructed, my arms at my sides as his mouth meets my shoulder. His movements are languid, his fingertips slowly trailing down my spine until he reaches the zip of my dress. I suck in a breath, hot and hurried, as he nips my shoulder, and the sound of my zipper being dragged down cuts the silence in the room.

The cool air hits my bare skin, and I shiver as his fingers continue their path down my back. I turn my head, and his lips are on mine again. It's a different type of kiss than before. It's still restrained, but barely.

And that rain cloud of guilt passes over me again as his fingers trace my skin. I don't want to be with him like this. I don't want him to think that I'm all in when the contract is on its way.

It isn't fair.

"Owen." I step out of his touch and hold my dress against my chest.

His brows knit together. "Is everything okay?"

I shake my head. "I have to tell you something."

He looks at me with his beautiful, selfless doe eyes, and I feel like the smallest person in the world.

"Okay."

"Max offered me a job," I say. "In Boston."

Owen stills, one hand in my hair and the other on my waist. "Oh."

His hands slide off me, and I'm instantly cold. "I'm so sorry."

"Don't be sorry. Is it a good job? I mean, I'm sure it's a good job, and I'm sure you'll be great at it."

"It is good. Beat reporter for the *New England Tribune*. And I've got a lead on an apartment. It's this little one-bedroom on Beacon Street, and it has a fireplace. I'm not sure if it's operational, but it's really cute."

Owen smiles. "This all sounds amazing, Spence. I'm so happy for you."

I look down at his hands. His fingers are thick, and his palms broad. He's so warm and kind. I know I will truly miss him.

"I didn't know how to tell you. I care about you, and I'm certain the only reason I stayed at *TGP* as long as I did was because splitting a turkey sandwich with you was the best part of being in that building." My voice shakes, and he pulls me into his chest without hesitation.

"Hey, hey. It's okay."

"It's not because I'm going to miss you so much."

He presses his forehead to mine. "You've gotta do this, Spence. This job is perfect for you, and if it's on the other side of the country, it only adds to the adventure."

He lifts my hand to his mouth and kisses my knuckles. From there, I'm done for. I sob, my breathing ragged as all this change catches up with me. I want this job, and I want Boston. I want something for myself, and I want space from my past and all the things I used as an excuse to hold myself back.

"I'm gonna see you all the time." He leans down and kisses me. "I'll be over there so much, you'll be sick of me."

"Don't take out a second mortgage on your house to pay for all those flights. Phones exist."

He lifts my chin with his finger. "I'm serious, Spence. I'll visit you. I'll call you. I'll do anything you need me to."

He searches my face, his eyes asking a pressing question that has no logical response.

"Are you sure this is what you want?" I ask. "The distance is a lot."

His brows draw together, and he looks at me so deeply that I can see every ribbon of color in his gray eyes. "Don't ask if I'm sure I want you. I will always want you."

The confession is heavy, but he seals it with a kiss that makes me certain we'll figure it out.

CHAPTER FORTY-NINE

"Boston?" Eve looks at me with wide, unblinking eyes. "You're moving to Boston?"

Miles is sporting the same confused expression as we gather in my living room. In the interest of not keeping any more secrets, I decided to tell them as soon as the contract came through. Which it did—thirty minutes ago.

"So it was a good meeting, then?" Miles takes a swig of the preemptive apology beer I provided and drags his hand through his wayward dark strands.

"A great meeting, and the job is perfect. I'm doing local news coverage, and it's a huge publication, so there is a lot of room for me to grow."

Eve looks down at the corn chip in her hand. "Boston?"

"Yeah. Boston." Miles takes the chip and shoves it in his mouth. "Keep going past New York, and if you hit New Hampshire, you've gone too far. Do you need me to get you a map?"

Eve slaps him on the shoulder. "I know where it is, you asshole. I just can't believe Spencer's leaving us for Boston."

"It's really nice there," I say. "And I'd love to have you come and visit."

"Of course I'll visit. But I'm not happy that I won't be able to see you every day."

I put my arms around Eve's shoulder and pull her into my side. "We'll talk all the time. I promise."

She looks up at me. "Boston?"

I smile. "Boston."

Her grin matches mine. "Okay. Boston."

After extricating myself from Eve and Miles, I stop by the rink to tell Kit and Danny about the move. They're a little shocked but supportive, and Kit talks about having one last family dinner before I move. We agree on a date, and she immediately starts hammering out some initial plans to be emailed out for approval. I stop by Doug and Elaine's places respectively to share the news as well. They both grin from ear to ear and offer the proud parental reaction I know I won't get when I tell my own parents. They ask to see photos of my new place and agree as a family to fly via Boston when they head to London to see Bea in a few months.

I'm elated after spending time with the Reillys, but all the joy and love that fills my heart leaches out of me on the drive to my parents' house.

Dad isn't home, and after the scene I caused by chasing Miles out of the house when he caught me with Alex, Mom isn't pleased to see me either. I never gave her an explanation, but her displeasure with discussing embarrassing social situations means she hasn't asked for one.

"Spencer," she says when she opens the door. "Can I help you?"

A door-to-door vacuum cleaner salesman would receive a warmer welcome.

"I got a new job, and it's in Boston."

She folds her arms across her chest, not moving from the threshold. "Another one of your little misadventures, then?"

"Sure. If that's what you'd like to call it."

She huffs. "I thought you'd finally settled down."

"It's a great job, and I'm looking forward to getting set up over there." My tone is dry and clinical, like I'm reading off a teleprompter.

"I suppose you'll be needing money?"

I shake my head. "I have some savings, and the salary for my new position is pretty good. I came here to let you know I'll be leaving in a week."

She cocks a brow, and as she studies me with those judgmental eyes, I realize I truly do not give a fuck about the words that I predict will come out of her mouth next.

"You'll have to explain this to your father."

"No, I won't, so pass on the information. Or don't. I really don't care what he has to say on the matter."

Mom's mouth slackens. "Spencer."

"I mean it, Mom. I'm tired of trying to live up to his expectations. I'll never be enough for him, and I'm fine with it." I tuck my shaking hands into the pockets of my trench and do the best I can to hold my head high.

This is the final nail in the coffin of my relationship with my parents, and Dad isn't here to witness it. Part of me wonders what he would do. Would he berate me, spraying insults like bullets? Or would he let me walk away with nothing left to say? I'm not sure which is worse.

"Bye, Mom." I pull her into a brief, stilted hug that she doesn't return, and her jaw tightens. She says nothing, only watching with her narrow, feline gaze as I walk away.

A small part of me breaks when she doesn't call after me. It splinters even further when I hear the door close before my foot touches the pavement. *I wonder what they'll say to their friends?*

What rumors will do the rounds in their social circles? Do I really care? I hate that I've inherited Mom's obsession with what people think of me. Our neighbors don't care that I left *TGP*. And I'm sure the hostess at that waterfront restaurant doesn't remember me dripping marinara sauce on my dove gray pinafore when I was eight, though it doesn't stop me from avoiding all talk of my career and never returning to that restaurant because I was an embarrassment.

I turn to look back at the house with its heavy and imposing craftsman style. The garden, with its flowers that aren't built for this climate and require ten times the upkeep. The windows with their lacquered frames and fine curtains. It doesn't feel like a home. It doesn't feel like *my* home, making it easier to say goodbye to. Still, I shed an obligatory tear, not for my home or my parents, but for the street I grew up on and all the memories I'm leaving behind.

It turns into more than a single tear on the drive to Owen's place, and when I arrive, he pulls me into a hug and kisses the top of my head.

"Tell me what you need," he says as he releases me.

There is such warmth and care in his expression that it dulls the pain of leaving Bristol Court behind. It clouds the memories and everything I experienced there, both good and bad. Whether he means to or not, Owen's presence paints the future I want. The future I need.

"You," I say. "I just need you."

I wrap my arms around his neck and press a kiss to his jaw. His cheeks flush, and he turns his head, his lips pressing against mine softly. *I feel safe, seen, and wanted when I'm with him. What could be more perfect than that?*

He kisses me again with more feeling until my back is pressed against the wall. My heart races, and my fingers claw at his clothing, tearing his shirt over his head and feeling the heat of his skin against my palms. I miss him already, and I haven't left yet.

"Can we go upstairs?"

He nods, takes my hand, and leads me up the stairs to his bedroom. His room is sunbathed with the smell of clean linen hanging in the air. I'm already convinced I'm not good enough for him, but seeing his expertly made bed and the classic taupe color palette of his room has me convinced that no one is good enough for him. He's too put together. Too perfect.

He's not what I'm used to, and against my better judgment, I'm waiting for the other shoe to drop. For his faults to be spelled out. I push the thought away as his fingertips find the hem of my dress. He pulls the loose fabric up the length of my body and discards it on the floor. My breath catches, and suddenly, the sunbathed room doesn't feel like a warm embrace. I wrap my arms around myself, covering the curve of my stomach. Owen doesn't draw attention to this action. Instead, he puts his hands on my cheeks and kisses me deeply. From there, we step back, my hands finding his belt. By the time we reach the bed, there isn't a stitch of clothing between us. He holds my gaze as we lay down on our sides, our bodies pressed together. We have a million things to say to each other. *How is living apart going to work? Are we making a mistake?* Suddenly, the future I saw with him seems harder to achieve than I thought.

"Stop thinking," he says as he uses the pad of his thumb to smooth away the crease between my eyebrows.

"I can't."

He stares at me for a long moment, his fingers tracing slow circles down my side and over my hip. I lean in to kiss him, and when I do, his hand moves. It slides over my thigh and between my legs. Now, those slow circles leave me short of breath, and I hold him tightly, my fingers digging into his back.

"Owen."

His name leaves my lips in an embarrassing whimper, and he smirks at the way my body tightens. His touch is dizzying, and I moan softly before his mouth crashes against mine. Still, he doesn't stop, and the only sound in the room is our ragged breathing.

"Owen," I say again, my body ready to break apart.

He presses his forehead to mine, his voice a deep rumble. "I know, baby. I know."

At his words, I'm done for, and I pray to whoever will listen that Boston doesn't ruin us.

A week and a six-hour flight later, I'm standing on Beacon Street, staring up at the mid-19th-century brownstone that hemorrhaged most of my savings. It's four stories tall, classic red-brown brick with a cloudless blue sky behind it. When the landlord deposited the key in my hand and told me the rent was due on the first of the month, my wide smile unsettled him.

The apartment is tiny and awkwardly shaped. The bathroom is off the galley-style micro kitchen, and the long, rectangular bedroom has a queen bed that touches both walls. The hardwood floors creak, and the blind on the window to the left of the fireplace looks like it's barely survived a hurricane.

I drop my bags, step into the middle of the living space, and throw my hands above my head. Because even though it's small, old, and impractical for modern living, it's mine, and I can't wait to start my life here.

After a call to Owen and then to Eve, I lift both my suitcases onto the bed and start ferrying clothes to the tiny closet. I didn't bring much with me, and when I reach the bottom of the second case, I stumble across a few things that Seattle-based sentimental Spencer wouldn't let me leave without. Alex's hoodie and my journals.

I put the hoodie to the side and open the top brown faux leather book. I read all the things I wanted to say to him but could never bring myself to. I reminisce, smiling at the good times and cursing the bad until I'm emotionally spent. When I close the last word, I put all my journals and the hoodie beside my front door. I'll call Kit and get Alex's address in New York because it's about time I returned his hoodie and my broken heart to him.

CHAPTER FIFTY

Three months into my tenure at the *New England Tribune*, I was called into my boss' office for a casual chat to see how I was settling in. Neil Meyer, the city editor, is the polar opposite of Max Marlow. He's an empathetic teddy bear, and I wonder how he has been in journalism for close to forty years. He starts all meetings with a quick discussion about the weather, the upcoming weekend, or something new I've done with my hair. On that day, however, he cut right to the chase. I wasn't going to be a beat reporter anymore. I was moving into investigative journalism, and he was sending me to Miami to investigate a clothing company that folded after a series of suspicious financial transactions.

That was five months ago, and between out-of-town assignments and West Coast visitors, I've barely had a moment to myself at home. Not that I'm complaining about having Owen here almost every other weekend. We both signed up for airline credit cards and have been putting the free airline mile promotions to good use.

It hasn't been all sunshine and rainbows, though. At the

end of a long day, when I'm exhausted from work or frustrated with a piece I'm working on, I wish he was here. We could cuddle on the couch, watch murder documentaries, and he'd cook something spectacular for dinner. Still, we're doing our best, carving out time for each other, and never missing a video chat date. Unfortunately, he isn't here, and from time to time, we both get frustrated with the distance.

I was vocal about my need for him last night, and before I fell asleep, he texted to tell me he got an early flight and he'd be waiting for me when I got home from work today. My cheeks hurt from grinning as I look up at the neat row of brownstones and the sidewalk covered under a thick blanket of snow. The evening air is cutting, and I hurry to my apartment to find Owen buzzing around my tiny kitchen, wearing a dark blue apron dusted with flour.

"I'm home," I call out, and Owen's eyes snap to mine. He tosses my cheap plastic measuring spoons on the bench like they've stung him and lifts me off my feet.

"Aren't you a sight for sore eyes?" he says as he adjusts his grip.

I kiss him hard and wrap my limbs around him in an absurdly desperate manner. "I miss you. I miss you so fucking much."

"I miss you too." He lowers my feet back to the floor, takes my face in his hands, and kisses me again. "And I'm making you waffles."

"You're too good to me." I press my face into his chest and breathe him in. "Have you been waiting long?"

"Only an hour. Flight was delayed out of Chicago. Otherwise, I would have made you something more impressive than waffles."

"Your waffles are very impressive." I grin.

Together, we move around the kitchen, Owen guiding me

on how to use the waffle maker for the tenth time while he chops up fresh strawberries and whips cream by hand because he insists it tastes better that way.

I set the reclaimed timber coffee table, fetching the silverware and some orange juice from the fridge. As I reach up to get two glasses from the cupboard, Owen's hands slide under my shirt and across my stomach, moving up to my ribs and gently pressing into my bare skin.

"I got you some groceries as well. There was nothing in your fridge."

"You're definitely too good to me." I lean back into him, and he kisses my neck.

"I can be even better." His voice is low, and my fingers tangle in his hair, holding his head against my neck.

"How so?"

He unties the apron, pulls it over his head, and drops it on the kitchen floor before he throws me over his shoulder and carries me into the bathroom.

"I fixed the towel rail, and now you have no reason to leave your towel on the floor anymore."

"You know I'm pushed for time in the mornings."

He pulls me off his shoulder and boops the tip of my nose. "I also cleaned up all the clothes you left on the floor."

"I was in a rush this morning," I say as I hold my arms over my head. He pulls my shirt off.

"You're in a rush every morning."

"I like to sleep in," I huff as his shirt joins mine on the floor, and he steps me back toward the bedroom.

"Are you sure it isn't because you've been at that bar in Brookline?" He kisses my neck, his hands deftly removing the rest of my clothing before he gently guides me to the bed. "Because I see everything you're tagged in."

"Oh, you want to talk about going out? I know you and

Dale spend more time playing golf than refinishing your second-story floors."

I drag my hand down his stomach, and his eyelids flutter.

"The floors are done." He struggles to get the words out as my hand moves further south.

"How do they look?"

"Like new, but do we have to talk about this now?"

Owen strips the rest of his clothes off, and I take a moment to appreciate him. The first time we were together, I was self-conscious about my thirty-year-old body compared to his twenty-five-year-old one. It didn't take long for that to subside because he wanted me so badly that he could barely speak.

"You know I love you, right?" I say as he hovers above me and drags the tip of his finger down the side of my body.

"You know I loved you first." He leans down to kiss me, and I can't remember the last time I was this happy. My skin feels warmer, my sheets softer, the air sweeter. I feel like I'm in a Disney movie, and we're at the scene right before the happily ever after.

"I've been thinking about something," he says between kisses. "About us, actually."

"This sounds serious." I bury my fingers in his hair. "We're too naked to focus on serious things."

He takes my wandering hand. "It is kind of serious."

His playful smile is gone, and there is a deep line between his brows. I press my thumb to the spot and smooth it out. I don't like that line. I never want him to be sad, stressed, or concerned. I want him to be as happy as he makes me.

"Is everything okay?"

"Yeah." He inhales deeply. "But the reason I got the floors finished was so I could put the house on the market, which I did last week. And I accepted an offer before I boarded my flight today."

"You sold your place?" My mouth goes dry, and my skin tingles, hoping this means what I think it does.

"I had to, otherwise I'd never be able to afford a place in Boston."

My heart swells, its rhythm almost audible. "You're moving?"

"Yes, Spence." He laughs. "As soon as I can."

I throw my arms around him, forcing him onto his back and burying my face in his neck. It feels like a dream, and I'm so excited that my response is a garbled mess of big emotions that he laughs way too hard at.

For over an hour, we stay tangled together in the sheets, limbs intertwined and my head on his chest, listening to his steady heartbeat while he draws little circles on my shoulder. We talk about the future. Getting a bigger place, maybe a dog. Owen insists he can handle the occasional blizzard and agrees to Sunday strolls through The Common whenever we can. I close my eyes and see our life so vividly. It stretches out before me, and my chest flutters.

I wasn't even looking when I found him, and that's the best part.

The waffles are cold when Owen crawls out of bed and slips into the shower. I consider joining him, but a knock at the door has me throwing on his oversized sweatshirt in a panic and finding my neighbor on the threshold.

"This came for you." The elderly woman gives me a sinister glare before she shuffles off down the hall, leaving a cardboard box at my feet. I take it inside, placing it on the coffee table amongst our abandoned waffle set up, and notice the New York postmark on the top corner. Curiosity rips me apart at the seams, and I tear into the box like it's oxygen and I'm drowning.

"Oh," I say to myself as I pull out a hardshell case with a

portable turntable inside. I already know who it's from, and my muscles tighten when I see the other part of the gift.

It's a record, a first pressing of Alex's latest album. And there I am on the sleeve. And it's titled 'Spencer'.

The cover art is me lying on the couch, a pencil between my teeth, and Alex's songbook on my chest. I turn it over to read the track listing, realizing they're all named after my journal entries.

"Do you remember when we listened to *Tapestry* on vinyl?"

"Do you remember when you kissed me?"

"Do you remember those Malibu Sunsets?"

"Do you remember when you broke my heart?"

I take a deep breath, tears in my eyes, and press it to my chest. As I do so, a note falls out, and I recognize Alex's handwriting.

Be free.

The shower is still running as I set up the turntable and queue up the record. I'm on the second track, tears streaming down my face when Owen joins me. He immediately realizes what's going on and walks to the couch, holding me while we listen to every bump in my road spelled out in soulful detail.

It's exactly like his old stuff, and I wonder what the purpose is. *Is it cruel to have me relive this heartbreak when I've finally made it to a good place? Or should I be honored that I am once again the subject of his art?*

As the tracks continue to play, his melodic voice filling my Bostonian apartment, I listen to the lyrics and realize exactly what it is. It's an apology. An admission of guilt. It's him taking accountability for his actions the only way he knows how.

When it finishes playing, Owen lifts the needle and rests it gently back in the cradle. My cheeks are flushed and eyes wet as he pulls me into his arms and kisses the top of my head.

"How do you feel?" he whispers into my hair.

I hold him close, watching the snow flurries outside the window illuminated by a car driving through my perfect neighborhood.

"Free," I say. "I feel free."

ACKNOWLEDGMENTS

I have to start with a big thank you to my husband, Callan, for his love and support. After twenty years together, you are still my favourite person in the world and I couldn't be more grateful to have you by my side through yet another book publishing journey.

I also want to give a shout out to my author friends, who understand how equally painful and joyous writing a novel can be. Thank you Demi, Mel, Allison and Kaitlyn for your encouragement and friendship. I am slightly less thankful for the amount of procrastination you all let slide at Writing Friday. If you were harder on me, this book would have been out in March.

A thank you to my number one fans, Nicole Radonich, Judy Williams and Anita Womersley, who will once again finish a book that took 18 months to produce in a matter of days and be asking for more. Hearing you say you can't wait to read more brings me so much joy.

Shout out to Kim, because she wanted a mention in the acknowledgments. I hope it's everything you dreamed it would be.

And of course a BIG thank you to my family. I love you guys so much and thank you for everything you do for me.

And lastly, I want to thank Pop. It's not the same without you here. You taught me everything I know about tractor maintenance and diesel engines. I'm sorry I've forgotten all of it. You were the number one customer at my pretend hair salon, bookstore, and cafe. You gave me your blue eyes and a wonderful childhood. I miss you every day, Peanut.

ABOUT THE AUTHOR

Lauren Jones grew up in North Queensland and now lives in Brisbane with her graphic designer husband and two mini dachshunds. She started writing stories as a kid and thought time-travelling high fantasy was an easy place to start, she was wrong. Since then, Lauren has worked on her craft, gravitating toward contemporary fiction. She can be found in her little library, rearranging her books or having an afternoon nap.

To stay up to date on new releases you can follow Lauren on Instagram **@laurenjoneswrites** or sign up to her newsletter at www.laurenjoneswrites.com.au.

ALSO BY LAUREN JONES

Tell Me How It Ends

The Place We Were Made

Milton Keynes UK
Ingram Content Group UK Ltd.
UKHW030833021124
450571UK00015B/187/J